AF541221

CYBER DIPLOMACY

Navigating the New Digital World Order

CYBER DIPLOMACY

Navigating the New Digital World Order

Preethi Amaresh

Pawan Anand

Vineet Kumar

CyberPeace

First published in 2025 by
PENTAGON PRESS LLP
206, Peacock Lane, Shahpur Jat
New Delhi-110049, India
Contact: 011-26490600

Typeset in Palatino, 11 Point
Printed at Aegean Offset Printers, Greater Noida

ISBN 978-81-984458-2-7 (HB)

Disclaimer: The views and opinions expressed in the book is the individual assertion of the Authors. The Publisher does not take any responsibility for the same in any manner whatsoever. The same shall solely be the responsibility of the Authors.

www.pentagonpress.in

This book is dedicated to the often-unheralded diplomats and cyber security professionals working behind the scenes to navigate the intricate, ever-shifting digital terrain of global affairs. It highlights the hard work of diplomats, policymakers, and cyber security professionals that goes on behind the scenes, often in relative seclusion, where there is little public oversight, to protect national interests, maintain global standards, and prevent major cyber hostilities. Though their contributions often go unrecognized, their work is vital in maintaining global stability and security in an age of unparalleled technological progress. It also brings together researchers, scholars and students dedicated to exploring the complex nexus between technology and international relations. Research, analysis and knowledge transfer are the building blocks of successful cyber diplomacy. They explain why they are important, helping policymakers understand the kinds of information and frameworks that are needed to navigate the often-complex and elusive context. We hope that this book serves as a cornerstone for the continuing foundations for safe and secure cyberspace in the future for all cultures and societies.

Contents

Preface

In todays interconnected world, diplomacy has transcended traditional boundaries, entering the expansive realm of cyberspace. This evolution, known as **cyber diplomacy**, involves using digital platforms and technologies to conduct diplomatic relations, allowing real-time communication and collaboration between governments, diplomats, and the public. This shift has fundamentally transformed international relations, intertwining technology with global policy.

Cyber Diplomacy: Navigating the Digital World Order delves into this dynamic landscape, where governments, policymakers, and cyber security experts work to establish rules of engagement in the digital domain. The stakes are high, encompassing the prevention of cyber conflicts, protection of critical infrastructure, establishing global digital norms, and assurance of data sovereignty. Recent developments underscore the growing importance of cyber diplomacy:

> The U.S Department of State launched the Bureau of Cyberspace and Digital Policy (CDP) in April 2022, integrating various cyber initiatives to promote U.S. interests in cyberspace, including cyber security, internet governance, and digital policy.
>
> The European Union established a legal framework to sanction individuals and organizations responsible for cyber attacks, information manipulation, and sabotage on behalf of other nations.
>
> The Global Conference on Cyberspace (GCCS), initiated in 2011, serves as a forum for states, industry, and civil society

to discuss and advance norms of responsible behaviour in cyberspace, emphasizing cyber capacity building and international cooperation.

This book aims to provide a clear and engaging exploration of how cyber diplomacy transforms international relations. It highlights the intersection of technology and foreign policy, addressing cyber security threats, misinformation, and digital sovereignty. The role of global powers in shaping the new rules of cyberspace and the impact of emerging technologies on cyber strategies are examined in depth.

The contributions of researchers, scholars, and students are vital in this field. Their insights equip policymakers with the knowledge to navigate the ever-changing digital landscape. Through these pages, readers will explore the evolution from reactive cyber security measures to proactive strategies that shape international standards and guidelines. Discussions include the role of cutting-edge technologies in supporting diplomatic activities, aiding decision-making processes, and facilitating predictive modelling in the cyber domain.

This book is intended for the next generation of diplomats, tech policymakers, and cyber security professionals who will lead efforts to create a secure and resilient digital future. Their ability to balance innovation with security and cooperation with competition will define the digital world order of tomorrow. Understanding cyber diplomacy becomes essential as we enter an era where digital threats can destabilize economies, influence elections, and challenge national security. We hope this book serves as a guide to this new frontier, where nations negotiate across borders, networks, and algorithms.

Preethi Amaresh
Pawan Anand
Vineet Kumar

Chapter One

The Cyber Frontier: Reshaping International Relations in the Digital Age

Cyber power is the name given to the growing centre of power that will completely restructure global politics through many digital technologies in both offensive and defensive manners either through states or non-states. The influence of cyber power extends to all kinds of levels and aspects of discourse, from basic infrastructure up to higher political discussions. The birth of cyber power will hence lead to an inevitable reconsideration of an old notion about power, which is the military and territorial dominance. Drawing lines between the traditional orthodox power and the real world, as a small player now puts heavy pressure on a bigger state in the presence of increased awareness of the technology, the states were formerly considered to reflect brute power.

Nevertheless, the overall implications of cyber power bring up an issue of sovereignty, that, again, with respect to digital access and information manipulation, have a bearing on national boundaries. Confidential government information is obtainable, through cyber-snooping, by exposing them to varying degrees of risk, through cyber-attacks the states critical infrastructures (power systems and financial networks) can be interrupted. Such vulnerabilities fundamentally undermine state sovereignty over its territory and resources and thus pose threats to state viability itself in this digital age. Further complicating the whole issue is the attribution problem. Very often, it is impossible to ascertain the country of origin of a cyber attack, making it difficult to determine on whom to lay the blame and how to respond. Such uncertainty can lead to many escalatory spirals wherein states are trying to determine both the aggressor and how to retaliate for their actions. Cyber options are now used more and more by governments in furthering their foreign policy pursuits. The proverbial needle-in-a-haystack cyber tools that can still breach the highest fortified digital security have established a new hierarchy for spying, hitherto the forte of human intelligence operatives. Well into the 21st century, stealing intellectual property, military secrets, and other sensitive bits of information about each other is now as common as breathing in international political relations. Coupled with that, cyber attacks have morphed very much from mere vandalism into a systematic yet calculated anarchistic approach to intrinsic infrastructure breakdown just to wield a political end.

Countries have employed cyber attacks to disrupt or influence rival elections, spread disinformation and crack societies apart. The attack of NotPetya in 2017 is one of the significant exemplary cases showing how awful mass cyber attacks are to an economy. The cases of Stuxnet and SolarWinds reflect increasing international cooperation to address an emerging set of state-sponsored cyber threats. The rise of cyber power first of all will have to mean a re-interpretation of what national security actually is. While at times it is defined mostly in military terms, this should take on some digital dimension by now.

Cyber attacks may disrupt basic services and bring about severe interruptions of economic activity and societal instability and pose threats to national security, in essence, an equivalent risk to that of traditional war. The broader this definition of national security gets, the greater would be the required integration of all elements into national defence, blending the traditional armed services with sophisticated cyber capabilities. This also widens the potential of attack surfaces targeted by threats through increasing dependency on interdependent systems like the Internet of Things (IoT). Cyber power, by itself, would introduce consequences to order and stability. So there would be ample room for miscalculation, escalation, and unintended consequences. Thus, such basic problems as the lack of consensus or rules for engaging in cyberspace, together with the difficulties of attribution could provide ample material for the ignition of a full-blown open conflict. Indeed, these struggles are ideal but expensive. On the other hand, it also touches upon monetary evaluation and public trust issues, as well as the goodwill of international partners. The cyber attacks during the 2016 US presidential elections are an ideal example of such moves capable of interfering with a democratic process and, hence, disrupting society and world stability. In the Washington debate over the integrity of elections and foreign interference in the internal political sphere, particularly when it comes to cyberspace, the geopolitical stakes of that power are high, if not a level of magnitude higher. This has increased the number of actors who have developed ever more powerful cyber capabilities. This microscopic complexity in cyberspace adds another layer of problems to classical architectures of geopolitics, which require new modes of cooperation in international politics. Such actions were developed mainly by the leading powers like the US, China, Russia, and others with high-powered cyber capabilities: it becomes more difficult and less effective to set a limit for such interactions with further proliferation to coincide with increasing importance of non-state actors.

International norms and legal frameworks around responsible state action in cyberspace would be a helpful way to mitigate some of the risks associated with cyber power. Countries, multinational organizations, and the business world must cooperate to lay down clear rules for those laws of participation, as well as for drafting those procedures, in the digital domain. Strong attribution mechanisms would need to be established to dissuade bad actors from performing their actions and to hold them responsible afterwards for what they have done. The work of the United Nations (UN) and other international organizations in uniting states and forming norms would be invaluable. But it shares space with some geopolitical struggles where rapid changes in the landscape of cyber warfare present further challenges along the road that limit ambitions to have robust global governance for cyberspace. To sum up, however, the rise of cyber power has brought about phenomenal changes in the sphere of international relations. From national security and state sovereignty to international stability, the concomitant effects cannot obviously be over-exaggerated. On the other hand, a great revision of the traditional paradigms of geopolitical thinking is a must: different states and non-state actors should be allowed to capitalize on cyber capabilities, using them both for offensive and defensive goals. The challenges cyber power creates go across international boundaries and, consequently, need a multipronged approach that includes setting up international standards; tightening cyber security defences; and putting in place more effective diplomatic mechanisms for the resolution of disputes and the avoidance of escalation in cyberspace. It will be how the states are able to navigate this elaborate landscape that will shape international relations in the future.

It is imperative that established theories of international relations are put into context in order to understand cyber diplomacy in a more nuanced manner, given the rise of cyber power. Traditional frameworks developed in the context of physical interactions will have to be adjusted to accommodate the peculiar characteristics of the digital domain. Well-known theories of international relations including but not limited to constructivism, liberalism, and realism inform the approach to unpacking state behaviour, cooperation, competition, and conflict in the cyber realm.

Realism further provides quite a stable ground for all this because of its usually strong emphasis on state power, security, and self-interest. A lot within cyberspace can manifest into power itself, from military capabilities to scientific, financial, and information flow. Realist theory contended states would act in the best self-interest towards their own cyber security, triggering an arms race in both offensive and defensive capabilities. To make matters worse, the further ambiguous nature of this makes states more or less unwilling to proceed into counter-retaliation against directly suspected aggressors over competing uncertainties as to guilt of the aggressor and room for escalation. When that does not happen, lack of clarity creates a security riddle that a state pursuing security presents when it causes insecurity in other states. From a realist standpoint, this would continue with states focusing on developing newer offensive capabilities that would make strikes and vulnerabilities more attractive and thus their military capabilities would be constantly increasing. The rivalry for supremacy in cyberspace is generally envisioned as a zero-sum game, whereby every victory for one state represents an inevitable defeat for the others. International order cannot be granted any due acknowledgment or credited with validating norms and rules by realists since it aims only at identifying the selfless nature of world systems, as well as the power extension of any state in cyberspace from the others viewpoint. In the competition for digital resources like the intellectual property, sensitive data, or skilled cyber security personnel, it is likely that assumptions of a zero-sum game would prevail, even perhaps leading to some conflicts over scarce resources.

An alternative viewpoint that emphasises collaboration, interdependence, and international institutions is offered by liberalism. Liberal theorists contend that governments have an incentive to cooperate because cyberspace is linked and shares vulnerabilities. There is also overwhelming support for international cooperation in the development of standards and norms, and the establishment of regulatory frameworks and dispute-resolution mechanisms, owing to the global scope of the Internet, the risks of devastating attacks on critical national infrastructure, and the extensive flow of information across national borders. Liberal institutionalism focuses on how global bodies such as the UN facilitate cooperation through forums for discussion, compromise and the formation of global norms of behaviour. They contend that in order to prevent violence and preserve stability in the cyber world, international cyber regulations must be put in place. These regulations ought to be the same as those that govern real warfare. Asymmetry in cyber capabilities, attributability, and non-state actors participation may hinder the influence of liberal policies in cyberspace, in contrast to international standards for the responsible behaviour of state and non-state actors. The application of international norms is challenging in a decentred setting where attribution is unclear and state control over online activity is contested. Thus, the liberal approach might be more effective in a setting like this, where mutual benefit is obvious and trust can be built. Common values, reciprocal benefits, and sufficient trust are essential for international cooperation to succeed under a liberal framework.

Another useful theoretical framework for understanding cyber diplomacy is constructivism, which stresses the part norms, ideas, and identities play in determining state behaviour. Constructivists hold that expectations of state behaviour in cyberspace are socially created. Therefore, actions performed in cyberspace are decided not only by a states governmental identity and the way in which it views other states but also by the already existing international community norms. Common norms, where they exist, can help to control state behaviour (for example, law can control criminal behaviour) and promote cooperation by means of their prohibition of some kinds of cyber attack. Still, the evolution of such standards has to be maintained by ongoing debate and government give-and-take. Establishing a shared knowledge of what behaviour is regarded as acceptable or unacceptable in cyberspace is a difficult exercise complicated by different opinions on national interests, security, and sovereignty. Constructivists stress the need for conversation, communication, and confidence-building techniques in order to establish these standards. Depending on who they are and what interests they have, different people will consider cyber attacks either acceptable or unethical. From this point of view, diplomacy and the influence of communication on norms, perceptions and promotion of cooperation is highlighted. State-to-state interactions and ongoing debates about what behaviour in the digital sphere is appropriate or inappropriate are hence gradually changing cyber norms.

Nonetheless, using these three theories helps one to realise that cyber diplomacy is a complicated interaction between conflict, competitiveness, and cooperation. Realism is mostly concerned with the possible arms race and security issues. While a liberal viewpoint values the advantages of cooperation and international society, constructivism highlights the socially created element of online norms and behaviours. To grasp this interaction, however, calls for a thorough approach combining elements of the three theoretical models.

Outside of these major paradigms, critical theories contributed important concepts for the study of cyber diplomacy. Critical theory has shown how the power regimes that exist within the layers of the digital space are reflections of the larger global injustice. And to buttress their own power and maybe even capitalize on compromised regimes, they mirror how great powers use their technological edge. One challenge is the digital divide between states that do and do not have advanced technical capabilities. This split impacts a states susceptibility to attacks, as well as its ability to conduct cyber diplomacy. Critical theorists emphasize the role of cyber power as a means of exacerbating pre-existing injustices and hierarchies, a feature that raises questions about the legitimacy and fairness of existing inter-state institutions and norms. Central to that critical perspective is examining the power that larger companies have and their interactions with state actors.

Where actors can literally cross national borders, there are very real concerns about governmental control. Those risks including state secrets being stolen, critical infrastructure shut down and elections through cyber means smudge old notions of the territorial. It calls for a deeper examination of how states are recalibrating their visions of sovereignty in a digital era, and how they are evolving their visions and tactics in a world of emergent power aggrandizement. Thus, the time has come to revisit international law and diplomacy in the face of the new order of state sovereignty. Cyber diplomacy concerns an effort to comprehend the uniqueness of the digital domain and to transcend conventional frameworks of international engagement. This makes it distinct from diplomacy, which is mostly about in-person contacts and territorial boundaries, and takes place in a circumscribed world of sovereign states. Its coverage extends to a broad range of activities that need to be managed, prevented, and resolved sensibly in cyberspace. This includes norms on responsible behaviour, enhancing predictability in cyberspace and expanding structural stability to cover cyber, responding to cyber attacks and broadening the technology envelope to international relations as a whole. It is a rapidly changing area, which must be kept up to date for the fast pace of technological development and a changing cyber threat environment.

Cyber diplomacy has a more complex and wider alternative set of actors and interests beyond the usual state-centred framework. It is states, after all, that are still the key players in the national pursuit of goals, on offence and defence, with its technology. By diplomatic apparatus, we mean a multi-layered, nuanced approach to diplomacy, richer than the past, state-to-state model, particularly since the stage has now been opened to multiple non-state actors, including hacktivist groups, terrorist organizations, and multinational corporations. These non-state actors frequently possess strong cyber capabilities that they use across the spectrum of their activities, from disruption of critical infrastructure to espionage. Their transnational work challenges traditional norms of state sovereignty and demands creative, new forms of diplomacy to engage and respond to them. International organizations like the UN are also essential for constructing cooperation, creating standards, and offering places for dialogue among various actors. The agenda is to prepare the questions concerning incident response coordination for the international law on cyberspace. Last, but not least, the private sector is a necessary partner to cyber diplomacy with not only expertise on cyber security technology in either defensive or offensive capacity but also a seat at the table for shaping and maintaining critical infrastructure. Often, to implement and react to cyber security measures necessarily, cooperation of organization between the private and public sector is required.

Cyber diplomacys instruments are as diverse as its participants. Conventional diplomatic instruments like bilateral and multilateral discussions are still crucial. However, new tools created especially for the online environment frequently complement them. In addition to creating uniform standards of conduct and dispute resolution procedures, international treaties and accords also serve to lay the groundwork for collaboration. As in the case of the Budapest Convention on Cybercrime, one of the few legal agreements supporting international cooperation in the prosecution of cybercrime, so-called legally enforceable agreements can offer a framework for action. In order to achieve an effect, these treaties need to be widely ratified and efficiently practised by the signing governments, which is often a challenging proposition. Confidence-building measures, or CBMs, are also critical to fostering transparency and reducing distrust among states. (Examples: organisational knowledge, work games, internal communication system for possible emergencies, etc.) The creeping national interests and the fundamental difficulty of attributing cyber attacks often erodes mutual trust and a common desire for de-escalation that are vital preconditions for meaningful CBMs. Incident response systems are important for mobilising responses during a cyber attack. Information protection procedures, cooperation investigation teams, and the creation of communication hotlines are a few examples of these systems. Clear guidelines and a high level of trust and cooperationpossibly from all parties involved are necessary for a successful incident response; however, national sensitivities and the requirement to protect sensitive data make this impracticable, particularly in these situations. Through Track-II diplomacy, other actors such as development agencies and professionals and practitioners from non-governmental organizations offer avenues for communication and understanding in addition to those formal tracks. These kinds of discussions can aid in the development of common standards and make it easier to solve challenging cyber issues. Actually, the task at hand determines how effective these tools are. Treaties, for instance, can be useful in establishing broad guidelines for behaviour, but they might not be able to keep up with the quick advancements in technology and subtleties of attribution. Although CBMs can help establish trust, their effectiveness is limited unless they are used in conjunction with a more comprehensive commitment to norm construction and cooperation. Although they necessitate quick information exchanges and trust between various organisations, physically based incident response systems can be crucial for handling crises. Thus, cyber diplomacy must be a multifaceted strategy that incorporates both formal and informal toolkits.

There are many case studies of the successes and failures of cyber diplomacy. Thus, while the Tallinn Manual on the International Law Applicable to Cyber Warfare is not an internationally legally binding document, it is nevertheless a significant step forward in the application of relevant international law principles in cyberspace. It was created after expert consultations, suggesting that there might be a way to work together to define legally ambiguous areas and establish consensus regarding suitable state regulations. However, the difficulty of converting expert opinion into legally binding international agreements is demonstrated by its limited legal enforceability. One example of the difficulties around attribution and whether to coordinate a global response is the 2017 NotPetya cyber attack, which was widely credited to Russia. The absence of a unified global response even though many other countries condemned the attack highlighted the inadequacies of the existing framework for responding to major, state-backed cyber attacks. The lack of coordinated action suggests that greater cooperation and better protocols for responding to crises are needed on an international level. Without clear international legal frameworks to regulate such activities, states could launch clandestine cyber attacks, as was the case with the Stuxnet worm, a widely publicised cyber weapon claimed to be the work of the US and Israel that targeted Iranian nuclear installations. This case study illustrates the need for more precise laws that define cyber warfare while also showing that escalation is likely due to attribution issues and the potential for error. Ultimately, cyber diplomacy is a dynamic field that necessitates creative solutions to the particular problems posed by the digital world. It includes a wide range of programs aimed at enlisting a large number of players, managing and preventing conflict in cyberspace, and using a variety of instruments to encourage collaboration and set standards. The success of cyber diplomacy relies on the ability to set strong conflict resolution protocols, clear behavioural norms, and build trust. Despite the strategic order in a completely different ecosystem, the great technological challenges to face are there (in particular, attribution tests), as well as non-state actors, and in order to ensure in this field, you must often find the right combination between new diplomacy and tactics tested to respond to the issues of the digital space.

In order to successfully manage the complexities of cyber power and create a more secure and stable international order in the digital world of the 21st century, it suggests a mix of treaties and accords, CBMs, incident response procedures, and unofficial diplomatic channels. The usefulness of these tools must be further assessed in future research, and best practices and methodologies must be modified to handle a shifting threat and new technologies. To guarantee a safer, more tranquil Internet, strong enforcement measures and strong international standards will be essential unlike in previous eras of international relations, where unipolarity or bipolarity existed and where the norm, the digital environment, is marked by global multi-polarity and reflects the dispersion of technological capability, the emergence of new economic powers and the interconnectedness of global society. While the US has dominated cyberspace for decades, a host of actors with diverging capabilities and goals are increasingly threatening US dominance.

One significant counterbalance to US dominance is China. Its rapidly evolving technology sector and significant state investment in offensive capabilities and cyber security make it a major player in forming the global cyber environment. China frequently takes this stance, which is typically more concerned with securing and insulating its own cyberspace through strict domestic regulations and efforts to establish national standards. But this is often inconsistent with the Internets open and interoperable nature, creating tensions in discussions and agreements over international cyber security norms. The country to promote its geopolitical and economic goals while also protecting its critical infrastructure, which raises major concerns regarding national-level financial manipulation and cyber espionage, has used Cyber capabilities both offensively and defensively. Traversal of the multi-polar nature of cyber power therefore necessitates an awareness of Chinas cyber ambitions. Russia also plays a prominent role, with a strategy characterized by aggressively deploying cyber operations and contesting weaknesses for tactical advantage. Russia has good human resources and, unlike the US and China, is prepared to use cyber attacks as a weapon of state policy, hence closing its gap in technological sophistication. (Although the NotPetya attacks attribution is still up for debate, it serves as an illustration of how Russia might carry out extensive cyber operations to inflict serious financial harm.) The UN and other multilateral organisations have started looking into the need for stricter regulations and procedures to deal with state-sponsored cyber attacks as a result of this confrontational stance, which has alarmed people around the world.

The complexity of the cyber landscape is being increased by a few emerging powers in addition to the established ones. With its technological edge and talent reservoir of well-trained cyber professionals, Indias capabilities are soaring. A further sign of its burgeoning economic power is its growing involvement in the swirling international debates around cyber security with the intention of shaping the behavioural norms for the online environment. As a tech-savvy citizenry with a sophisticated digital economy, South Korea has long played an active role in international efforts to enhance cyber security cooperation. Its experience in responding to cyber attacks, and especially attacks on its critical infrastructure, provides it an insight into the challenges of international cooperation in this area. However, the multi-polar environment is not exclusively a phenomenon of nation-states. Whether their goals are economic enrichment, political revolution, or ideological promotion, important non-state actors such as hacktivists, criminal organisations, terrorist groups, and many others frequently use cyber capabilities to accomplish their goals. The fact that their acts frequently cross national boundaries makes attribution and retaliation more difficult. The fact that advanced ransomware attacks frequently target businesses and critical infrastructure that impact multiple nations, however, highlights the limitations of responses that are limited by national borders and the pressing need for international coordination. Due to their role, the conventional state-oriented paradigm of international relations is essentially unstable, necessitating the use of creative diplomatic strategies for conflict resolution and negotiation. The landscape is made more complex by the nature of cyber power. Cyber power is far more challenging to measure than traditional military power, which is readily measured in terms of troop numbers and armaments. Less obviously, this makes the international systems ingrained distrust and uncertainty worse. A states technological infrastructure, skilled labour force, offensive and defensive capabilities (some classified), and leaders willingness to use cyber attacks as foreign policy tools are the first steps in determining its cyber capabilities. It makes it more difficult to properly advance diplomacy, particularly when it comes to the participation of other nuclear-armed nations in arms control agreements or cyber confidence-boosting initiatives. An additional challenge to international cooperation is the speed at which technology is developing and changing. New vulnerabilities will be found, and new offensive tools will be created. Diplomatic tactics that can adjust to and react suitably to new threats are necessary in light of the changing climate. What we agree upon today might not be applicable tomorrow, so we need to keep talking about it and making adjustments to stay impactful and relevant. The economic effects of cyber power are equally potent. The increased reliance of supply chains, financial institutions and critical infrastructure on digital technologies makes them vulnerable to targeted attacks. By impacting trade, output and investor confidence, the attacks could inflict serious economic harm. To address the risks of potential attacks in this domain, there should be a positive incentive for cooperation, because the interconnectedness of the global economy can exacerbate the economic consequences of these attacks. Divergent national interests, however, often hinder progress on such cooperation, including on safeguarding sensitive information and economic competitiveness. The implications of cyber power on human rights cannot be ignored. Cyber attacks can violate fundamental rights, such as freedom of speech, right to privacy, and the right to due process. Cyber technologies can also be used to conduct surveillance, censor and repress, which raises serious ethical and legal issues.

This is only possible in the digital age, if governments, international organisations, and civil society work together to address these issues and create international human rights legislation that protects human dignity and fundamental rights online. It is easy to argue that global cyber power depends on both state and non-state actors, and that this is complicated because state and non-state actors have different needs and capacities. Multipolarity of this kind threatens global peace and necessitates creative diplomatic solutions. It will take a sophisticated grasp of the capacities and intentions of different actors, robust international standards, and efficient dispute resolution and incident response procedures to bring some order to this unstable environment.

Rapid technological advancement combined with the economic and human rights ramifications of cyber power creates a complex and vital environment that necessitates a vibrant process of communication and adaptation focused on cooperation and establishing trust. The course of international relations in the digital age will depend on the capacity of states and other actors and willingness to cooperate in order to handle the opportunities and difficulties presented by this multipolar cyber environment. The previous debate used this competitive cross-section of organisations, interests, and agendas to highlight how multipolar global cyberspace is. Due to its intrinsic complexity, international cooperation necessitates a strong architecture that mainly depends on the efficiency of multilateral platforms and international organisations. Norms and mechanisms to promote cooperation may be established because cyberspace is becoming more interconnected and interdependent, but the anarchic nature of international relations frequently guarantees that legally binding agreements have multiple layers of political, historical, and technical flaws. The UN itself, with its large membership and responsibility for preserving world peace and security, is at the vanguard of these initiatives. But the difficulties in striking a balance between conflicting national interests, as well as the difficulties with attribution and enforcement in the digital sphere, frequently compromise its efficacy. The UN has been actively involved in cyber security because cyber attacks can transcend national borders and endanger international peace and security. The UN has many tools at its disposal like diplomacy, capacity building, norm-setting, and the development of international law. The General Assembly passed an array of resolutions on a range of cyber safety concerns, including preventing cybercrime, fostering global collaboration, and putting regulations in place that boost confidence. Despite not being enforceable by law, the resolutions constitute significant declarations of values that influence global standards and government conduct.

However, the UNs ability to efficiently manage cyberspace is restricted by its inherent drawbacks. It makes it difficult to enforce legally binding state regulations because it maintains state sovereignty as one of its fundamental tenets, particularly for those in positions of authority who are immune to external criticism. It is an ongoing attempt to achieve a balance between a broad spectrum of technological knowledge and the international ambitions of its significant membership. The UNs sometimes challenging and sluggish administrative procedures hinder swift actions regarding arising cyber threats. As states may be unwilling to accept accountability for an attack, even when evidence suggests their involvement, attribution of cyber attacks continues to be an important challenge. It is often both technically and politically difficult to determine the attacks origin. This opaqueness makes it more challenging to bring those accountable to justice and prevent future events of the same form. The UN has significance because it promotes collaboration and debate about cyber security standards, regardless of these drawbacks. This is the responsibility of several UN agencies, such as the International Telecommunication Union (ITU), the UN Office on Drugs and Crime (UNODC), and the International Criminal Police Organisation (INTERPOL). Creating technical standards and promoting the safe use of information and communication technologies are the two main tasks of the ITU, for example, to assist member-nations investigate and prosecute cyber criminals. INTERPOL facilitates cross-border collaboration in cybercrime law enforcement efforts. By means of its training and capacity-building programs, the UNODC enables nations to create domestic legislation and capabilities that enhance the international regulatory framework on cybercrime.

A number other global organisations, besides the UN, play a vital role for developing cyber security policies and encouraging cooperation. The Organisation for Security and Co-operation in Europe (OSCE), for instance, has an extensive record of supporting systems that boost trust in the military and security domain. A number of efforts that bring member-nations together to share information and work together on cyber threats and challenges are among its cyberspace endeavours. The OSCEs geography of engagement in Europe, and its pursuit of confidence-building measures, makes it particularly well-placed to work on regional cyber safety issues. The Association of Southeast Asian Nations (ASEAN) and the African Union (AU) are two regional organisations increasingly involved in addressing cyber security issues in their regions. Such organizations serve an integral role in enabling international cooperation on cyber security threats, harmonizing national approaches and building capacity. Their tailored approaches might be less futile than the one-size-fits-all solutions attempted by large institutions such as the UN, since they look into the specific cyber security needs and challenges found in every place. Regional organisations, however, typically do not have the necessary authority and funding needed for successful enforcement of rules and regulations.

This will require multilateral cyber security treaties and accords to set the stage for global governance in cyberspace. One explanation for this is the considerable advance in international cooperation against cybercrime in the form of the Budapest Convention on Cybercrime. With the goal to enhance global cooperation in the investigation and prosecution of different kinds of cybercrime, the Council of Europe adopted this treaty. In order to encourage global collaboration in the investigation and prosecution of all types of cybercrime, the Council of Europe put forward the Cybercrime Convention. There are certain shortcomings inherent in the Convention, particularly with the struggle to extradite cybercriminals abroad when implementing its laws. In order to encourage accountable government conduct in cyberspace, an array of additional multilateral efforts has been implemented. The goal of creating such diverse CBMs (such as information-sharing, technical assistance programs, etc.) is to reduce the risk of escalation and miscalculation while also opening the door to transparency. These CBMs, however, frequently lack enforcement mechanisms and are voluntary. States must be willing to meet, coordinate, and share in order to be effective, but this willingness is frequently predicated on power politics and mutual trust.

The process of creating international standards is crucial but challenging. There is still debate over the precise definition and application of responsible state behaviour in cyberspace, despite the fact that there is now a renewed consensus on the concept. Following global disputes over what constitutes appropriate cyber behaviour among states, the first deals with the use of offensive capabilities, and the second deals with the targeting of vital infrastructure. Furthermore, because technology is advancing so quickly, it is nearly impossible to establish standards that will endure and be flexible enough to accommodate a changing cyber environment. Because norms that are applicable today might not be tomorrow, facilitators must continuously review and update them. Furthermore, the power structures of multinational corporations have a significant impact on cyber security standards and cooperation. Therefore, the most technologically advanced governments may have a ruling effect that hinders decision-making and marginalises the weaker party. The creation of inclusive standards that represent the interests and concerns of all pertinent stakeholders may become more difficult as a result of this discrepancy. The governance of global cyber security is facing challenges not only from state actors, who frequently create hostile environments for civil society and non-state actors, but also from a lack of participation in certain decision-making processes.

Finally, the worldwide complexity of the cyber environment gives international organisations a major role in shaping cyber security norms and aiding collaboration. However, despite the great strides of the UN and other international organisations in terms of standards setting, communication enabling, and cooperation easing, there are still many hurdles to overcome. Differences in power in the realm of international organisations, the difficulty of attributing blame when attacks happen, and the ineffectiveness of some enforcement mechanisms each impede effective global cyber security governance in different ways. To face these challenges, we must deepen international collaboration, promote confidence among countries and adapt regulatory benchmarks to the rapidly changing nature of technology. Thus, in order to build a more secure and safe digital environment, global governance on cyber security requires sustained and concerted efforts of all parties.

Chapter Two

Cyber Engagement across Various Domains

International organisations perform an integral role in traversing the complex waters associated with worldwide cyber issues, as previously demonstrated. In simple terms, the effectiveness of these multilateral efforts has an immediate connection with how various national governments view cyber diplomacy as an important part of bigger foreign policy strategies. With an emphasis on embedded seamless integration, digital diplomacy transforms the interoperability principle from a secondary consideration into a key consideration when structuring international affairs systems. An ever-growing foundation of state power that influences the strategic decisions that determine foreign policy decisions and engagement worldwide is cyber capability.

Cyber technologies are employed by states to achieve a range of foreign policy objectives, which range from impacting political outcomes to growing economic interests. There are multiple ways to use cyber capabilities to advance diplomatic goals. For instance, countries can use their cyber capabilities to gather intelligence that can assist them make prudent decisions during diplomatic talks. By employing cyber espionage to uncover an adversarys shortcomings, a state may bolster its hand in negotiations. Cyber capabilities may be utilised to analyse the actions of other states enabling systems to alert countries for prospective risks and forward-thinking diplomatic responses. Cyber capabilities can consequently boost conventional diplomatic attempts and provide a strategic edge in accelerating national targets.

The association between cyber capabilities and diplomatic efforts is not always mutually strengthening, though; offensive cyber strategies can have both short-term strategic advantages and long-term instability; cyber attacks, especially those that emphasize essential national infrastructure or cause substantial disruption, may lead to disputes and long-term relationship damage; failing states are seldom successful in their worldwide diplomatic engagement; and countermeasures may undermine global cooperation and security through establishing a self-perpetuating dynamic of escalated situations. Cyberspace renders it difficult to know if a state is responsible for the attacks and if it is, in what manner and such attribution difficulties are obstacles to appropriate diplomacy and on the whole, result in mutual accusations of failure and mistrust that inhibit confidence building and productive dialogue.

The 2017 NotPetya cyber attack serves as an unsettling example of how inadvertent cyber activity can impede diplomatic aims. The attack is believed to have originated from Russian sources, and may have been specifically targeted at Ukrainian enterprises, despite being so infamously credited, as it is. Nevertheless, the attack quickly spread over the world, affecting both companies and governments in many different countries and incurring substantial financial losses. In addition to putting Russias ties with various countries to the test and hindering its diplomatic attempts to create an image of accountability in the international arena, this side effect of the strike damaged Russias credibility globally. At the very minimum, cyber actors should be cognisant of how their actions can affect diplomacy. This scenario illustrates a cautionary flag concerning the utilisation of cyber capabilities without an understanding of what could result from their especially reckless usage.

Moreover, the concurrent nature of cyber operations and the asynchronous aspect of most diplomacy both impede the diplomatic process, especially when it comes to interference and adequate rehabilitation efforts. This frequently involves setting accelerated strategies, like establishing knowledgeable cyber diplomacy teams that are capable of responding quickly and effectively to changing situations as it is challenging for policymakers to navigate across the line between asymmetric warfare in operational cyberspace and traditional diplomatic statecraft. Effective policy development proves difficult due to the lack of clearly defined global standards and legal frameworks that regulate the actions of states in cyberspace. For cyber diplomacy to be integrated into the sphere of foreign policymaking, a comprehensive agenda-setting strategy will therefore be crucial. Governments must put comprehensive national cyber regulations that integrate overarching foreign policy demands while setting the boundaries of appropriate cyber power together. To determine the possible effects of the cyber activity on diplomatic ties, states should keep evaluating risks that are linked with their cyber operations. This requires an extensive examination of possible loopholes as well as an overall intelligence picture of the cyber capabilities of both allies and adversaries. In order to reduce the overlap between cyber operations and conventional diplomacy, it is essential that sturdy, open communication be both secure and readily available. Successful collaboration among agencies is required for this type of cooperation, for instance, between the departments of foreign affairs, defence, and cyber. This will assist states to better organise their actions regarding cyber threats while exchanging information in order to minimise the likelihood of escalation and miscalculation. Developing expert cyber diplomacy teams that coincide with state diplomacy missions can serve to establish a coherent and seamless approach. Additionally, a more secure and stable cyber environment still relies on global collaboration. The establishing of legally binding norms and regulations that regulate state activity in cyberspace is of paramount importance in order to minimise the possibility of disagreement and confusion. Multilateral discourse has to be maintained within the framework of the UN and other international bodies for the purpose to achieve this. With the goal to promote trust between possibly adversarial parties, transparency regulations encompass measures undertaken to enhance information exchange and reduce the chances of aggravation. In order to carry out capacity-building efforts, it is important to help nations that are developing to enhance their cyber security measures; while also lowering the risk of cyber threats, global partnership becomes necessary.

A substantial amount of thoughtful coordination of cyber capabilities with traditional diplomacy and international law is required for comprehending how to construct multifaceted approaches that incorporate cyber operations into overall foreign policy goals without unexpected repercussions and constructive associations on the functional fields of international relations. In order to establish a more secure cyberspace, strong cyber diplomacy needs to find a balance between clearly defined national strategies, efficient methods of communication, and global collaboration. This may be more than just a technological advances challenge; it could indicate an important shift in how international relations are carried out.

Cyber diplomacy can be an invaluable tool and will likely continue to be so in the years to come, but only if such approaches are periodically assessed for appropriateness and altered according to the cyclical advancement of cyber capabilities and the growing interdependence of cyberspace. If cyber diplomacy is not properly incorporated into global strategy, it could worsen conflicts, undermine global equilibrium, and make it more challenging for states to accomplish their foreign policy objectives. For this explanation, the near future is growing ever more digital, and the most effective means to boost broader cyber security is to begin thinking about cyber diplomacy broadly and constructively.

As the digital realm and cyberspaces availability expand, this approach should be ongoing and updated continuously to keep cyber diplomacy an appropriate and effective instrument of 21st century diplomacy with the objective of fostering security, peace, and cooperation across borders. When a cyber diplomacy approach is carried out inadequately, it merely serves to breed hostility and disrupt the international system, making it more difficult for countries to successfully achieve their foreign policy objectives. Consequently, in order to maintain a secure and flourishing tomorrow for the rapidly digitalised world, extensive and proactive cyber diplomacy actions are now demanded.

On top of that, the area is rapidly transitioning from being thought of as an open and uncontested sphere to an arena of strategic competition. To be able to station satellites for commercial, military, and scientific purposes, countries have made huge investments in space-based capacities. On the contrary hand, cyber attacks constitute an important danger to this development of space assets. Satellites, which are the basis of many essential infrastructure systems, are the primary objective of these cyber threats, which additionally encompass denial of service attacks, hacking, and even cyber-enabled sabotage that result in physical harm. From global positioning systems (GPS) and communications networks to weather forecasting and financial transactions, an effective cyber attack on a space-based system might have devastating consequences.

Due to the inherent interconnectedness of present-day infrastructure (such as communications, transportation, and banking), any glitch in a single field can have a detrimental impact on other sectors, leading to massive pandemonium and considerable financial damage. Consider the weaknesses of GPS systems. These systems, which are dependent upon a set of satellites, serve as crucial for timing, synchrony, and navigation in many different kinds of fields, notably banking, maritime transportation, and aviation. A comprehensive cyber attack that interferes with or even spoofs GPS signals might result in multiple collisions, navigational oversights, and monetary damage. Attacks on communications satellites have the capacity of disrupting vital communication networks, affecting emergency services, banking institutions, and commerce around the world. If prolonged outages bring essential facilities to a slow down there can be over time impacts on society and the economy alongside those that occur immediately.

When the militarys reliance on space-based capabilities increases, so does the possibility of safety concerns. Military satellites provide critical communications, intelligence, surveillance, and reconnaissance (ISR) operations. Thus, the ability to respond appropriately to cyber attacks on space-based infrastructure forms an element of national security. A concentrated approach to cyber diplomacy needs to be developed because of the special challenges caused by the space industry. It requires an effort to create certain standards, frameworks, and methods for dispute resolution due to the substantial distances, complications of attribution, and the likelihood of swift build-up. The dire situation is exacerbated by the dearth of a robust global legal framework that governs space activity. Even while the 1967 Outer Space Treaty was a breakthrough agreement, it lacks the level of detail required for dealing with the varied nature of cyber threats in the space domain. Still, the framework fails to sufficiently address international law because it makes inadequate mention of cyber attacks. The existence of ambiguity fosters uncertainty, promotes miscommunication, and amplifies the probability of confrontation.

States have to vigorously pursue space-focused cyber diplomacy with the objective to mitigate these risks. This requires encouraging communication, adopting laws, which increase confidence, and setting international guidelines for suitable conduct. Developing early warning systems about cyber threats attacking space interests will call for coordination. A terrific approach of strengthening this groups competence for identifying and responding to threats is working together and exchanging information, which reduces chances of misunderstandings and intensification. Developing technical ways for safeguarding against cyber threats in space-based systems necessitates collaboration between nations.

To be able to cope with cyber attacks perpetrated from space, international legal structures are additionally going to be established. Specific requirements for appropriate state conduct, such as the restriction on offensive cyber attacks against space resources, should be included in such a framework. Precise attribution techniques along with effective dispute resolution procedures are additionally necessary for the purpose to decrease the potential of ambiguities and aggravation. In reality, conflict is made feasible by the dearth of explicit rules regulating the implementation of cyber power in space. The formulation of global agreements and norms ought to encourage openness concerning space operations alongside prohibiting hostile cyber attacks. To foster shared comprehension and reduce the likelihood of confusion, states ought to be urged to offer information on their space capabilities. Building mutual respect and confidence between countries is necessary for implementing space policy into practice in order to encourage the building of a more secure and peaceful space environment.

Thereby, including cyber diplomacy into space policy requires a holistic strategy. One of the domains in which they must collaborate to form national policies is the safeguarding of space assets itself; another involves collaborating with global bodies to construct mechanisms for dispute resolution and promote appropriate space engagement. In order to assist developing countries protect their space facilities and decrease the international cyber security attack surface, states ought to promote efforts to build capacities. Understanding of the security consequences associated with space-based abilities and the importance of cyber diplomacy in minimising risks must be emphasised through educational efforts. Technical experts, policymakers, and diplomats must be trained in the nuances of cyberspace and space-based systems in order to make sound decisions and organise the global cooperation needed to establish this new sector. Future politicians and diplomats will be more effectively capable of addressing the more complex problems in this critical arena due to educational efforts that highlight cyber diplomacy in the space domain. As a consequence, to effectively integrate cyber diplomacy into the space domain, one should fundamentally analyse the point of view and approach needed in this critically important field. The space setting and the terrestrial cyber environment are closely linked, and conflicts in one stage have a ripple effect on others. Companies and nations must engage actively and jointly in establishing precise standards, even inclusive procedures, and efficient constitutional frameworks, in order to ensure a secure and foreseeable space future. By promoting the militarisation of a hazardous space domain, failure to act puts at risk international security and stability. For every nation to have a secure and economically viable future, competent cyber diplomacy in the space sector is vitally crucial. Agreements between nations may be undermined, conflicts may come to pass, and wars that ruthlessly devour more than the atmosphere of Earth could break out if this difficulty is not properly addressed.

The deployment of military cyber strategies will change the essence of disputes and entail the establishment of novel approaches for preserving peace and security worldwide. A new form of conflict is cyber warfare. (Contrary to traditional battle, internet conflict occurs in virtual space with previously unprecedented speed and scale, without clinging to borders of geography, deferring physical strength and engagement.) Without any real troops or weapon deployment, a single successful hack has an opportunity to demolish vital infrastructure, alter whole economies, and even inflict fatalities.

Nevertheless, the fundamental concepts of cyber warfare are inherently at variance with our traditional approaches to settling disagreements. It is difficult to figure out with precision on who is accountable for an attack because attribution is extremely challenging in cyberspace. Still, this type of uncertainty may give rise to nations interpreting the cause of an attack and responding effectively, thereby raising the possibility of unanticipated escalated situations, inadequate thinking about strategy, and even a conflict between states. A constantly evolving and pre-emptive approach to developing cyber security solutions must be taken since the frequency and rapidity of cyber attacks currently are too tremendous for conventional defence systems founded on a prehistoric perspective. This is the third aspect of the equation.

Taking into account the blurred boundaries between state and non-state actors makes matters more complicated. While state-sponsored cyber attacks are a major concern, there are also chances of cyber attacks by non-state actors, such as terrorist and criminal organisations. It is very difficult to keep a watch on them, ensure that they cease to exist and respond to the actions of these actors because of the obscurity of cyberspace and their dispersed architecture. As cyber security is complicated we must not only create channels for communicating intelligence but we must additionally work together with nations around the world in creating regulatory structures that will dissuade and combat cybercrime. Instances of violence on the cyber frontier are one of the key concerns. The conflict can quickly transform from a comparatively minor cyber attack to a counter-attack. Since systems are intrinsically linked together, the detonation of a particular system may quickly propagate throughout the same infrastructure, generating mayhem and upheaval. In fact, it is primarily the likelihood of accumulating impacts that highlights the significance of de-escalation and control measures in cyberspace. Setting standards for appropriate government conduct in cyberspace is a prerequisite to preventing inadvertent or deliberate escalation.

Cyber warfare involves more than the militarys objectives. Critical national infrastructure, such as transportation networks, banking institutions and power grids, are becoming increasingly vulnerable to cyber attacks. An attack against these systems, if effective, would have orders of magnitude leading to a higher impact on society and the economy and casualties that dwarf those of a typical military operation. Adequate cyber security is becoming increasingly crucial both domestically and internationally, as demonstrated by the likely outcome of broad disarray and instability. If countries are to mitigate the potential hazards of cyber warfare, international diplomacy is essential. Error and significant uncertainty become more prevalent when there is no defined global legal framework regulating the implementation of cyber capabilities in conflicts between nations. New rules and standards should be developed for regulating state activity in cyberspace due to the distinctive hazards of cyber warfare that are so unusual in present-day global humanitarian law and are either entirely inept at tackling them or inadequately competent in doing so. This demands global collaboration as well as a preparedness to come to an accord amongst nations that have distinct cyber security capabilities and goals.

Yet, decreasing the probability of cyber warfare necessitates the establishment of CBMs. In broad terms, government CBMs could encompass communication, teamwork, and information exchange in order to promote confidence and mutual comprehension. These types of activities enable improved openness, cyber security operations and aid, and prevent errors and misunderstandings. Nevertheless, for such CBMs to be effective, governments have to be willing to participate in serious discussions and comply with the established regulations. Subsequently, if states are to be held responsible for offensive cyber behaviour, appropriate attribution instruments must be developed. Nevertheless, it is widely difficult to assign responsibility for cyber attacks because cyberspace has distributed components and hackers implement highly sophisticated tactics. Despite the challenges, strengthening attribution capacity, strengthening the inhibitory impact on cyber attacks, and expediting the accountability of illegal cyber activities all rely upon global collaboration. Obtaining it through partnership between countries with greater capacity, intelligence, communication, and the growth of knowledge in technology is both desirable and necessary.

Since cyber conflict hinders worldwide peace and stability, the UN ought to keep playing an instrumental part in encouraging global collaboration and establishing a common ground on cyber security regulations, decreasing the potential hazards brought about by cyber conflict, and enabling the establishment of a peaceful and solid cyberspace where all people can take advantage of it with integrity and stability. However, for the UN to achieve its objectives in addressing this issue, member-states must be ready to work together with the UN in establishing global standards, as well as the legal framework and concepts that the UN provides; establishing national policies for cyber defence of critical infrastructure and preventing cyber threats. These comprise both offensive (counter-attack) and defensive tactics such as constructing defences to mitigate attack severity.

Moreover, there is a need to formulate national cyber security strategies aligned with international norms and rules, which restrict state action in cyberspace and foster a more peaceful international environment. It is a fast moving, high-stakes field with diplomacy, cyber warfare and military strategy all in play. In the light of the current lack of clear international norms and the challenges associated with attribution, this raises an elemental question regarding global security. State-sponsored cyber attacks by unconventional state actors threaten the stability, security and peace of the world system. To ensure a secure and peaceful cyber environment, this situation calls for international cooperation, confidence-building measures (CBMs), meaningful attribution and a global legal framework.

In a bid to move freely without anxiety regarding corruption or cybercrime, a careful balance of contending national interests conceals actors who are threatening us with safety and partnership in the path of our unblinking sight. States are required and ought to rethink their viewpoint on security, transitioning from one-dimensional nationalist in nature to largely multicultural circumstances to global in scope, collaborative approaches in the area of cyber security. Such an action plan is the only means to safeguard equilibrium of global climate and prevent an imminent build-up of cyber warfare. The capacity of states to successfully tackle these issues through a meticulously planned and hostile cyber diplomacy agenda will influence the trajectory of international security. In turn, this demands a commitment to the kind of accessibility that encourages confidence and a common comprehension of appropriate state conduct in cyberspace, both of which contribute to predictability and equilibrium in the international framework. Failing to do so could bring about an era when the digital world evolves into an ever-present battlefield, threatening the safety and security of the world.

As was pointed out in the sections earlier, cyber diplomacy provides both substantial possibilities and challenges for an array of fields, from the more thoroughly intertwined realm of international relations to those related to space and military operations. Following that, its essential to concentrate on education, which is the fundamental component required to thrive in this digital age. The continued growth of the cyber ecosystem is contingent upon an overwhelming agreement on appropriate cyber behaviour in conjunction with cyber diplomacy, advanced technological abilities, and an explicit framework of globally binding rules. This includes a particular emphasis on technological proficiency and cyber security understanding, both nationally and internationally. Education affects the way individuals think and their interactions with this digital ecology in an abundance of aspects. Digital literacy provides citizens the understanding and resources that they require to effectively use the digital realm as individual actors in an efficient and productive way. This encompasses safeguarding ones own sensitive information, detecting phishing attempts, and being mindful of fundamental Internet security. People must be able to safeguard themselves against cyber attacks if a country is to be less susceptible overall. This is how an entire nation can be safe online. Nevertheless, the underlying theme in national cyber security will be complete safeguarding at the level of the individual. In furtherance of safeguarding individuals, understanding technology enhances the countrys cyber security standing. By enabling the quicker identification and reporting of cyber threats, digital literacy additionally assists in helping people become better prepared. This is an essential advantage for systems for early warning and rapid reaction measures. This general comprehension lessens the detrimental impacts of cyber attacks and enables rapid recovery. It suggests that the wider population is less vulnerable to misinformation attempts and other measures that hinder online interaction. Any national cybersecurity strategys effectiveness depends heavily on the populations level of technological understanding. Indeed, a digital nation cannot tackle its national security problems within the same digital realm until its citizens have the requisite skills, expertise, and determination.

Education in the general training of security personnel is just as pertinent as individual safety. Recruiting appropriate cyber safety professionals is becoming increasingly important in the constantly developing digital marketplace. The next generation of cyber defenders will continue to be taught in schools with the technical expertise, capacity for critical thinking, and ethical awareness needed to effectively navigate the complicated terrain of cyberspace. Additionally, such experts are required for both national defence and global cyber security collaboration. As a result of the modifications made in the geopolitical scenario, a balancing education must be provided in both technical knowledge and strategic perspective. Teaching striving diplomats is an additionally likewise significant task. Diplomats need specialised instructions on cyber issues as cyberspace becomes increasingly pertinent to global affairs. With knowledge of how to understand and navigate the complicated nature of cyber diplomacy, they should be ready to represent their countries at global forums and discussions. In addition to the technical facets of cyber security, they need to understand its political effects. This requires one to be aware of the global treaties, conventions, and laws pertaining to cyberspace as well as the strategic goals of different governments. The global collaborative frameworks must be established in the training as the most efficient way to deal with the issues surrounding cyber security and develop the capacity to work together and come up with mutually beneficial solutions.

Nevertheless, the function of regional and international organizations including the UN is essential in increasing understanding and education on cyber security. Their position to set global standards, exchange information and assist capacity-building for developing nations is paramount to making cyberspace protected and long-lasting. Other actions include UN cyber security understanding, training and capacity-building activities that are crucial enablers for governments to construct strong national cyber security strategies. Those measures should be maintained and scaled globally. Curriculum formulation is also one of the greatest influences that will set the future of cyber security education. But cyber security, and technological ability, should correspondingly include geopolitical ramifications, legal frameworks and ethical matters. Incorporating and adding all these numerous factors jointly guarantees students will come away with a comprehensive knowledge of cyber security and its position in international relations. Moreover, the curricula are required to be active and responsive to the rapidly transforming technology setting. Awareness campaigns are important in raising understanding of cyber security along with formal instruction. This might remind people of their accountability for their online conduct, educate them on curricular cyber threats, and provide safe navigating recommendations. For this reason, outreach efforts can be set up and carried out by governments, businesses, and non-profit organisations to reach a broad demographic. These campaigns have to be tailored for each audience because every target has unique requirements and limitations.

Yet, there are still impediments in the path of advancing significant digital literacy and cyber security knowledge. Another significant problem is the technological gap, which hinders access to scientific information and resources in a world that has become more and more centred on the realm of virtual reality. In spite of providing affordable Internet access and educating digital literacy, narrowing the digital divide requires expenditures in infrastructure and global cooperation. The rapid pace at how quickly technology is evolving is another challenge, as training strategies and the curriculum must be altered periodically to take into consideration emerging hazards and breakthroughs. While doing so, it will also make an important contribution to national security, which is where cyber security advancement is an important objective for national educational initiatives in the years to come. In order to enhance the nations comprehensive cyber security stance through raising awareness and digital competence, cyber security organisations, education ministries, and other appropriate parties need to create an integrated strategy. For the global battle against cybercrime to promote cooperation and seamless integration, national plans should be in accordance with global norms and guidelines. In order to improve subsequent efforts, it is imperative to determine the impact of awareness-raising and education efforts.

This requires the development of accurate measurements along with assessment techniques that can be implemented to assess how outreach efforts and educational campaigns impact cyber security and digital proficiency levels. The findings drawn from these evaluations ought to provide direction for future strategy and execution initiatives. In a nutshell, technical training is essential for national and international activities; however, it must be put in the framework of a society of appropriate cyber usage and collaboration in order to combat cyber threats internationally. Creating a more secure and safe digital future for everyone demands this comprehensive and inclusive strategy. It is now crucial to understand the complex interconnections between cyber diplomacy, technology, and the global economy, an intersection of heretofore-unimaginable complexities and effects. Virtually every element of the international economy, most importantly trade, finance and business, rests on an immense network of undersea cables, which possess a primal relationship with information technology. Nevertheless, there is a further danger associated with this reliance; it opens economic systems to various dangers that might cause catastrophic consequences. In order to promote financial stability and advancement, nevertheless, an innovative collaborative effort in the realm of cyber diplomacy needs to be undertaken because this is a flowing stream with extensive and rapidly changing potential hazards.

From sophisticated systems, which facilitate cross-border financial transfers to complicated supply chains that regulate the transportation of goods and services, contemporary economic activity is heavily dependent on integrated digital systems. The prevailing marketplaces fundamental component, e-commerce, relies completely on secure digital infrastructure. As a consequence, the ongoing exchange of financial data that facilitates both private and institutional commerce is subject to strong cyber security specifications.

As digital technologies become increasingly integrated into their operations, even standard sectors are becoming more vulnerable to cyber attacks. A disruption to these digital networks has an opportunity to cripple entire industries and undermine national economies.

There are numerous risks in this networked digital space. Cyber attacks aimed at essential infrastructure such power grids, transportation networks, and communication systems, can have an enormous effect on the global economy. Production ceases to exist, supply chain delays, along with substantial financial losses, can result from the disruption of these systems. For example, a cyber attack on a major port might hinder international shipping lines that affect sectors of the economy that are dependent on timely commodities deliveries. Furthermore, shortages, increases in prices, and widespread financial instability might ensue from this. This complexity of cyber attacks poses a risk to the financial sector. Cyber criminals continually devise new ways to bypass security measures, procure sensitive information, and disrupt financial activity. Such attacks target individuals, businesses, and even central banks and pose a risk to financial stability and undermine confidence in global financial institutions. Because cyber attacks on the national financial infrastructure might affect the monetary policy of a nation or the overall state of its economy, they can have especially significant consequences. The pace and extent of the harm these attacks inflict may be too much for even the strongest national response strategies to cope with. Thus, international cooperation is crucial because of this particular reason.

Leaking of information is an important worry regarding financial fragility in the age of technology. Personal or commercial information when stolen can cause the victim millions in financial loss, reputational destruction, or even criminal penalties. While individuals could become vulnerable to identity or financial theft, businesses could encounter customer attrition, losing an edge over competitors, and high dispute resolution and cleaning expenses. Many instances of the serious consequences that massive amounts of data breaches can have on multiple sectors show that the monetary consequences of data breaches go well beyond the breachs targeted victim. Remediation from such breaches is very costly and, more importantly, impacts the confidence of investors, investment choices and, consequently, future growth of the economy.

Theft or cyber espionage of the trade s private information, intellectual property, and private company data of competitors is a serious threat to the economy during a time of global competitiveness in the marketplace. Such theft can be devastating to an organization financially; it disrupts the ability to compete, and hampers innovation. Of course, the economic impact of industrial espionage can be quite evident, repressing economic growth but no doubt also calling into question the global financial structure and power groupings. Active cyber diplomacy is also needed to counter such nefarious activities, and international treaties and conventions need to be in place to ensure prevention and governance of such acts. Nations must work together to mitigate these risks and safeguard the global economy. For routing regulations, disseminating best practices, and effectively coordinating responses to its existence, cyber diplomacy offers a crucial foundation. This calls for an integrated strategy from governments, business sector players, organisations around the world, and civil society. To ensure that different systems are able to collaborate and that data can be sent securely between them, it is essential that international regulations and processes for cyber security be developed. This will act as the foundation for a secure international digital ecosystem. By establishing incident response procedures, nations can effectively respond to cyber attacks that will assist in preventing these kinds of incidents from becoming greater and from having detrimental consequences.

The UN and other international organisations play an essential function in advancing global standards and collaboration in cyberspace. These can indeed make a difference, at least in the short term, if only individual nation-states are willing to cooperate and abide by existing regulations. To protect against malicious cybercrimes and pave the way for a more secure world, there must be a clear legal framework that leads to state accountability for actions undertaken in cyberspace. However, without global cooperation, cyber warfare could escalate in both retaliation and targeting of major infrastructures, with the potential to affect the world economy negatively. Protracted political and social divisions may be deepened by the resulting upheaval in the economy, creating a climate of uncertainty and instability. In furtherance of strengthening cyber security, investments in cyber diplomacy also help promote global stability and sustainable development.

Consequently, there are multiple obstacles in the path of anyone seeking to establish effective cyber diplomacy. The varied character of cyberspace, which is made up of many actors and overlapping law enforcement, hinders the development of consistent norms and standards. Furthermore, competing national agendas and interests frequently hinder understanding and productive international agreements. A flexible and adaptable strategy to cyber diplomacy must be adopted due to the cases increasing complexity and the rapid pace at which technology is evolving. However, the challenges involved in establishing effective mechanisms for international cyber cooperation are significantly outweighed by the potential drawbacks of doing something. Key components that would increase the effectiveness of cyber diplomacy in addressing economic vulnerabilities can be given more attention in the future. First, we must strengthen international legal frameworks with clear expectations around the behaviour of authorities in cyberspace and effective accountability mechanisms. Second, its members also need to improve their cooperation and exchange of information to build trust and enable a better-coordinated response to cyber threats. Third, any agreement that supports developing nations in improving their cyber security capabilities while actively engaging in international cooperation initiatives has to involve capacity building. Last, but not least, because public-private partnerships (PPP) leverage the expertise of both sectors to address worldwide issues in this sector, they can be highly significant for enhancing cyber security.

Considering that the new economy relies progressively more on elusive information technology, the entire world is susceptible to cyber threats, requiring the need for steadfast cyber diplomacy. The cyber economy and its operators will therefore be defined in the near future by a collaborative process, which includes cooperation between governments, intergovernmental organisations and business. This kind of international cooperation, establishment of comprehensive norms and promotion of capacity building can mitigate the threats posed by cyber attacks and provide a safe and sustainable digital environment. How effectively cyber diplomacy functions is intrinsically linked to the global economys continued stability.

Chapter Three

Beyond the Algorithm: Ethical Frameworks for Protecting Human Rights in Cyberspace

The previous discussion highlighted the important connection between economic security, cyber security, and the need for collaborative international solutions. Yet, utilising cyber capabilities, even for defence, presents significant ethical dilemmas that should be carefully thought through. The following part explores the ethical frameworks necessary for governing state conduct in cyberspace, recognising the difficulties of establishing widely accepted norms in an area that is shifting rapidly. There is an outstanding opportunity for escalation and poor decision-making in the absence of clearly defined standards of conduct, which might certainly represent significant hazards and jeopardise global peace and security.

The ambiguity surrounding proportionality is the greatest obstacle in setting ethical standards for cyber operations. In practice, proportionality in the usage of force is regulated by generally accepted internationally recognised laws and is remarkably simple. This evaluation is made more challenging by the Internets illusive character. It is even more difficult than judging the proportionality of a conventional military response to decide on an appropriate response to a cyber attack. Estimating how often and how bad a cyber attack is likely to be is difficult because it involves factoring in not only the immediate impact of a given operation, but also any potential knock-on effect. An action that seems acceptable in and of it may have disproportionate, unanticipated consequences when examined in the wider context of a strategic setting. The dearth of measures for assessing the degree of severity of a cyber attack makes this assessment challenging. For this explanation, novel approaches to determine the relative importance of cyber measures must be developed, ones that take into consideration the immediate as well as long-term implications across areas.

When looked at within the context of an overall strategic environment, a move that is considered appropriate in the context of itself may have disproportionate and unanticipated implications. The dearth of reliable criteria to gauge the intensity of a cyber attack makes the decision harder to make. This requires new models for assessing the impact of cyber reactions to ensure that they are distributed equitably while considering the short- and long-term effects across a wide variety of sectors. The fact that even the best attribution systems have drawbacks highlights the importance of carefully thinking through any unintended things that could happen. Bias in cyberspace can be related to a wide disregard for ethical standards; this would be addressed through creating standards that govern cyber operations to steer clear of collateral damage and ensure that they are centred on appropriate targets for military purposes.

If examined in the context of a larger strategic environment, an action that seems judicious in isolation can have unintended and outsized effects. The absence of reliable signals to measure the severity of a cyber attack complicates the decision. This requires better methods for assessing the proportionality of cyber responses, considering both immediate and lasting impacts across several sectors. The fact that even the best attribution systems have limitations emphasizes how important it is to carefully think through any unintended consequences. Potential bias in the virtual world of cyberspace can come from an attitude of disengaged ethical relativism; the answer to this would be guidelines, which channel cyber activity away from generating negative responses, as well as help ensure that operations target appropriate military objectives.

Government cooperation and building consensus are required for effective frameworks of ethics. Due to substantial disparities in national interests, advances in technology, and viewpoints on the rules of international law, this is a difficult effort. A destabilising arms race in cyberspace might arise through misconceptions and aggravation driven by the absence of stated ethical guidelines in this interconnected world. Since they offer a platform for the purpose of discussion, compromise, and the establishment of norms that both parties may agree upon, the UN and all other international organisations serve as crucial to this approach. Nevertheless, these initiatives depend on every nations commitment to respond constructively and conform to internationally recognised norms.

Mechanisms for responsibility and implementation must also be an integral component of ethical frameworks of cyber operations. Standards of ethics remain merely aspirational in the absence of such systems. Establishing systems that are either adequately effective or respect the independence of states is difficult. This could encompass the development of international investigative organisations, reporting on events platforms, and a system of sanctions for violations of generally accepted standards. In establishing such procedures, care must be taken to avoid the possibility of misuse, to call for accountability and to guarantee suitable process.

Another beneficiary of ethical considerations of cyber operations extending beyond state actors are non-state actors made of civil society organizations, private firms, terrorist groups and criminal networks. These actors offer major barriers to global responsibility as well as cooperation and are growing increasingly susceptible to cyber attacks. The appropriate extent of participation, authority, and responsibility constitute some of the ethical issues encompassing non-state actors. Global collaboration and the development of effective platforms for halting and responding to acts of violence by non-state actors will be required for addressing these problems. Some instances of such approaches involve improving global capacity development, sharing of information, and law enforcement partnership.

In the end, establishing ethical guidelines for conduct on the web is a crucial initial step towards establishing a more stable and secure Internet community. Dealing with issues of requirement, bias, and proportional representation requires a holistic approach, which involves the establishment of precise norms, strong accountability infrastructure, and multilateral cooperation. Without these structures, cyber warfare might spiral out of hand and have unexpected, possibly disastrous consequences.

Governments, international organisations, and civil society have to collaborate together in order to tackle these challenging moral problems while promoting ethical conduct in the world of technology. For the advancement of diplomatic interactions in cyberspace, instruments for developing and implementing these rules of conduct into operation must be efficient. The progress of modern technology calls for an adaptable approach that enables continual modification and improvement of regulations associated with issues of ethics. This process of continual modification means that rules of ethics remain relevant and productive in the ever-evolving landscape of cyber operations. To address the risk of cyber war and build a safer, more stable international order, it should be recognized that we are in such a long-term endeavour.

Standards regulating government conduct in cyberspace are essential, as was discussed in the earlier part. Nevertheless, relationships between states are solely one component of the ethical issues. In order to address ever more complicated cyber attacks, which have obvious consequences on individuals and communities, safeguarding human rights, is crucial. Violations of human rights in space are increasing in frequency, regardless of the fact that digital technology offers previously unattainable chances for development and interaction. This requires swift action and robust security measures. In addition to the rapid nature and confidentiality of cyberspace, perpetrators tend to be resistant to punishment, making responsibility challenging and putting both individuals and organisations at risk.

Individuals may be targets of attacks via the Internet, which result in fairly grave violations of privacy or serious infractions that cause significant damage. For instance, theft of identity leads to financial loss, and harm to ones reputation may ensue from the theft of sensitive data. These kinds of assaults could impact individual ability to obtain employment, medical care, and other basic needs, which have far-reaching effects. The disclosure of sensitive data can additionally result in more serious attacks, such as assault with intent, extortion, or harassment. These violations could result in severe psychological effects that range from anxiety and depression to a decrease in faith in technology. Full safeguarding remains vital as children and young people are increasingly vulnerable to harassment online, abuse and grooming. Its this absence of identification that allowed predators to target more vulnerable people, with disastrous consequences for their mental and physical health. A lack of effective means to pursue and apprehend those responsible is part of the reason for the increased demand for international cooperation and the strengthening of legal frameworks.

Focusing on specific populations, which include media professionals, political dissidents, or individuals of any ethnic or religious minority, offers unique challenges, nevertheless. Cyber attacks have the capacity to undermine cohesiveness in society, cause resentment, and circulate misleading information. For instance, the widespread dissemination of photo-shopped photographs and fabricated articles can incite phobias and xenophobia leading to actual physical assault against those being targeted. These kinds of assaults have the capacity to shake up entire populations, contribute to already-existing disputes, and deteriorate the confidence in institutions. The leveraging of advanced hacking and surveillance innovations to zero in on human rights defenders obstructs their right to freedom of speech and association, while assaults like denial-of-service that interfere with essential services can impact the capacity of the general public to gain access to assets and fulfil their most essential rights. The surveillance of these journalists and activists by cyber espionage also constitutes a severe infringement on freedom of expression and fundamental human rights. Considering the interdependent nature of the digital realm, cyber attacks have far-reaching consequences. Such disinformation attacks stand a chance of eroding citizen confidence in voting, polling and democracy itself. Attacks on critical infrastructure, like health-care centres or electric power lines, can lead to catastrophic impacts that can traumatise entire communities while placing lives at risk. The digital divide or the technological gap leaves some parts of the population more vulnerable than others, particularly those who lack access to technology and have low levels of digital literacy. Given that they lack the ability to defend themselves or to pursue damages, these individuals tend to become the disproportionate ones of cyber attacks. In order to ensure that all individuals receive equal safeguards against infringements on rights of humanity, which the Internet allows for, the technological gap must be closed.

This calls for a broadened analysis encompassing legal frameworks, programs for learning, innovations in technology, and additional information. In actuality, there is an element for safeguarding global human rights laws, however it must be constantly updated and altered in order to account for the distinctive features of cyberspace. Recognising and using present regulations and agreements will be essential, as global cyberspace grows increasingly complex in its daily activities. This will assist in understanding how cyber activity influences more conventional violations of human rights of confidentiality, freedom of expression and life. The creation and subsequent execution of international agreements and guidelines aimed at fighting cybercrime and safeguarding human rights in cyberspace demand collaboration as well as coordination between states, global organisations, and members of civil society. In order to encourage the responsibility and hinder subsequent violations, effective mechanisms for looking into and pursuing criminals ought to be set up. Cross-border cyber attacks produce jurisdictional difficulties and call for collaboration across borders in order to plan legal action, share intelligence, or collect documentary proof.

To be able to mitigate the consequences of attacks via the Internet, advances in technology are also crucial. Greater precautions for safety, like robust encryption and digital safety methods, may decrease an individuals or a companys risk preferences. To detect attacks via the Internet and allow immediate prevention and action responses, systems for early warning ought to be generated and carried out. The algorithms for machine learning (ML) and artificial intelligence (AI) can also be used to recognise and prevent the spread of fabricated data. They may additionally draw attention to fabricated media reports along with content that may have been manipulated. But technological advances have to be used ethically, protecting the confidentiality of individuals and preventing unforeseen consequences. In order to make sure technological safeguards are efficient and do not adversely affect the freedom of expression or other fundamental liberties, they ought to be continually assessed and assessed.

For efforts to protect people and their communities from online-facilitated human rights violations, education is crucial. Comprehensive programs for digital literacy provide individuals the understanding and skills required to protect themselves with a single click. This involves telling individuals about widespread risks that include malware, phishing schemes, and disinformation campaigns along with providing recommendations on how to protect themselves effectively via the Internet. Education may additionally be an effective instrument to foster analytical thinking and ethical conduct on the Internet. People require having the capacity to differentiate reality from fiction in order to safeguard themselves from the manipulative and fixated elements, which frequently accompany cyber attacks.

For the purpose of fostering a more educated and safer Internet population and to balance the power movement between technological companies and people in general, it is crucial that we integrate cyber-safety education into community initiatives and educational institutions. The consequences on human rights and the transnational nature of cyber attacks demand global collaboration. To be able to establish regulations, coordinate responses, and aid in dialogue, the UN and other global organisations are essential. Effective structures for global collaboration between law enforcement agencies, intelligence, and legal institutions must be put into effect in order to prevent cybercrime that puts people in danger and violates their rights. The first step in empowering people to stand up for their individual freedoms and rights in the age of technology and encouraging a more watchful and secure technological society is by integrating cyber-safety education with social gatherings and educational institutions. The transnational character of cyber attacks and their effect on human rights necessitate international cooperation. The UN and other international organisations are essential for establishing standards, coordinating responses, and facilitating communication more than for their actual capabilities. Effective systems of international cooperation in law enforcement, intelligence sharing, and judicial cooperation must be established in order to combat cybercrime and defend human rights. Given that cyber attacks and technology are constantly evolving, it creates an advantageous spotlight on the establishment of a flexible and adaptable plan for preserving human rights in the realm of technology. The best way to stop new threats is to improve up-to-date defences and come up with innovative concepts. In order to ensure a safe and secure online environment for all, the worldwide community ought to continue to be vigilant and actively engage in protecting both individuals and organisations against the increasing dangers of violations of human rights made possible by technological advances. The sections above placed emphasis on the numerous ways in which cyberspace allows human rights violations and the susceptibility of both individuals and organisations to such infractions. That is just a single component of this vulnerability, which also encompasses the complicated connection between the right to free speech and ever-more-advanced methods of restricting dissent and regulating data available on the Internet.

Once a tool that ensured a freely accessible communication between individuals, the internet has since become a tightly regulated, controlled private tool for communication. To attempt to regulate data stored on the Internet, governments employ several kinds of tactics. They encompass more discreet censorship techniques like specific search term blocking or search engine result tampering, in addition to more explicit restrictions on specific internet pages and social networking platforms. Attacks like these frequently affect reporters, human rights supporters, dissenters, and minorities who voice opinions that are critical of the administration or its decisions. Enforcing those restriction strategies can be challenging due to the anonymous nature and reach of the web, developing an unending game of rivalry between those who would like to regulate data and those who attempt to bypass the limitations. Online expression is made more challenging by the use of highly sophisticated technologies for surveillance. Governments and business organisations rely on sophisticated techniques to track variations of the online conduct of individuals, investigate online correspondence, and obtain an enormous amount of personal data. Free speech may be suppressed by this kind of oversight as individuals might be discouraged from communicating their views online by the possibility of retaliation recognizing and targeting a person for intimidation, harassment, or even imprisonment which can also be achieved by gathering information and evaluation. With the rapid development of these surveillance devices, individuals now mostly have difficulty to safeguard their personal information and exercise their fundamental right to free speech without being concerned about being monitored.

Non-state actors additionally contribute an important part in restricting internet freedom of expression along with governmental actors. Dissident voices can be dismissed and the exchange of information halted by cyber attacks aimed at news organisations, online communication platforms and other online platforms. From simple denial-of-service (DoS) attacks that overload internet pages and make them ineffective to advanced hacking operations resulting in theft of information, content alterations, or even failures in the system, these kinds of attacks cover an extensive spectrum. By encouraging an environment of fear as well as self-censorship with such incidents may suppress the freedom of speech. Moreover, it can be tough to track and hold non-state actors responsible for their freedoms and actions due to the degree of anonymity that the world of internet offers. The right to free speech is seriously jeopardised by propaganda on the internet and disinformation. The swift dissemination of incorrect, deceptive, or inaccurate data online has rendered it more accessible for unethical behaviour and manipulation to take place, and also for trust among individuals to be undermined. Full safeguarding remains vital as children and young people are increasingly vulnerable to harassment online, abuse and grooming. Its this absence of identification that allowed predators to target more vulnerable people, with disastrous consequences for their mental and physical health. A lack of effective means to pursue and apprehend those responsible is part of the reason for the increased demand for international cooperation and the strengthening of legal frameworks.

Cyberspace regulations concerning freedom of expression continue to be scattered and often fall short of dealing with the challenges of todays technological world. Due to many up-to-date regulatory structures having been developed for offline situations, they are unequipped for dealing with the distinctive features associated with digital life. Given that national regulations and laws vary significantly, the global character of cyberspace that provides the legal framework is increasingly becoming complicated. This makes it harder to hold perpetrators accountable for the infringements of worldwide freedom of expression. In order to ensure that the fundamental right to free speech remains adequately protected in cyberspace, explicit, legally enforceable global agreements and guidelines must be set up. In order to protect the fundamental right to free speech online, we need to employ a holistic approach. Reducing the risks to free expression can be greatly supported by innovations in technology. Better cyber security protections and instruments for detecting and countering fraudulent data are two instances. However, effective implementation of these technological advances is essential for safeguarding peoples right to confidentiality while avoiding unanticipated consequences. Cross-border authority, the lack of non-state actor responsibility, and safeguards for whistle blowers are only a few of the problems that have rendered the law at times undoubtedly outdated in todays world. Global collaboration is required for everything from defining consistent guidelines and requirements to overseeing measures of enforcement and sharing strategies that work.

To be able to allow people to effectively understand the complicated data terrain and distinguish reliable sources from misleading data, it is also essential to cultivate analytical skills in media literacy. Students may acquire knowledge from educational initiatives on how to recognise inaccurate data, how to critically assess the data that they come across online, and how to behave effectively as they utilise online resources. The most important factor to ensuring access to reliable and goal information is diverse media, which is solely accomplished through promoting ethical journalism while guaranteeing the continued existence of autonomous media consumption. For the purpose to continue keeping a tab on online restrictions, defend those who face persecution for their views, and encourage freedom of expression, organisations representing civil society are crucial.

In the present world around us, where information is fed into a machine until it gets to a peak and the Internet eventually finds itself at the crossroads, this struggle has become so prevalent. A comprehensive and sophisticated examination needs to be conducted given the intersection of shifting political backdrops, advancements in technology, and the fundamental complexity of the digital realm. Maintaining equilibrium between the legitimate goals of states in adhering to order and security and the fundamental entitlement to freedom of speech calls for steady discussion, creative approaches, and an ongoing commitment to safeguarding human rights in the age of technology. The freedom of expression in cyberspace ultimately relies on governments, global organisations, non-profit institutions, and technology firms coming together in order to establish a more open, secure, and equitable online environment for all people.

Yet, the widespread nature of surveillance, the decline of privacy, and the shortcoming of data security have significantly influenced the digital worlds aesthetic and human rights domains. The problems at hand are not merely related to technology; they are essential for both diplomatic relationships and cyber diplomacy, and they deserve thoughtful investigation and collaborative approaches. In the age of technology, surveillance throughout all of its indicators has become crucial. Governments are increasingly deploying advanced technologies to track movements of individuals, observe Internet activity, and gather information about their citizens as an outcome of growing concerns about national security and regulation. The tangents of this include facial recognition technology deployed in public places, the analysis of social networking data to spot future risks, and extensive surveillance applications. There are still worries about potential violations and infringement of fundamental liberties, but some believe this sort of public scrutiny is essential in stopping criminal activity, terrorist activity, and other threats. Several programs for surveillance are not properly regulated, which increases major issues about the responsibility and likelihood of unrestricted authority by the government. Monitoring involves the collection and evaluation of private data. Intentional or not, data breaches are a near certainty, threatening the privacy and security of individuals. A marketplace for highly confidential information has been established by the growth of data brokers and the relatively simple nature of which sensitive data can be obtained and shared online, leaving individuals exposed to fraud, identity theft, and other different kinds of abuse. The scenario is made more severe in numerous countries by an absence of robust information security rules and laws, which demonstrates to citizens the improper use of their sensitive information. Global collaboration is necessary to promote the movement of data across borders and assure consistent protection of information guidelines.

The notion of privacy is being rethought as a consequence of a movement regarding privacy in the age of the internet. Conventional notions regarding confidentiality are severely questioned by the widespread collection and analysis of private information by corporations, government, and other organisations. The accessibility with which individual browsing habits and personal information can be monitored contributes to significant worries about how much authority people truly have over their personal information. Fairness, order, and accountability are further moral concerns with computational decision-making processes, which relies on the evaluation of enormous quantities of private information. The choices that impact the lives of individuals, such as those comprising criminal justice, possibilities for employment, and requests for loans, are increasingly employing algorithms that may inadvertently bolster prejudicial views and make distinctions against specific demographics.

A further essential aspect of the problem of cyber diplomacy is data security. Cyber attacks on government departments; businesses of all kinds, and key infrastructure offer severe risks to national security, the economy, and the safety of the public. Highly susceptible data is today more prone than at any time to theft, manipulation, and destruction because of the sophisticated nature of online assaults and the increasing interconnectedness of digital systems of all kinds. Therefore, enhanced technological safeguards are essential, such as facilitating the development of robust cyber safety regulations, the dissemination of information about threats, and global cooperation in the fight against cybercrime. Still, efficient solutions for cyber attacks and preventing the development of future developments depend on the existence of open channels for interaction and measures that promote confidence between states.

Yet, the widespread nature of surveillance, the decline of privacy, and the shortcoming of data security have significantly influenced the digital worlds aesthetic and human rights domains. The problems at hand are not merely related to technology; they are essential for both diplomatic relationships and cyber diplomacy, and they deserve thoughtful investigation and collaborative approaches. In the age of technology, surveillance throughout all of its indicators has become crucial. Governments are increasingly deploying advanced technologies to track movements of individuals, observe internet activity, and gather information about their citizens as an outcome of growing concerns about national security and regulation. The tangents of this include facial recognition technology deployed in public places, the analysis of social networking data to spot future risks, and extensive surveillance applications. There are still worries about potential violations and infringement of fundamental liberties, but some believe this sort of public scrutiny is essential in stopping criminal activity, terrorist activity, and other threats. Several programs for surveillance are not properly regulated, which increases major issues about the responsibility and the likelihood of unrestricted authority by the government. Monitoring involves the collection and evaluation of private data. Intentional or not, data breaches are a near certainty, threatening the privacy and security of individuals. A marketplace for highly confidential information has been established by the growth of data brokers and the relatively simple process with which sensitive data can be obtained and shared online, leaving individuals exposed to fraud, identity theft, and other different kinds of abuse. The scenario is made more severe in numerous countries by an absence of robust information security rules and laws, which demonstrates to citizens the improper use of their sensitive information. Global collaboration is necessary to promote the movement of data across borders and assure consistent protection of information guidelines.

A further essential aspect of the problem of cyber diplomacy is data security. Cyber attacks on government departments, businesses of all kinds, and key infrastructure offer severe risks to national security, the economy, and the safety of the public. Highly susceptible data is today more prone than at any time to theft, manipulation, and destruction because of the sophisticated nature of online assaults and the increasing interconnectedness of digital systems of all kinds. Therefore, enhanced technological safeguards are essential, such as facilitating the development of robust cyber safety regulations, the dissemination of information about threats, and global cooperation in the fight against cyber crime. Still, efficient solutions for cyber attacks and preventing the development of future developments depend on the existence of open channels for interaction and measures that promote confidence between states.

The innate complexities of the digital setting and conflicting interests of states hinder global agreements and partnerships in the digital age. It makes it hard to give precise instructions for collaboration since essential terms like cyber attack, cyber warfare, and cyber espionage does not have a standard tough explanation. It is made even harder by distinct national legal systems, which make it more challenging to hold international attackers on the Internet responsible for their actions. The lack of a commonly accepted notion of state accountability for cyber operations renders it challenging to determine who is responsible for attacks and what could be done about them. For the establishment of an accepted norm for responsible government conduct in cyberspace, more work requires to be carried out in creating agreements and contracts. One of the primary duties of regional security organisations and global organisations like the UN is to promote global collaboration in cyberspace. These types of organisations have the ability to promote partnership, ignite initiatives with the objective of encouraging trust, and set standards for appropriate government conduct over the Internet. Yet, the efficiency of these organisations is frequently hampered by the lack of ability of member-states to come together on important matters, the divergent objectives of states of power, and their lack of support. Additionally, the pace at which technology continues to advance often far exceeds the capacity of these organisations to respond to new risks and challenges.

In the modern age of the Internet, the private sector is very effective. The overwhelming majority of the technology that enables our Internet communication, along with gathering of information and surveillance has been developed and put into effect by major technology firms. More transparency and responsibility arise from combining the likelihood of data misuse with the need for the enormous quantities of private information that these firms generally collect. Thus, it must be done to establish industry-best requirements and self-regulation mechanisms in order to ensure ethical conduct in the realm of the internet. Nevertheless, self-regulation could prove to be inadequate enough to address the issues that are triggered by the overwhelming power of digital enterprises. Last, but not least, within the larger framework of cyber diplomacy, data security, privacy, and surveillance are not just technical problems but also have a close connection with fundamental moral and human rights problems. The rich process of establishing global norms along with partnership calls for the collaboration of governments, both multilateral and bilateral international organisations, firms, and grassroots organisations. Important to this endeavour are a mutual dedication to safeguarding rights for humans in the digital age and a willingness to work together with the goal to create solutions that address the complicated issues that the age of technology presents. The concept of transparency, responsibility, and the establishment of effective channels for handling problems and offering compensation to victims of cyber crimes and human rights violations constitute every part of this.

Establishing confidence and fostering an atmosphere of cooperation is crucial if one desires to effectively navigate the ethical challenges of the Internet age and ensure a secure and fair Internet access for everybody. The eventual development of cyber diplomacy itself will be heavily influenced by this coordination, which will help states to accomplish the appropriate equilibrium between their national interests and the fundamental liberties and rights of their citizens in a world that is growing increasingly more interconnected than ever. The writings that followed earlier highlighted privacy, security of information, and monitoring, demonstrating the ethical and human rights difficulties posed by digital actualities. Nevertheless, a key component of any preventative measures contrary to fraudulent online behaviour is responsibility and the process of attribution The combination of anonymity, dispersed networks, and the capability to hide ones origin in cyberspace makes it highly challenging to locate and bring charges against an offender.

The very structure of the Internet makes attribution difficult at times. Cyber attacks may originate from any part of the world and usually navigate numerous networks and jurisdictions, which is one of the primary reasons they are so easy to understand. Although an attacks geographical basis can be identified, sophisticated strategies like botnets, proxy servers, and virtual private networks (VPNs) cover the perpetrators correct location and personal identity; determining the specific individual or organisation behind an attack calls for an extensive investigation that usually uses electronic forensics and intelligence-gathering endeavours. This procedure frequently does not have the specialised expertise and global collaboration it requires owing to its intricate nature, commitment to time, and demand for resources.

The problem is made more complex by the absence of constitutionally recognised guidelines or requirements. What is a cyber attack? What differentiates cyber crime from cyber warfare? In addition, it can be challenging to establish effective regulatory structures for addressing these issues since they remain subject to discussion and continue to be causes of dispute among nation-states. Holding offenders liable can be rendered more challenging by the fact that various legal systems and even jurisdictions interpret pertinent laws in various ways. The establishment of a robust accountability structure is impeded by an absence of an integrated, globally standardised strategy, regardless of the fact that it is crucial.

Attribution is a technical subject as well as one of politics. Governments may be unwilling to publicly identify cyber criminals for fear of diplomatic repercussions or escalated tensions, or due to the anxiety that doing this might demonstrate their own shortcomings. Allegations, especially those that do not have definitive proof, are likely to cause global conflicts as well as severe punishments. Intentional and opaque attacks, for which responsibility becomes possible after taking many different shapes, are a particular approach employed by state-sponsored groups to gain an unfair advantage without placing blame. This ultimately results in an environment of apprehension and uncertainty that hampers efforts to create an adequate responsibility structure.

How tough is it to assign blame when important infrastructure is attacked? Figuring out the perpetrator can be extremely difficult, but an effective assault, particularly on a grid, may result in disastrous outcomes. The attacker could leverage multiple types of compromised networks, take full advantage of network shortcomings in the system being attacked, and perhaps use equipment and resources from other organisations in order to conceal their activities from detection. Even when investigators have the ability to determine the computers location or even the network that was the target of an attack, determining the specific perpetrators frequently requires an in-depth digital forensics analysis, frequently carried out jointly with multiple partners in the private sector and other nation-states. In this process, months or years may pass, and the harm done may already have broad and long-lasting consequences. The use of persistent and advanced threats (APTs), nevertheless, makes this considerably more difficult. APTs are often defined as sophisticated, long-term hacking operations that are supported by governments. Because these attacks are made to go undetected for long stretches of time, the attacker can destroy a significant amount of private information or take down vital systems without being detected shortly thereafter. For example, it can be difficult to place blame on APTs because of their long lifespan and stealth. The perpetrators might have long since concealed their movements by the time an attack comes to light. Since such incidents are hard to recognise, there is a probability of serious and long-lasting impact before anybody can be held responsible for their actions.

The attribution problem solving is made more complex by the involvement of non-state actors. Although cybercriminals are an important danger, whether they function on their own or in collaboration with criminal organisations or groups, attribution is made more difficult by their movement. In the light of their lack of relations to any state, it has grown more and more challenging to use conventional diplomatic mechanisms to deal with the problem, thus leading to an entirely novel approach concentrated on global collaboration and regulatory cooperation.

Additionally, it has grown harder and harder to make a distinction between state and non-state actors. It can sometimes be hard to differentiate between cyber attacks sponsored by the government from those that are launched by independent war makers who lack an obvious legally binding authorisation stamp but may nonetheless benefit from government assistance or implicit authorisation. It can be challenging to figure out who should be held liable and what sort of response could possibly be needed with regard to this lack of clarity. Disagreements usually develop in this grey area, requiring meticulous investigation and an intricate hold on the political and technological backdrop for the purpose to set up accountability structures. The international regulatory framework for combating cyber attacks is still in stages of development. Although there are a number of internationally recognised treaties and regulations which encompass numerous facets of cyber crime, an adequate international framework for law that precisely defines state responsibility, establishes attribution procedures, and provides individual effective solutions is still being developed. Unilateralist acts and retaliatory measures that run the risk of escalated disputes often fill this regulatory vacuum.

Effective methods of dispute resolution are further hindered by the dearth of an easily understood and binding legal structure for international law. In the wake of an attack, actions taken unilaterally that heighten tensions and cause additional instability could arise from the absence of an established resolution of dispute procedure. Internationally dispute resolution procedures have to be put into effect if there is to be a predictable and secure global system in cyberspace. Establishing mutual trust and confidence between states therefore becomes crucial to overcoming these challenges. The concept of transparency, exchange of knowledge mechanisms, and mutually beneficial development of shared requirements for responsible government behaviour in the cyber realm are also indispensable. Global bodies like the UN can play a crucial role for fostering partnership and developing norms, though their success depends on the readiness of states to make compromises and collaborate together. Accountability and attribution on the Internet involve complicated processes. It would call for an integrated approach, which involves bolstering international laws and regulations, developing digital forensics instruments, and the sincere commitment of nation-states to willingness and working together. If the responsibility question remains unanswered, the ethical and rights-related concerns brought up in the earlier sections of this work will not be addressed, the world of technology will stay open to abuses, and victims of cyber attacks will have limited options for looking for redress. Cyberspace responsibility, or more particularly, the requirement for a secure and equitable cyberspace for all, is not merely a technical endeavour if we take lessons from the lessons of the past.

Chapter Four

The Cyberspace Chessboard: Case Studies in Strategic Cyber Diplomacy

Specific cyber incidents and the diplomatic responses motivated by great force attract attention to the difficulties of attribution and responsibility in cyberspace already under discussion. These events highlight the difficulties of negotiating the international situation in the information age since they show both amazing achievements and major shortcomings in a framework unable to meet the demands for global action and cooperation. Understanding these answers will help one to put things into perspective and develop improved future solutions. One clear illustration of this is the anticipated billion-dollar global damage resulting from the 2017 NotPetya cyber assault. Other notable incidents of cyber attacks include the 2011 PlayStation Network hack, 2012 attack on Saudi Aramco, 2013 and 2014 Yahoo hacks, 2007 Estonia cyber attacks, 2024 Disney attacks and more. DoD and NASA hacks also abound.

Established by Israel and USA in 2010, the highly sophisticated Stuxnet worm used a malware program designed to attack Iranian nuclear facilities. However, the incident reminds us of the multifaceted nature of technological warfare and its propensity for magnitude regardless of whether or not its cause of action has been widely reported and widely acknowledged. While the attack was deemed to have succeeded in accomplishing the goal it set, it also ushered in an important increase in the digital weapons race. Iran replied to an advanced cyber attack on its critically important infrastructure by making significant investments in its own cyber capacity, which impacted the regional security setting. In the meantime, Stuxnet was an unambiguous indicator of possibility for national governments to conduct severe cyber attacks as well as the layered nature of conventional military that could be probable over cyberspace. Though less about international diplomacy than a direct, if covert, dispute, the response showed how unambiguously implemented actions could strategically backfire over time.

Impacting many companies, which include multiple US government agencies, the SolarWinds attack of 2020 was a wide compromise of the software, SolarWinds Orion. Broadly, it was believed that it might have been carried out by Russia; this attack triggered American and European leaders to respond immediately with sanctions and diplomatic expulsion. Once more, nevertheless, the response was limited, with countries functioning in somewhat different capacities. This volatile response emphasises the difficulties in maintaining national interests with synchronised opposition to large-scale, scattered strikes.

A common instance of how cyber attacks may result in physical damage as well as disruption of essential amenities is the 2015 attack against the Ukrainian power grid attached to groups backed by Russia. Huge power outages that were brought on by the cyber attack conveyed the actual impact of cyber warfare. The response showed up during an era characterised by increasing global recognition that cyber attacks compromising critical infrastructure could be addressed with the same response exhibited by conventional warfare. The occurrence, nevertheless, had instead, obvious proof attached and less mindful attribution might have helped facilitate a more immediate and unified reaction. More than in other instances lately allowing greater collaboration global responses, the simple nature of responsibility highlights the necessity of solid evidence to establish a more resilient diplomatic reaction.

These case studies demonstrate an array of cyber attacks and the spectrum of diplomatic responses they inspire to learn more. In certain instances, diplomatic opinions have been effective in averting additional incidents or assigning the accountability of the perpetrators. In other instances, nevertheless, an absence of governments acknowledging specific responsibility, their unwillingness to act collectively, and shortcomings in international law has impeded a swift response.

Assessing these incidents allows one to recognise a number of recommended procedures for following reactions that occur.

1. Much quicker along with more precise attribution may arise from more resources in technological forensics and intelligence exchange between different countries. That would also request global recommendations for collecting data and evaluation.
2. Enhancing international law is essential so that there be precise international law on the responsibility of states for disputes and target execution. That calls for both international collaboration and a willingness to provide certain national interests alterations.
3. A greater effective response to cyber incidents calls for enhanced mechanisms for around-the-world collaboration and knowledge exchange, which includes joint task groups as well as early detection mechanisms. This emphasises bilateral confidence building and confidence to promote global communication and openness.
4. Establishing robust cyber defensive structures along with promoting standards of excellence for important infrastructure will contribute to reducing the adverse effects of incidents and reduce the importance of reactive diplomatic relations. This ought to include public and private sector participants collaborating in tandem.
5. On a regular basis, diplomatic participation and dialogue on cyber security issues can help states determine guidelines of responsible state conduct, build confidence in one another, and prevent cyber disputes from becoming progressively worse. This encompasses being part of UN-style international bodies.

Essential components of an effective multi pronged approach for establishing an even more secure safe cyberspace are advancements in technology, modifications to legislation, and more collaboration across borders. As case studies demonstrate that creating a legal framework bolsters the rule of law, attribution, and partnership in response to cyber events is important. The digital age remains free to exploit without these developments, in doing so reducing global safety and equilibrium. A more secure international cyberspace requires not only ongoing diplomatic review but also additionally a dedication to forward-thinking and collaborative strategies since the landscape of cyber risks is always transforming. Though it is not an intended outcome, a framework in which accountability regulations must be the ultimate objective. In addition to developments in technology and state goodwill to work together when faced with prevalent threats, this makes room for substantial changes to global norms.

Both these case studies point out challenges and additional complexity associated with global cyber security cooperation. Looking at cases where such cooperation brought about favourable outcomes is equally important so that one can utilise the information acquired from past errors and the lessons gained to influence existing regulations. Examining the factors behind these distinctions offers substantial insight of what drives or hinders operational online collaboration.

Working at the creation and implementation of worldwide cyber security standards and regulations has been a significant achievement. While international cooperation is, by need, a prolonged and often divided affair, it brought about numerous significant breakthroughs. As shown by the Budapest Convention on Cybercrime, international collaboration has enabled cybercrime to move forward rather substantially. Without a doubt, nevertheless, the effect it has on national laws and global collaboration extends beyond its limited consent. Although it is not commonly recognised, it provides proof of the effectiveness of multilateral diplomacy in addressing widespread cyber security problems.

This has its foundation on a concentrated approach striving at specific categories of crimes and which includes widely recognised methods both for overseas cooperation and legal action. Within specific global organisations and businesses, additional growth has been accomplished. Established in 2015, the United Nations Group of Governmental Experts (GGE) on advancing responsible state behaviour in cyberspace represents one of the best illustrations of these efforts to promote discussion and seek ways for common alignment on guidelines for accountable government conduct in cyberspace. While the GGE has produced no constitutionally binding agreements, its dissemination of information has at least contributed to clarifying the challenges and established a consensus at least that will influence national policy and the worldwide conversation on accountable practice in states. However, the GGEs success is limited and is primarily reliant on its inclusion, bringing together multiple states to participate in open dialogue and mutually beneficial search. Though difficult to regulate, this encompassing strategy demonstrated it was vital for establishing a framework for ongoing interaction and the gradual advancement of shared expertise. Without a system of law, nevertheless, it is challenging to put into effect these voluntary regulations and their drawbacks are apparent.

A number of regional organisations have additionally been engaged in progressing cyber security by working together. One such actor is the European Union (EU), which has seen some active participation of its member-states in the development and adoption of wide-ranging cyber security strategies and policies, thereby enhancing overall cyber attack resistance across the Union. The European Union novel approach in the Network and Information Security Directive (NIS Directive) foresees the specific cyber security necessities of the operators owning such significant infrastructures across the countries of the Union. The extensive reach of the bloc as a watchdog over its constituent member-states has been credited with the EU achievements given that it facilitates the adoption and execution of policies that would be difficult with just multilateral treaties.

In addition to legally binding agreements and organisational arrangements, nevertheless, much not officially recognised collaboration among governments has also been effective in addressing particular weaknesses in cyberspace. For example, a countrys ability to recognise and combat state-sponsored doxxing and cyber criminal organisations relies much on the sharing of information between different countries. Successful actions against cyber threats are dependent on well-functioning sharing of information systems, regardless of their bilateral character and at times ineffective interest. Depending on the degree of confidence and trust, which lessens as time passes with ongoing interaction and organised goals among the parties, is the most significant factor in informal collaboration. The lines are drawn, however, as it is unofficial and it becomes difficult to demonstrate uniformity and accountability.

Actually, numerous instances indicate gaps in collaboration for worldwide cyber safety. The absence of common understanding on key concepts like cyber attack and cyber warfare, hinders the development of an in-line constitutional structure. As previously touched upon, disagreements over attribution at times get in the way of the kind of integrated reaction needed to hold perpetrators accountable or r such future attacks. Unique cyber security skills, and national interests over information sharing in conflict, geo-political agendas, etc., have resulted in division in cyber incident opinions.

A particular issue with the entirety of this is that no single global organisation is present currently with the capacity to set up cyber security norms. Although it does not have mechanisms for monitoring legal compliance, the UN is an organisation to establish standards as well as encouraging interactions. The absence of a powerful centralised power with the capacity to exercise control over cyberspace allows states with liberty to act independently of one another, which could worsen disputes and threaten the fragile equilibrium of world law and order. And that makes global efforts crippled with no supranational power or a way of effectively settling disputes between nation-states. The digital gap exacerbates the challenges of world technological partnership further. Far smaller relative assets and capacities as a consequence of heavy-handedness of developer countries resulted in fallacy and distortion of regulations, so exacerbated by the imbalance in power and compromising the efficacy of collaborative initiatives. Developing nations frequently lack the resources and expertise required to comply with conventions agreed upon in such discussions or engage actively in them. This is undoubtedly an issue in the generality and effectiveness of shared efforts and hinders the development of a fair and secure digital age that is actually international. Additionally, cyber dangers are changing more quickly than international legal systems and diplomatic pathways of action. Cyber security global collaboration calls for a flexible and adaptable approach since contemporary technologies as well as potential attack routes continue to evolve. The currently functioning legal system is unable to meet the demands and remains perpetually behind the reality of the attacks since technology rapidly evolves and always leaves an enormous gap between readily accessible legal instruments and cyber reality.

In this regard, though certain progress is being achieved in terms of multilateral cooperation in cyber security, numerous obstacles remain to be addressed while indeed there has been a certain establishment of norms, guidelines and collaborative methods, particularly in some geo-political domains and organisational structures. Still, the absence of a unified worldwide governance construction, battling national goals, disparities over attribution, and the growing technological divide still hinder the establishment of a really successful and comprehensive approach to international cyber security. There is no redeeming aspect to this; therefore, future efforts ought to concentrate on tackling significant issues in order to establish a more secure global internet seamless integration. Being able to reach this requires calling for improved mechanisms for attributing attacks via the internet, more potent legal frameworks, increased intelligence sharing, and efforts bridging the digital divide and promoting greater participation in across-the-globe cyber security projects.

Unique geopolitical settings, technological instruments, and national priorities influence the various ways in which various cyber diplomacy techniques show themselves. While some states give collaborative efforts and the establishment of guidelines the greatest importance, others are unilateralists about cyberspace, concentrating greatly on the immediate benefits associated with aggressive acts and strategies. Examining these distinct approaches additionally demonstrates the complex relationships among power, partnership, and competition in cyberspace. The US makes use of a multipronged method with certain components of competition along with certain aspects of cooperation. In addition to multilateral forums such as the UNGGE, the USA has worked together with key supporters to establish bilateral treaties enhancing intelligence-sharing and organised reactions to cyber attacks. The above strategy reflects that the US will continue to maintain its technological edge and goals to impact worldwide cyberspace standards. Nevertheless, particularly among countries with less advanced technology, such an approach has additionally drawn criticism for possibly levelling the playing field. Despite concerns with transparency and the potential for escalated situations, the US approach to hindering cyber attacks sponsored by states through the use of public condemnation and undercover operations has proven effective in some cases. China, on the other hand, has adopted cyber diplomacy with a more enthusiastic, but at times, an obfuscatory mindset. Along with its role in global discussions, it has also been accused of conducting major cyber attacks and cyber espionage aimed against both private and government actors all around. The above strategy reflects the desire of China to be an important player on the global Internet setting through integrating financial rewards with coercive methods. But such an approach has at times generated accusations of infringing global laws and destroying the confidence of the public. The strategy taken by China highlights even more the challenging task of establishing shared norms for conduct in cyberspace that will garner every individuals acceptance while key stakeholders are not entirely committed to accountability and forthrightness.

Russia has officially denied accountability for numerous cyber attacks; however, it has been frequently associated with tasks striving at foreign institutions, rivals in politics, and critical infrastructure development. In this regard, even at the possibility of inciting a strike from the global community at large, the strategy indicates its desire to tap flaws in cyberspace for strategic benefit. Russias approach relies on ambiguity and a lack of willingness to conceal attribution and generate unrest. Confidence-building efforts have been undermined as global efforts to reach an understanding on cyberspace rules and regulations disintegration. Through exchange of data, law coordinating, technology resilience as a whole bolstering, etc., the EU has an unparalleled strategy regarding cyber diplomacy efficiently setting up partnership between its member-states. Based on the concepts of collaborative governance and mutual assistance, this has been a somewhat beneficial strategy to boost the capacity for recovery of critical facilities within the EU. However, the wide range of issues facing the EU and the ongoing commitment of its members to voluntarily work together limit its ability to address these difficulties and impact cyber norms around the world. Additionally, considering the challenging task of accomplishing common ground on the inside, the EUs approach might prove inefficient in identifying the lightning-fast speed of technological advancement and cyber threat evolution.

By the technique for evaluating these different approaches, certain substantial elements of understanding are accessible. First, an important indicator of the effectiveness of cyber diplomacy is the extent to which nations adhere to accountability and transparency. In states where opaque approaches are employed, CBMs and actual partnership may cause challenges. Second, even though actions that are unilateral might pay off for a while, over the course of time they are frequently implemented at the cost of broader global cooperation and equilibrium. Third, efficient cyber diplomacy is about balancing the two rather than about only partnership or competition as both defence in cyberspace and engaged participation with global agenda-setting are inevitable requirements. Lastly, disparity in access to scientific information and technology reinforces inequality in power and reduces the broad appeal of multilateral initiatives; so, the technological divide is a major threat to international cyber diplomacy.

The capability of states to align national objectives with shared goals will eventually characterise the sustained effectiveness of cyber diplomacy. Countries pushing towards improving international legal frameworks encasing attribution, responsibility, and accountability in the digital age are hoping to promote collaboration via the implementation of these bolstered frameworks. This includes defining essential phrases while developing effective conflict resolution systems, therefore embarking on the legal framework for advancing global norms and standards. Establishing an ethos of responsible behaviour in cyberspace among governments, businesses, and the public relies also on promoting education and understanding of those same cyber risks and highlighting the importance of ethical conduct in the digital realm. Important techniques for consolidating global cooperation systems involve further information exchange along with capacity building, within others. This includes helping nations, especially underdeveloped ones, to exchange intelligence, efficient procedures, and technological strategies to strengthen cyber security via means of exchanges of information. This can include the establishment of worldwide initiatives designed to enhance the ability of countries to deal with cyber potential risks while providing adequate technical and monetary assistance for those countries that require it. Not only do international initiatives ensure that the most advanced nations do not impose regulations and norms but they also guarantee that important players have a say when deciding the future path for cyberspace oversight.

Given the changing nature of cyberspace, cyber diplomacys future years will demand continuing development and adaptation mechanisms. Past achievements and shortcomings will inform the ongoing modification of these approaches. Establishing mutual trust and confidence among governments in order to foster interaction and reduce the likelihood of mistakes and escalated situations would be primarily significant. The development of forward-leaning dispute resolution and negotiation ways in cyberspace could aid in reducing the potential risks of state-sponsored cyber operations and technological warfare.

When all factors are taken into account, the juxtaposition of cyber diplomacy strategies demonstrate intricate and diverse events influenced through numerous geopolitical factors, national interests, and ability. Making choices in cyber diplomacy encompasses the pursuit of national interests and the promotion of global equilibrium, accountability and safety cooperation and rivalry; hence the requirement of a sophisticated strategy is much enhanced. To accomplish this and build a safer cyberspace emphasizing on strong laws and regulations, global collaboration, and constricting the digital gap, an integrated worldwide effort needs to be made. A really secure and collaborative digital world cannot be attained without such sincere relentless efforts.

Governments do not, nevertheless, have only jurisdiction over the technological field. The proactive participation of non-governmental organisations is one crucial yet frequently overlooked component of international cyberspace. In reality, the development and implementation of cyber norms, rules, and practices are greatly impacted by multinational corporations (MNCs), civil society entities, and individual hackers. Their profound impact influences the structure of international relations in addition to the successful outcome of personally overseeing cyber diplomacy efforts.

On a global scale present in the world of technology and with an extensive internet infrastructure, multinational organisations play a crucial role in determining cyber security requirements. Through conduct of cross-national boundaries, consequently they are both subjected to and able to unveil cyber attacks. Large multinational companies therefore have an interest to promote worldwide cyber security partnership as well as in accordance with laws and regulations that maintain their assets and business operations. Organisations such as Google, Microsoft, and Amazon, for instance, have substantially funded cyber security research and development (R&D). They also trade efficient procedures and information about threats with other governments and companies. Leading experts in cyber security effectively engage in international forums and industrial initiatives, actively shaping cyber security policy, developing standards for technology, and so boosting legal protection at all levels of cyberspace. MNC impact has shortcomings as well. Profit motivates several of their decisions, which may contribute to disputes between their business goals and those that benefit society as a whole. The imbalance in power between large multinational corporations and lesser known companies or nations with poor infrastructure demands challenges regarding the just and fair advancement of cyber security regulations. Given how complicated the dilemma of corporate responsibility becomes when addressing cyber hacks, it is subsequently essential that we find an appropriate equilibrium between developing a robust worldwide legal structure that calls for companies to take into account their financial objectives while preserving the interests of others against cyber attacks.

MNCs go beyond simply technical requirements. They additionally contribute to create world data protection regulations and establish standards on safety and confidentiality for other consumers. Organisations belonging to civil society greatly affect the arena of cyber diplomacy as champions, watchdogs, and agents of mediation. Along with promoting greater accountability and willingness in organisations and governments in the first place, one also significantly assists individuals to be aware of cyber safety concerns and act ethically online. Moreover, highlighted by organisations from civil society are the human rights consequences of cyber safety measures and processes alongside the monitoring of cyber attacks and actor accountability. They assist and determine the general consensus about issues and oversee discussions about policy. The Electronic Frontier Foundation (EFF) and Access Now are two organisations tracking government actions in cyberspace, documenting violations and advocating robust defence of online freedom.

Still, the financial backing readily accessible to civil society organisations and the need of obtaining financing usually characterise their constraints. The wide range of voices in the nonprofit sector may additionally render it difficult for it to communicate a uniform perspective on current events worldwide, hence jeopardising its impact in developing international norms. Frequently splintered in different points and opinions and objectives, civil society groups make it challenging to offer an overall position on essential cyber security issues. Additionally, the power balance is affected by how certain contents determine engagement in global forums. If credibility is to be bestowed and a worldwide equitable cyberspace continues to exist and flourishes, cyber diplomacy procedures call for an extensive and multifaceted involvement that includes numerous civil society opinions that must grow to be normative.

Though they seem to be minimal, players, individual hackers may also significantly impact cyber diplomacy. From demonstrating shortcomings to unveiling highly sophisticated cyber attacks, organisations at the more advanced end of the spectrum often influence the narrative and demonstrate reaction. As firms translate their cyber security efforts into the cyber akin of military manufacturing facilities, MNCs and governments may additionally find guidance in their efforts of white hat hackers, who in an ethical manner. see flaws and report them to the appropriate agencies in order to avoid their nefarious exploitative practices. These outcomes promote the better securing of ones employment opportunities. On the other hand, black hat hackers acting out of political or monetary gain have the capacity to undermine critical infrastructure, pilfer confidential data, and threaten national security. Such actions might set off global disturbances requiring diplomatic responses, test responsibility and attribution.

The narrowing gap between state-sponsored and independent participants and the increasing scientific abilities of individuals hinder this and make it harder to pinpoint accountability and react effectively. The combination of technical, legal, and political endeavours with the objective of enhancing cyber security, consequently bolstering global partnerships against cybercrime, and thereby encouraging ethical behaviour in the world of technology, calls for numerous approaches for tackling the problem at hand. In closing, it is also unquestionable that in the regulatory environment of cyber diplomacy, national security agencies (NSAs) have readily apparent and multiple impacts. These valuable contributions start from many different kinds of actors; all of which contribute to the development and implementation of cyber norms, policies, or practices. Grasping the complicated dynamics of cyber diplomacy and developing complex tactics for fostering a more secure, reliable and collaborative cyberspace, one would have to rely on having an understanding of their accessibility.

There are multiple fundamental developments reconsidering the landscape of cyber diplomacy as the world continues to evolve at an ever-quickening pace and advances in technology race far ahead of the establishment of global standards and legal systems. States and global organisations must therefore keep novel regulations and strategies under assessment. One pattern is the sophisticated and widespread integrity of hacking attempts. In modern times, cyber attacks target critical infrastructure bolstering fundamental amenities like transportation systems, medical facilities, and electrical power lines. They extend beyond mere theft of information or sabotage. Among possibilities for catastrophic consequences are public disruption, monetary damage, and even fatalities. Although the identification of them has grown more challenging, such attacks typically constitute the primary catalyst for a diplomatic reaction that occurs.

From national governments to well-organised criminal networks to solitary predators, sophisticated methods consist of botnets, polymorphic malware, and zero-day vulnerabilities that hinder responsibility as actors participate within obscure surroundings. Diplomatic efforts towards accountability and a deterrent have proved difficult in this state of uncertainty. Attribution devoid of any kind of proof will only result in errors in judgement and escalated situations affecting international relations. The third primary challenge is the obscuring of disparities between state and non-governmental participants. It can be difficult to make a direct connection for those individuals to specific hacks given the degree of possible denial with which government-backed actors at times function. This is made more severe by the rise of actors with relations with the government who employ sophisticated strategies to conceal their original sources or oversee in intermediary firms. A keen capacity to recognise the difference between attacks sponsored by governments and of autonomous actors forms the backbone of entirely successful states, particularly in terms of diplomatic methods for dispute resolutions. To improve attribution and accountability, it is necessary for greater international cooperation, advanced forensic techniques and more gathering information capability. While harder to accomplish, achieving equivalent responsibility guidelines and requirements enables to minimise the likelihood of incorrect interpretation and escalated situations.

One of the most significant difficulties is that there are numerous IoT devices. The distributed and often unregulated nature makes it challenging to figure out who holds responsibility and who is liable; attacks will have cascading repercussions potentially affecting crucial infrastructure and impacting individual systems; there are additionally an excessive number of devices that are connected and many of them with little or no protection. Thereby an important attack appears open to exploitation. Being responsive to this test will require global cooperation, developing all-encompassing norms for resilient IoT security, bolstering responsible production methods, and improving consumer understanding.

Cyber diplomacy thereby faces possibilities as well as obstacles with the advancement of ML and AI. While AI and ML can significantly improve cyber security and determine the capacity to identify and prevent attacks, they also present new flaws. AI-based incidents can be more complex, flexible and challenging to identify. Additionally, the employments of AI in autonomously targeted weapons systems foster deep ethical and safety challenges that ought to receive worldwide discussion and the advancement of suitable regulating establishments. It is essential, consequently, to look thoroughly at how AI may contribute to up-to-date power disparities in the digital age by highlighting nation-states with more substantial resources, understanding, tools, and training foundations. Therefore, the building of global norms and laws should be carried out at the global level in order to control the potential risks of AI accessibility in the digital age.

Additionally, greater consideration ought to be given to the connection among cyber security and human rights. Attacks by hackers may interfere with putting together confidentiality, and freedom of speech among other fundamental freedoms. National security concerns are employed by lawmakers often to oppose tracking and even limitations, which restricts fundamental liberties. To ensure that human rights are protected in cyberspace, new global laws hindering measures to safeguard cyberspace from obliterating basic freedoms must be created. It demands an orderly strategy to protect human rights while paying close attention to legitimate security concerns. It highlights the need of recourse through global legal channels, open dialogue, and the establishment of worldwide regulations giving human rights the greatest importance in the age of technology. Particularly challenging for cyber diplomatic efforts is the growing reliance on the Internet for computing. A Cloud environment raises issues related to authority, sovereignty over data, and data movement across borders connected to such private information being processed and stored. Since there really is an opportunity for international issues caused by foreign governments with regard to international data and agreements, regulating and safeguarding information and collaboration across borders must be established. Two of the most challenging diplomatic tasks are making arrangements for cloud providers to follow important global standards and regulations and encouraging worldwide cyber security collaboration.

Given the dynamics of war, cyber, the next phase of conflict is turning into an increasingly important problem. While disseminating conflicts in addition to the boundaries of the internet, cyber attacks might additionally constitute an innovative instrument of war. Essential measures to avoid unintentional escalated situations must guarantee that the deployment of cyber weapons adheres to international regulations and complies with the proportionality standards with discussions on regulations and standards of commitment on digital operations. It calls for collective action in order to establish a global structure for dispute resolution and mediation in cyberspace and boost the understanding of what cyber warfare could potentially mean for global peace and security.

Dealing with these latest developments and problems calls for a broad approach. Building up multilateral negotiations and collaboration relies on categories of this form; therefore, new dialogue and collaboration mechanisms are urgently required to improve exchange of knowledge, set up prevalent norms and regulations, and offer effective methods of resolution of conflicts and disagreement shifting. In addition, a clear international law framework that involves responsibilities and obligations in addition to policies for containment are essential that encompass both governments and non-state players.

Positive reinforcement of assistance in technology along with capacity building for countries that are less developed so that they have an important part in global cyber diplomacy efforts is another crucial stage. Lastly, an extremely significant approach to avoiding cyber threats while developing a safe and feasible digital environment is the support of a secure digital citizenship society by awareness-raising and education efforts. Cyber diplomacy is by nature itself always shifting, responding to the rapid advancement of innovation and evolving geopolitical issues. The eventual development of international relations in cyberspace will be determined by the ability of nations to acknowledge and respond to these frameworks. Henceforth, setting up a secure and steady cyberspace is crucial to foster cooperation and competition to the favourable advantage of all.

Chapter Five

Decoding Cyber Diplomacy: Emerging Trends and Strategic Foresight

Considering that AI has an important influence on both kinds of cyber threats and the techniques needed for dealing with them, it serves as an emerging transformative factor in the discipline of cyber diplomacy. The consequences are intricate, presenting both huge hazards and heretofore-unimaginable opportunities, demanding preventive measures and thoughtful consideration from the worldwide population.

The potential of fortifying technological defensive structures is among the most important ones that machine learning presents. Now, far quicker and with greater efficiency than individual analysts, systems using AI can navigate through huge amounts of statistical information and uncover patterns and deviations, which indicate acts of hostility. This enhanced identification capacity may contribute to reducing the detrimental effects of cyber attacks and assist in preventing substantial damage by greatly reducing the speed of response to them. The majority of cyber security tasks, like risk fixing, software enhancing, and reactions to more prevalent threats of harm, can be automated by machine learning, thereby opening human professionals to focus on challenging and serious problems. In addition to growing national technological infrastructure resiliency, automation enhances productivity. For instance, real-time analysis of network traffic powered by machine learning systems for intrusion detection makes it possible to recognise and prevent malicious activity before it can inflict substantial damage. Moreover, learning algorithms may facilitate the establishment of more advanced and flexible security mechanisms that incorporate lessons learnt from previous breaches and evolution as they confront new obstacles. In comparison to unchanging and rule-driven infrastructure, this dynamic approach significantly enhances the effectiveness of information technology security solutions.

AI algorithms, which at first can search vast databases gathered from numerous sources including leaked data, dark web discussions, and free and open-source intelligence to find potential weaknesses and anticipated future attacks symbolises yet another ground-breaking use for machine learning in intelligence about threats by collecting samples. This preventative strategy reduces hazards before they show up, consequently enabling mitigation measures. Examining past strategies of attack helps machine learning to find potential targets and flaws so that preventive measures could potentially be set up before the attack commences. This is subsequently critical for the preservation of vital facilities as it assists firms to bolster their defences against potential dangers. Deterring attacks before they even commence has the potential to drastically reduce the cost of attacks on computers, which includes the loss of monetisation, harm to credibility, and legal consequences.

The altering power of machines with intelligence, likewise, has its limitations. Using the same capacity that enhances cyber security defences, malicious actors can also produce more intricate and swift attacks. Trojan horses can be consequently developed and transmitted by AI systems, which may impede recognition and responses. Attacks can be extremely modified given that they seek specific individuals or organisations by employing malware created specifically to take the benefit of known shortcomings. In addition, AI may generate hyper realistic deep fakes to be able to undermine political settings by enabling the propagation of disinformation and misleading information. Social security and trust are under severe threat by the growing number of credible deep fakes and technological advances that are capable of modifying both video and audio records or impersonating individuals.

More specifically, with the advancement and implementation of autonomous weapons systems (AWS), which typically is fueled by machine learning, the possibility of harm is significant. Deep ethical and safety uncertainties encircle the prospective existence of machines that are autonomously made attainable by machine learning, which makes life-or-death decision-making without human intervention. The absence of human oversight of these advancements boosts the likelihood of errors of judgement, errors in calculation, and escalated situations. Perhaps still harder is figuring out who bears the burden of inadvertent damage. Developing international regulations and legal structures for the application of machine learning in combat will contribute to avoiding a global arms race in AI applications and decrease the possibilities of unforeseen escalated matters. If there are no clear guidelines of participation for powered AI weapons, the ineptness of a states artificial neural network underestimating the circumstances could set off devastating findings. Therefore, creating tenets for the responsible and legitimate creation and utilisation of powered AI equipment calls for forward-thinking global collaboration.

Relevant furthermore is how machine learning may entrench previously pronounced power inequalities in cyberspace. States with sophisticated infrastructure and sophisticated machine learning ability in their toolboxes will likely continue to have an overwhelming edge in cyberspace, perhaps leading to an entirely novel kind of digital imperialism. This disparity results in different countries with fewer capabilities to struggle to defend their technological structures and contend with on the Internet, subsequently perhaps distressing the international framework. It is crucial to bridge this gap in technology so that nations worldwide may be efficiently and effectively secure and participate in the technological landscape given that the worldwide web enables individuals by enabling them to feel the existence of other people wherever they are and whether highly technologically sophisticated or undeveloped, nations of all sizes ought to come together for the exchange of resources, technological advances, and information so that these deprived regions could possibly have cyber security capacity utilisation constructed.

The multiple challenges that AI generates in cyber diplomacy call to mind a varied approach. First, and most importantly, global establishment of standard parallels as well as guidelines on the moral and ethical growth and implementation of AI in the field of cyber security has been done. The ultimate goal of this shared endeavour must be to foster the creation of regulations for the appropriate use of machine learning that are not incompatible with either international legislation or human rights that are fundamental. This ought to encompass developing safeguards for innovation and dissemination of AI-powered armament structures. Second, particularly among developing nations, additional funding has to be provided to strengthen cyber security ability. These nations should consequently be able to take a better part in global cyber diplomacy initiatives and reinforce their security measures against AI-powered attacks. Thirdly, it is also extremely important for expanding understanding among people on the opportunities and dangers of AI. Experts are going to advocate appropriate AI regulations and discuss the intricate nature of the digital domain more effectively. Fourth, additional research needs to happen to remain pertinent against a constantly transforming risk setting. Funding powered by AI cyber security techniques can help in developing more effective identification and mitigation tactics given that the challenges that AI presents in cyberspace must be dealt with; governments, researchers, and the private sector need to interact and work together.

The way different countries control the revolutionary implications of AI will be extremely important when deciding cyber diplomacy developments in the decades to come. This calls for a team-based, proactive approach that reduces the potential danger of AI and produces the advantages it brings. Nations in collaboration can make sure that AI improves cyber security and increases global equilibrium, consequently creating opportunities for a more safe and cooperative digital future. The question at hand is how we could employ AI for good as the world of technology gets increasingly more intricate, therefore promoting its development as well as implementation while promoting an equitable and peaceful international system. Only steady collaboration as well as commitment to ethical creativity is going to allow us to effectively navigate the uncertain flows of AI in cyber diplomacy thus ensuring a more secure and more equitable future for everyone. While great progress has been accomplished, an increasingly worrying propensity in cyber warfare advancement is the elimination of boundaries between standard and unconventional conflict as well as higher levels of complexity and fatalities. Since the beginning of time, when independent hackers or loosely organised teams often carried out relatively straightforward attacks and data theft, the field of cyber attacks has grown significantly. Now the province of government-backed actors is all the most recent cyber warfare, misinformation initiatives, multifaceted malicious software, and misuse of critical infrastructure. The discipline of cyber diplomacy itself encompasses the growth in line with the present scenario and engages in a more proactive process in order to encompass a global synchronised approach to combat these increasing risk factors.

The collateral harm feasible from cyber attacks have grown exponentially as numerous facets of contemporary existence are more dependent progressively on the global web. Since so much cutting-edge critical infrastructure is dependent on related information systems, cyber attacks might result in disruption or even a complete breakdown of this network of systems. These cover electric power lines, financial institutions, public transportation systems, and healthcare facilities. A possible outcome could be a successful cyber attack on a national power grid that makes crucial infrastructure ineffective, leading to huge economic disruption, turmoil in society, and even fatalities on the adversary. In a similar direction, the general population can be impacted significantly when healthcare systems cease while national economies may be thrown off when attacks focus on institutions of finance.

The recent development of AI further complicates this already challenging environment. Given that systems powered by AI generate and propagate malware more and more on its own, its becoming increasingly hard to identify and prevent them. With specific vulnerabilities noticed specifically in wireless networks or infrastructure, these AI-augmented incidents can be quite specific and centred. AI to identify targets might also handle enormous volumes of information and organise strikes much more particularly and enhance its achievement rate. States that have sophisticated AI capacity have the opportunity to collaborate with those without it to narrow the technological innovations disparity while ensuring fair distribution of cyber security resources given their various levels of capacity.

Using AI in cyber warfare also demands significant ethical concerns. One very concerning potential is the development of AWS, typically fuelled by the use of AI. Deep ethical and safety concerns encompass the likely outcome of it being driven by AI weapons making lethal decisions without human intervention. Establishing stringent regulations to restrict the development and use of such weapons calls for collaboration between nations as human supervision is not present and there is an option of unforeseen consequences. The absence of an easily understood set of regulations boosts the possibility of an uncontrolled machine learning arms race growing, thus adding conflicts and maybe resulting in unfounded disputes.

The more general geopolitical setting in which these breakthroughs in technology occur additionally influences technological warfare. Rising competition among super powers, especially between the US and China and between the USA and Russia and other developing cyber powers is leading to extremely unpredictable constraints. Considering it as a means of statecraft, cyber attacks have been carried out in order to achieve either financial or political objectives. This could encompass anything from technological warfare and monetary disruption and sabotage to covert operations. These organisations obscure the divide between combat and times of peace, thus raising the likelihood of uncontrollable escalated issues and complicating the choice of appropriate alternatives. Lack of clarity regarding global regulations and laws renders this environment even more complex in nature. The inevitably dynamic nature of cyber warfare further offers traditional thoughts of escalated situations and deterrence current understanding. Briefly as cyber attacks are more covert and harder to associate with than most other kinds of attacks, that is at times tough. Additionally, a small cyber attack could trigger off a more high degree reaction, consequently offering ample room for escalated issues. An effective cyber attack against a state may set off an immediate response swiftly intensifying with the inclusion of conventional military forces. Although all of them could cause early damage, they need much better lines of communication and de-escalation techniques in order to remain under control.

The manner in which international relations operate in the age of technology has to be altered primarily if we are prepared for the new obstacles brought about by the development of cyber warfare. Their quickness, opacity, and additional complexity make conventional diplomatic instruments at times incapable of dealing with cyber attacks. This requires a more stringent and flexible approach rooted in safeguarding instead of reactive response strategies. Creating global cyber space standards and guidelines is an essential step in this plan of action. Undoubtedly, regardless of the great progress achieved through international arenas like the UN, the need for more powerful and widely recognised regulations regarding behaviour has no end in sight. These recommendations ought to include safeguarding crucial infrastructure, using offensive cyber devices, and setting accountability for violations. Explicit, constitutionally binding standards could provide less chance of escalation and more cyber stability. Better worldwide cooperation is also absolutely vital. Several steps should be taken to build efficient cyber risk management: sharing of threat intelligence, establishing co-designed cyber security techniques, and carrying out de-escalation techniques. Under present-day geopolitical conflict, it calls for an important level of trust and openness between nations that might be difficult. Still, conquering these challenges is going to call for an integrated approach with presumably catastrophic outcomes.

Promoting national cyber capacity is an additional aspect of achieving effectiveness with cyber diplomacy. Nations heading towards collapse have no possibility than to make major investments in robust cyber safety systems, trained personnel, along with efficient emergency response mechanisms. In addition to the rapid advancement of technology, that calls for significant spending on the improvement of organisational capacity and workforce development. National policies have to be both offensive and defensive in nature, informing possible perpetrators that they are going to be strongly dissuaded regardless of how national interests are being maintained.

Cyber diplomacy has to be particularly inclusive of civic society as well as the business sector alongside government players. Frequent targets of cyber attacks and those containing vast volumes of sensitive data are private companies. Only public and private sectors collaborating in tandem create a strong cyber security posture. Additionally, organisations representing civil society can be extremely beneficial in promoting public understanding, appropriate technology use, and enforcement of more robust worldwide regulations and standards.

While it can be hard to make predictions about how cyber warfare will advance and what consequences it will have on international stability, certain trends are unquestionably going to continue. Both the complicated nature of cyber attacks and the gradual integration of cyberspace with essential infrastructure will keep expanding. Should AI be employed with greater frequency in cyber warfare, such dangers will only become increasingly possible. Political in nature competition will keep driving cyber warfare; therefore, it will be difficult to differentiate between traditional and non-traditional warfare. Beneficial cyber diplomacy is absolutely essential in this modifying terrain. Coping with a greater equilibrium in cyberspace and decreasing the threat of cyber warfare will depend on fostering collaboration across borders, norm generating, strengthening capacities, and multi-stakeholder engagement. Neglecting this will run the risk of cyber warfare turning into an existential threat to global security and safety that might have catastrophic implications on global stability and general human well-being around the world. Creating global frameworks to handle issues, settle conflicts, and foster confidence would be beneficial to ensure that cyber conflict stays confined and refrains from growing into traditional warfare.

More and more complicated and widespread cyber attacks continue to demonstrate the constraints of a merely government-led strategy regarding cyber security. None of them regardless of their strength has the finances or understanding needed to effectively safeguard against a broad spectrum of cyber threats by their own shortcomings. This fact requires an evolution of paradigms towards cooperative responses; consequently PPPs will grow ever more essential to both national and multinational cyber security initiatives. Bringing together the special strengths of the government and private sectors, PPPs generate an integrated approach that is far more effective than doing it by themselves.

Governments offer a specific set of capacities. They have the ability to build legal frameworks, determine recommendations, and set up country responses to attacks by hackers. Often with the use of data resources that might provide warnings in advance about these kinds of attacks, they are able to invest significant funding in developing national cyber safety and plans of action. Governments can occasionally be less agile, lacking private industrys specialised knowledge of technology abilities or an element of invention or looping back of acquiring knowledge. On the other hand, the private sector has been driving cyber security innovation in technology. The development and deployment of cutting-edge technologies and advanced approaches required to detect, prevent, and respond to cyber attacks rests on individuals and companies. In addition, they have a substantial pool of highly skilled cyber safety professionals covering incident response, electronic forensics, developing software, and network security with various backgrounds. Also, the competitive atmosphere in the business community often reinforces fast advancement and adaptation of both crucial elements in the newly emerging field of information security.

With their cooperation, collaboration between the public and private sectors addresses these issues. By making use of the private sectors expertise in technology and innovative thinking, governments can enhance existing defence abilities. This may include sharing information about threats, sharing knowledge on recommendations and norms for cyber security, and working together on scientific research. As an example, governments and individual companies may work together for the development and put into action leading-edge cyber security products like surveillance systems, malware assessment instruments, and emergency management systems. Governments can use the latest technology due to this collaboration, which additionally fosters creative thinking and competition in the information security market as a whole. In the form of PPPs, they may also assist private businesses and government agencies to make agreements for information sharing. The public and private sectors may respond to arising cyber threats far quicker when threat intelligence is shared. This may include developing standard intelligence on threat formats, putting forth secure platforms for transferring knowledge, and creating secure systems for collaboration and data exchange. More effective sharing of data has become crucial since numerous cyber attacks are taking advantage of shortcomings in frequently employed software or amenities. By allowing private companies to immediately address these flaws, notification systems may mitigate the harm that a security breach might bring about. In addition to creating operational iterant incident response methods, they will also need to counter defensive capabilities. Multiple consequences may arise from cyber attacks, which often call for an integrated response to mitigate harm and stop similar occurrences in the years to come. PPPs may assist in establishing cooperative emergency response strategies, which lay out the roles and responsibilities of private as well as public organisations. This includes setting up channels of communication, outlining the escalation approach, and setting up tasks during a crisis. A resilient response may mitigate the adverse consequences of a cyber attack while preventing it from getting direr. Government and private sector individuals could benefit from exercises and planning of scenarios to bolster crisis response expertise and boost their sense of trust.

PPP operations have been significantly affected by regulatory and legal structures. Players in both the governmental and private sectors must have their responsibilities, duties, and accountability lay out clearly. The above structures must ensure reliability, openness, and the safeguarding of confidential data. The private sector should be encouraged to take part in cyber security efforts by the government at large. Economic incentives like exemptions from taxes or additional assistance could be a means towards accomplishing this. A straightforward description of legal safeguards for companies engaged in cyber security efforts is also crucial, as it will reduce the unwillingness to work together and share data. This receptive method recognises the highly sensitive nature of information and national security challenges while fostering optimistic cooperation. Beyond partnerships at the state level, PPPs are a new element of international cyber diplomacy. Because cyber threats are transnational, international collaboration on cyber security is crucial. In order to combat particular cyber threats, PPPs can also encourage international collaboration and information sharing between nations. This entails exchanging threat intelligence, organising incident response efforts, and working together to create global cyber security standards and guidelines. For instance, multinational corporations that operate globally frequently have a wealth of information about threats that governments of other countries may be interested in learning about. One of the main objectives associated with global PPPs is the responsible, secure exchange of such information in accordance with national security policies and regulations. However, when trying to create effective global PPPs, there are important barriers that need to be addressed and overcome. The simple fact that various nations have different rules and regulations adds to the difficulties. The collaboration as well as knowledge sharing may be hindered by these differences in national laws, guidelines, and order of importance. This highlights how international cyber laws call for a cohesive strategy. Creating international cyber security guidelines and requirements that are recognised by major stakeholders could facilitate sharing information as well as cooperation quicker. International bodies such, as the UN and specially trained agencies can be crucial in this course of action. Specific guidelines on jurisdictional and data supremacy matters encourage confidence as well as promote partnership.

The prospective existence of conflicts of interest among public and private organisations presents a further challenge. Private companies may be hesitant to share knowledge that might undermine their worth as competitors in the marketplace or reveal their shortcomings. In return, governments could be unwilling to provide the confidential data of private sector organisations. For us to resolve these kinds of issues, we have to be upfront and interact forthrightly. Additionally, appropriate laws and regulations may decrease the potential hazards associated with sharing information while also encouraging collaboration. Furthermore, the mindset of trust and respect among each other within the government and private sectors is essential for the effective execution of global PPPs as well.

A complicated look at that involves many different parties that are necessary for developing robust international PPPs. This encompasses governmental organisations, business organisations, global associations, and educational institutions. For the reason of sharing data, organising activities, and crafting efficient cyber safety efforts, collaboration among multiple stakeholders is crucial. More profound partnership is made feasible by ongoing interaction, joint endeavours, and sharing of information channels, all of which assist in fostering mutual confidence. In furtherance of technical assistance, the contract proposes the dissemination of the latest developments in governance, laws and regulations, and ethical concerns.

PPPs are going to be increasingly significant in digital safety for future generations. A collaborative approach between the public and private sectors will be crucial in protecting critical infrastructure, adhering to national security, and ensuring stability around the world, as the spectrum of cyber threats grows more complex. How national and international lawmakers encompass PPPs into their information security plans is going to determine whether these efforts will continue to be adapted in the coming year or years. In order to ensure a secure and adaptable cyberspace, we ought to continually take steps towards developing strong and flexible PPPs at all levels. The setting up of international standards and regulatory structures that are essential for the achievement of this important interaction, the establishment of a common mindset of information sharing, and the financial support of cyber security infrastructure development all rely upon adaptability and dialogue. The coming years of cyber security and, consequently, global security will ultimately be decided by these kinds of partnerships.

The crucial role of such PPPs in enhancing national and/or global cyber security was the primary focus of the prior debate. Nevertheless, even the most powerful PPPs will not succeed if cyber diplomacy cannot be carried out in a truly multilateral way. Nowadays, nearly every aspect of the cyber diplomacy ecosystem is regulated by a relatively small percentage of major governments and large multinational companies. Given that various perspectives as well as abilities necessary for an integrated strategy to tackle cyber security have been overlooked, this focus of influence and expertise results in important blind spots. A major change that expands involvement to encompass members of civil society organisations, nations that are developing, and the entire international community would be necessary for more equitable cyber diplomacy.

The exemption of countries that are developing from genuine participation in cyber diplomacy is an important roadblock to successful international cyber security. Given that they frequently do not have the resources and ability to react appropriately to the increasing digital dangers they face, these countries have to be highly susceptible to cyber attacks. Their fragile position is further aggravated by their absence of engagement in global discussion and norm-setting methods. Measures that enhance capacity should be given top priority according to an inclusive strategy, providing IDLs the financial backing, guidelines, and technical support that are needed to build their own cyber security abilities and efficiently take part in global discussions. This might encompass aid for the development of cyber security facilities, financial assistance for cyber security instruction, and technical support efforts that enhance capacity for institutions for developing the governing bodies of nations.

In addition, due to its marginalisation as a consequence of the technological gap, the Global South lacks the capacity to participate in cyber diplomacy efficiently. Their ability to get involved in online conversations, share knowledge, and respond to cyber threats is severely restricted by inequitable availability of technology and connectivity to the internet. It will take partnerships to establish internet infrastructure, foster digital literacy, and ensure fair equitable access to technological advances in order to close this gap in technology. Collaboration across borders will be crucial to this endeavour; powerful countries can help less fortunate countries through providing them technical and monetary support to build their digital skills and infrastructure development. It additionally involves assisting to develop cyber security resources and instruments in languages that are suitable as well as culturally relevant ways to ensure everyone understands and contributes efficiently.

Apart from just state-to-state participation, an important increase in private-sector partnership between advanced and developing nations is required for fostering inclusiveness. The sensitive nature of cyber security solutions and associated services calls for the participation of the international private sector. Creating collaborative ventures or partnerships for dissemination of technology along with capacity building between private sector companies in both developed and developing countries may be part of the collaboration. Guidelines designed to promote responsible and ethical company behaviour in emerging economies ought to function as a framework for this. It must not just generate revenue but also involve regional knowledge and funding. Furthermore, importance is placed on the crucial yet usually disregarded role that nongovernmental organisations serve to encourage encompassing cyber diplomacy. Given that civil society organisations have firsthand understanding of local contexts, these organisations are able to identify the distinctive cyber security difficulties that different groups are facing. Establishing moral and successful cyber policy requires a variety of viewpoints on human rights, digital inclusion, and ethical issues. It takes some significant work to include civil society organisations in policy discussions, consultations, and decision-making processes in order to include them in cyber diplomacy discussions. To make sure that their contributions are acknowledged and equally taken into consideration when coming up with policies, this involves encouraging research in organisations from civil society, incorporating capacity building efforts, and officially incorporating their point of view into debates encompassing the development of global norms.

Additionally, the vital role of organisations representing civil society assures that cyber security ethics can be effectively addressed. Privacy, surveillance, and free speech are among the many ethical quandaries that are brought up by the development and implementation of cyber security technological advancements. Organisations representing civil society frequently provide similarly relevant representation as well as analysis on these significant human rights problems bolstering cyber diplomacy with more comprehensive ethical and human rights factors to consider. Their close collaboration with communities that were impacted makes certain that cyber laws adhere to human rights and fundamental liberties as well as remaining technically sound.

Looking beyond a state-centric point of view is also essential to a more broad strategy for cyber diplomacy. However, a multi-stakeholder method involving individuals, companies, governments, and civil society organisations will be necessary as cyberspace grows ever more inter-related. In an ever-changing, complicated risk environment, this approach puts the greatest emphasis on collaboratively solving issues and mutual responsibility. Mutual accountability remains dispersed and up-to-date with broad channels for dialogue, adaptable methods of decision-making, as well as inclusive procedures for governance, which take into consideration the different points of view of every individual. By providing an environment for beneficial discussions, fostering collaboration, and encouraging the establishment of international standards and guidelines, global multilateral agencies that include the UN can contribute significantly towards encouraging this multi-stakeholder discussion.

Concrete measures for fostering an all-encompassing cyber diplomacy are overdue. Governments ought to constantly search for techniques to communicate with nations that are developing and groups from civil society, provide funds to assist them to build capability, as well as set up procedures for official involvement. This kind of support might come in the form of funding programs aimed at advancing cyber security in developing nations as well as efforts from different organisations to assist in facilitating the development of national cyber security methods, or financial aid and exchange programs which enable employees from developing countries to acquire significant cyber security expertise while engaging in global cooperation.

Global organisations also contribute significantly to the cause of integration. Additionally, they may encourage more extensive dialogue and collaboration among different stakeholders and aid in facilitating the development of international standards and guidelines that take into account the priorities and interests of all parties involved. Last but not least, the UN could make significant contributions in building capacity, improving data exchange, and the establishment of platforms that allow countries with low incomes and organisations of civil society to contribute substantially in cyber debates and decision-making, by working with pertinent specialised organisations. For the same reason, transparency and responsibility are essential for guaranteeing that individuals consistently endorse the causes that they would like to aid. Being forthcoming additionally requires agencies and governments to recognise and make available data and information in an open manner while offering every stakeholder an opportunity to participate in how decisions are made.

But encouraging more equitable cyber diplomacy is not just an issue of fairness; it additionally serves as a strategic requirement. A more flexible and adaptable digital age that is more prepared to meet the difficulties of the 21st century will come about from the actors growth and diversifying their portfolios Working together will help make sure that cyber security strategies are not only more effective but also driven by an improved understanding of the different requirements and circumstances of different organisations. In the final analysis, a broader approach for cyber diplomacy will ultimately render the online realm safer and fairer for all. Our ability to embrace diversity while developing a truly international, shared approach to address common problems with cyber security will decide the next phase of cyber diplomacy. We have only the potential to establish a safe, proportionate, and advantageous cyberspace by employing a comprehensive strategy. The significance of including cyber diplomacy was made readily apparent by those aspects, which understood the drawbacks of a state-centric approach and highlighted the essential functions performed by nations that are developing, grassroots organisations, and the business community. The preceding information has to serve as the basis for any dialogue with regard to the future course of global cyber security requirements and oversight. Going ahead, there are far too numerous significant variables to take into consideration simultaneously, including developments in geopolitics, innovations in technology, and the constantly changing character of cyber threats.

The built-in challenges of creating widely recognised guidelines and standards to safeguard peace are an important barrier in establishing efficient global agreements for the digital age field. Implementing global agreements and laws can be difficult because of the internets centralised and interdependent nature, which renders it a free-for-all. Cyber security guidelines are an issue of contention since states that have different technological abilities and national priorities are frequently at odds about the best methods to regulate. A prime instance of how challenging it can be to arrive at a consensus on certain key points related to international cyber safety law is the contention over what is considered a cyber attack, who ought to be held responsible, and the best way to deal with the consequences of a cyber disaster. The efforts to create a predictable and secure digital age environment are hindered by this uncertainty and discrepancy.

Creating effective global cyber security guidelines can be difficult due to the increasing level of detail and incidence of cyber attacks. To cope with the dynamic threat surroundings created by state-run hacking, online crime, and electronic warfare tactics, institutions of governance have to constantly reinvent and evolve. The problem becomes more severe by the fact that cyber attacks often go beyond national boundaries, making it increasingly difficult for a particular nation to effectively deal with them on its own turf. This requires the establishment of multilateral structures to facilitate sharing information, crisis management, and capacity building as well as improved collaboration across borders.

Recent developments regarding technology present both possibilities and difficulties for international cyber security guidelines. Modern technologies like machine learning or AI and quantum computing may enhance cyber security procedures and technologies, but they additionally bring new hazards and weaknesses. For instance, AI-driven attacks will grow harder and more complicated to detect, enabling them to slip through present cyber security safeguards. Similar to this, the advancement of quantum computing might render present encryption methods obsolete, which requires the growth of new secure encryption methods that might alter the current security structure. In order to ensure that the development and implementation of novel technologies adhere to international regulations and human rights, global resilience in traversing these developments in technology is necessary. This could encompass urging open dialogue about the trade-offs of quantum technology, working globally to establish regulations, and advocating the latest developments in AI security and confidentiality.

Shifts in international relations are also expected to have an important effect on the governing of global cyberspace. The nature of cyber security cooperation will shift as a consequence of new cyber powers, greater rivalry among present mega players, and an evolving cooperation structure. When external actors like terrorist groups and organised crime networks have enormous power, it can be challenging to create systems of governance. Identifying how to continue operating in this highly complicated political climate, while maintaining a commitment to global collaboration and the administration of law, is a particularly challenging task.

In addition, the connection between cyber security and human rights is an important problem that ought to be meticulously taken into consideration as additional international regulations are put forward in the years to come. There are numerous ethical and human rights problems associated with the implementation of technology for surveillance, including the likelihood of discrimination, and the possibility of observation and suppression of disagreement. International frameworks ought to make sure that cyber security measures are suitable, necessary, and human rights-compliant. In order to accomplish this, cyber security policymakers will need to emphasise an effective structure, which incorporates human rights factors into the development, implementation, and evaluation of measures to safeguard the internet. In the unlikely scenario that cyber security-related human rights have been breached, it additionally calls for accountability and corrective actions.

Global organisations will develop mechanisms that will establish future cyber policies and guidelines. The UN along with other important international organisations has to continue the initiative to facilitate interaction, collaboration, and development of global norms. Nevertheless, the effectiveness of these organisations will depend on their ability to respond to the constantly shifting environment of cyber threats and encompass a broad spectrum of business, state, and humans who matter, including governments in the first place, along with civil society. For these organisations to adequately satisfy the demands of everyone involved and guarantee that every decision serves the different goals and perspectives of the global population, these types of organisations have to operate through greater transparency and accountability. It also implies that UN agencies can, in addition to establishing additional agreements, strengthen sharing of data mechanisms, promote a more cooperative outlook, and advocate initiatives that build capacity that help developing nations in bolstering their cyber security capacity.

Working together and competition will probably be combined when establishing global cyber security norms and governance in the future. A multi-stakeholder approach comprising corporations, governments, non-profit organisations, and global organisations will be essential to efficient governance systems. It calls on individuals with perhaps opposing viewpoints to create a setting of mutual respect and compassion, enhance openness, and build trust.

International cyber security standards should additionally not be seen in a state of nothingness, as the real world and cyberspace continue to meld into an independent dynamic environment. Critical infrastructure, including electricity networks and public transportation, rely substantially on digital technologies and have become vulnerable to cyber attacks that could have detrimental consequences in reality. International collaboration will be necessary for safeguarding such critical facilities from cyber attacks and to make sure essential amenities are not halted. In order to accomplish this, it will be essential to leave behind traditional state-centred security structures while acknowledging the mutual dependence of both the physical and digital domains.

Last but not least, substantial expenditures in the area of capacity development can lead to innovations in the global norms for information security. One major problem is that developing nations are frequently ill prepared or untrained in dealing with security threats. Further global collaboration will be required to bridge this technological gap, with higher-income nations helping less fortunate nations with monetary, technical, and instructional assistance. As a means to minimise this likelihood in the field of cyber security, this capacity building ought to emphasise suitable constitutional levers, policy-making expertise, and organisational scaffolding alongside improving technological capabilities. To be able to improve global cyber security requirements, we then require significant investments in building capacities. More specifically, countries that are developing are frequently short of the financial backing and specialisation needed for successfully combating security threats. To continue to address this technology gap, greater global collaborations must be created, and more prosperous countries have to offer the requisite funding, technological expertise, and practical expertise to help establish government entities. Yet, developing this capacity should involve more than merely improving technical expertise; it ought to include comprehending policy development with regard to those investigations, and also understanding institutional structures for managing risk and structural and legal structures of expertise. In the long run, this will call for a shift in mindset from a solely reactive strategy to one that can be more forward-thinking, preventive in nature, welcoming, and bound by internationally recognised standards and guidelines with the goal to guarantee a secure and just technological future for all individuals.

Chapter Six

The Compass of a Diplomat: Charting a Course for Effective Cyber Diplomacy

Given that it can be challenging to comprehend the complicated terrain of international relations in the age of technology, diplomats must be competent in information security. This demands a comprehensive approach in which, instead of simply understanding technical terms, one must also understand the strategically important reference of cyber security within the broader context of international legislation, economic diplomacy, and foreign policy. The educational and training initiatives of diplomats must be significantly revamped to accommodate their understanding of the possibilities as well as challenges related to information security.

The curriculum should, most importantly, consist of an essential understanding of cyber security concepts as well. As opposed to becoming solely technical, the course ought to include an assessment of strategy that gives diplomatic staff the theoretical framework they need to understand the risks, weaknesses, and prospective consequences associated with cyber-related incidents. Understanding basic concepts like safeguarding information, security of networks, the use of cryptography responding to incidents, and vulnerability oversight are part of this. However, one must consider the strategic implications of the above ideas instead of being bogged down in minute details. For example, diplomats require being conscious of how a carefully constructed attack on an investment firm might bring about a worldwide economic downturn or how shortcomings in a nation-states critical infrastructure might be exploited to achieve political ends.

In spite of a fundamental understanding, diplomats require instruction regarding particular domains that are specifically connected to their diplomatic responsibilities. This requirement necessitates the creation of concentrated instructional resources that point out specific cyber security issues that occur especially in diplomatic environments. For instance, diplomats establishing agreements regarding arms control need concentrated understanding of the information technology consequences related to defence infrastructure and weapon deployments, such as the possibility that compromises could raise tensions and spark conflict. Economic diplomats should further be mindful of the importance of cyber security in safeguarding national economic goals, regulating the risks related to international data transfers and e-commerce, and addressing cybercrime and infringement of intellectual property. In a similar vein, when ambassadors engage in rights-related debates, they have to understand the effect which cyber monitoring and gathering of information has on the rights of individuals to privacy, freedom of expression, and other basic liberties. Given that they effectively prepare diplomats for opportunity situations in the real world, scenario-based instruction and simulation-based instruction have to obtain greater emphasis. Realistic cyber threats, global legal systems, and the challenges of negotiations between nations ought to be included in simulated events. Diplomats may experiment with decision-making in secure circumstances while creating effective strategies for managing cyber security issues with this fully engaged approach. For example, diplomats might be required to communicate with different countries, private sector participants, and global organisations to coordinate the response and mitigation efforts in the case of a cyber attack in opposition to an essential infrastructure mechanism.

The promotion of a culture of continuing growth and instruction for employees is just as essential. Diplomats have to remain up-to-date on the most recent threats, developments in technology, and standards of excellence in the constantly developing area of information security. Ongoing training developments, involvement in industry events and conferences, and interaction with top cyber safety professionals are a few examples of how to do this. Distance learning programs, live webinars, and immersive learning platforms all provide outstanding opportunities for continuing education. Enabling them to pursue important credentials and educational possibilities in international relations or cyber security, with a Masters degree focusing on information security, would also substantially strengthen the abilities of diplomats.

For such training initiatives to be effective, both in regard to establishing security and essential information transfer, cooperation between both private and public industry is necessary. Research centres and universities are capable of offering academic expertise and scientific understanding. Government-sponsored organisations may provide the use of receptive information as well as hands-on expertise, while firms in the private sector can present knowledge about new dangers and industry standards of excellence. A mutually beneficial approach that emphasises on every sectors advantages can additionally develop as the outcome of instructional efforts and sharing of expertise projects. In order to ensure that the training reflects the different points of view and challenges of the global community, experts from nations that are developing must also be involved in this collaborative strategy.

Another essential component involves acquiring good cyber security methods for communicating. Useful technical knowledge and implication exchange for non-technical individuals, which includes officials from the government, the media, and the public, should have the ability to be provided by diplomatic officials. This encompasses having the capacity to concisely explain the technical aspects of challenges, translate challenging information into understandable narratives, and having control over the way other people see business responses to cyber security incidents. In negotiations abroad and collaboration, diplomats are also mindful of how to communicate effectively with multiple stakeholders from different backgrounds in order to find some mutually beneficial agreements. Instruction in interpersonal communication additionally focuses on relations with the media and public speaking in both written and spoken forms, and techniques for negotiation that pertain to technological problems.

Creating strong diplomatic technological capacity relies primarily on establishing sound global partnerships and cooperation. By means of cooperative responses to unexpected events, amalgamating data, and connection exercises, diplomats must foster the goodwill of their colleagues from other countries. This implies having great awareness of the several approaches of cyber security around cultural sensitivity, and cross-cultural communication abilities. Imagine such cyber security diplomacy training including components on international cooperation and discussion and the difficulties of trust and coordination in a hostile environment. Apart from mandatory courses, diplomatic institutions have been encouraging a culture in the understanding of technological safety. This includes creating clear guidelines for the arrangement of cyber security policies and actions; ensuring that resources are dedicated to preventing cyber security hazards; and encouraging a reporting and taking responsibility culture. They must understand that it is an operational requirement where the involvement of all employees is essential, in addition to an IT-related problem with the most technical significance in an educational institution. Eliminating the risk of error by humans, which is frequently considered as an important exploitable risk, is dependent upon conventional awareness sessions on cyber security for all the staff including managerial and technical staff at their place of employment.

Furthermore, it is essential that the effectiveness of diplomatic cyber security instruction be assessed frequently and modified in alignment. This might involve periodic evaluation of the fundamental elements of instructional initiatives, gathering remarks from diplomats and other individuals, and monitoring how training influences diplomatic behaviour. Learning to operate systems in cyber security has to stay up-to-date since the rapid move for advancement in technology requires it. Not only in reaction to responses but additionally considering most recent research on the dynamic issues they experience, diplomatic training in cyber security therefore needs to be frequently examined and enhanced. Systematic evaluation of the impact of such education is crucial in order to identify areas of growth and ensure that diplomats obtain lessons in the expertise and abilities that are essential for establishing the difficult landscape associated with global security measures.

The final approach for acquiring technological safety understanding for diplomats is a more restricted but nonetheless comprehensive one. Basic education, specialised instruction, case-based instruction, continuous professional growth, cross-sectoral partnerships, abilities to communicate, global connections, information security culture, and continuous evaluation make up various parts of this matter. Giving these areas the highest priority helps diplomats to better grasp and handle the cyber security challenges of the 21st century, so that they aid the building of a safer and a more secure planet. As countries look to send their best and most vibrant diplomats to take part in diplomatic moves for the benefit of their nations, it is consistent with the reality of the global community and the digital age every day being less expensive and constantly shifting. The effective implementation of subsequent diplomatic efforts in the age of technology is thus dependent upon having an adequately trained and thoroughly specialised diplomatic corps that has sophisticated cyber security accreditation.

Clarity about national cyber defence capabilities and strategies is also a necessity. Transparency may mitigate mistrust and miscalculation, but states have ample reason to fear disclosing sensitive information. These open discussions could also be related to national cyber defence systems, difficulties and capabilities, as well as national cyber security strategies that set free national strategies and policies. At this level of national goals and plans, publication should not be confused with sensitive information about company operations or weaknesses. By showing that there is a commitment to accountability about what governments does in the digital space, this transparency builds trust.

This trust is further built with the establishment of internationally accepted standards of behaviour in cyberspace. By articulating acceptable use of cyber capabilities, proscribing illegal acts, such as cyber attacks against critical infrastructure, and providing modes of accountability, these standards would apply to multiple forms of government activity in cyberspace. Those processes could not and would not happen overnight, but be the result of an extended period of international dialogue and cooperation. The crisis and survival of these multilateral organisations, such as the UN, hinges on these conversations and states having some form of agreement on how to tackle international issues. However, the effectiveness of these discussion boards depends on the willingness of states to engage in constructive deliberation and search for common ground. Treaties containing and ensuring such enforceable norms can and will be effectively complemented by more robust enforcement mechanisms, formalisation of such norms and evolution of international laws in the digital age. This could mean establishing rules for managing disputed behaviours as well as mechanisms for reporting and acknowledging cyber attacks.

Most importantly, these requirements need to make room for the various abilities and viewpoints of state governments. Building sufficient consensus among states to accomplish expansive compliance to digital standards seems unlikely to be a feasible option if an individual international agreement relies on a strategy that fits all. In order to establish an architecture that is simultaneously effective and welcoming, it is crucial to acknowledge that various countries have different levels of advanced technological capacity alongside their distinctive national security imperatives that exist. A receptive and complex look at this requires taking into consideration the distinctive circumstances of each nation. In order to guarantee that all states have the expertise and resources they need to take an active role in the development and implementation of global cyber norms while the primary focus ought to concentrate more on developing the capacity development of nations and assistance with technology.

In addition to communication being associated with standards set up, the development of CBMs is additionally important. CBMs are defined as measures taken by states to increase trust between individuals while decreasing the probability of disapproval, disagreement, and miscommunication. CBMs in the Internet age, for example, may include sharing of information deals, joint cyber security exercises, and the establishment of crisis-management hotlines. By evaluating their skills and abilities in secure conditions, states will be able to develop mutual comprehension and learn from the experiences of others. Any accord on sharing information might foster a more proactive approach to cyber security by aiding states in avoiding and reacting to cyber attacks. In periods of crisis, hotlines can serve as a vital route for immediate interaction where it contributes most and lead to hindering uncertain shortcomings that might result in escalated situations. Establishing confidence in how states maintain adherence to global standards and illustrating their willingness to abstain from hostile or negligent behaviour can be accomplished by establishing a transparent reporting method (while taking into account the consequences for national security). An essential basis of trust is this level of detail in the reporting of incidents, thereby rendering it far less probable that events are going to be dismissed and interpreted incorrectly, which could contribute to heightened conflicts.

Furthermore, international organisations will be important in promoting trust as well as confidence. Here, the UN may foster the establishment of global norms by enabling discussions, promoting collaboration, and establishing relationships with regional organisations and specialised organisations. Yet, the partisan readiness of member-states to engage firmly and endorse the efforts of these organisations is an essential requirement for their successful functioning. Improvement in the capacity of these organisations to effectively handle concerns regarding cyber security is essential, especially given the objective of providing technical assistance while promoting this type of development of capacity. These organisations may further serve as unbiased agents in disagreements and discussions about contentious issues in cyber security. Their credentials in diplomacy and rule of law can also be beneficial when setting and upholding novel standards of conduct in cyberspace.

Ultimately, it has to be essential that one fosters the mindset of ethical innovation in information security. This encompasses creating and implementing technologies in a manner that reduces risks and maximises equilibrium. The creation and implementation of machine learning and AI in cyber security requires concerns about ethics as these developments must be used responsibly and not be employed to increase existing holes or establish fresh ones. Being involved with the private sector as well as academic communities, carefully revealing shortcomings, as well as making sure that cyber security advancements conform to stringent guidelines for ethics are crucial. By promoting progress that contributes to stability and security worldwide, one can promote confidence while establishing responsibility to take action in order to avoid neglect and unexpected repercussions. At the corporate level, an approach to enhance present developments is now being created. An ongoing commitment to accountable innovation will act as an essential component for promoting mutual trust and confidence in the complicated and constantly shifting world of cyberspace. Creating a safe and secure future in the age of technology calls for collaboration. Besides bilateral ties, there are multiple pillars of shared international efforts on the IoT, and these will be understood as time passes by means of the establishment of internationally recognised guidelines and global structures. Stakeholders in the present structure interact mainly, but they do so in groups while reacting to challenges quickly instead of actively by developing solutions to them. Establishing a more robust better-performing system will call for focused broad efforts. With any hesitation, nevertheless, the UNs demand for overseeing cyberspace requires it to be expanded. While the UN has addressed cyber security in a variety of forums, a more concentrated and centralised method must be developed. Relevant committees and bodies, like the UNGGE and the First Committee of the General Assembly, could have their present strengths significantly enhanced, or a UN agency could be created. More than just diplomatic efforts must be the primary objective of this elevated UN participation; countries with low incomes must also continue to benefit from technical support as well as capacity building. Numerous countries do not have the ability or expertise to take part actively in global cyber security debates and pursue effective cyber safety standards.

A UN-led program that provides these countries the knowledge, equipment, and expertise they require to strengthen their cyber security defences while continuing to participate in global collaboration assignments could potentially fill this shortcoming. A fairer and effectively functioning international cyber security ecosystem could be achieved by making sure that the development as well as implementation of global norms are actually participatory and serve the needs and concerns of every nation.

Finally, the UN should also regulate and contribute to addressing challenges in cyberspace. It is exceptionally difficult to determine who deserves blame for a cyber attack, and disagreements over who carried it out may fuel conflicts and ignite repercussions. A credible and unbiased organisation like the UN could serve as an advantageous platform for states to debate and establish ways of settling dispute resolution, develop mechanisms for looking at and responding to cyber attacks, and have discussions. This renders it important to provide the UN an explicit purpose and adequate mechanisms to resolve conflicts along with strengthening its technical skills. Creating a transparent process for looking through and placing blame for cyber attacks would greatly reduce, if not entirely eradicate, the risk of miscommunication as well as escalated situations, considering that diplomatic neutrality might not constitute any enforceable power. This would require a coordinated scientific procedure facilitated by experts from various nations that are members, which would foster willingness while decreasing the risk of actions that are unilateral being carried out in the wake of partially created events.

It seems that there is also an essential function for regional organisations and other non-UN organisations. Member-states of regional security organisations, such as NATO or ASEAN, may work together more effectively by sharing techniques that work, conducting joint exercises, and implementing regional cyber security standards effectively. Finally, these organisations could collaborate with the UN in establishing a more comprehensive and successful strategy for international cyber governance. In particular, closer collaboration between NATOs Cooperative Cyber Defence Centre of Excellence (CCDCOE) and similar institutions internationally may result in greater standardised procedures of cyber security processes and the communication of expertise that is essential for activities. The establishment of shared threat intelligence systems would also enable coordinated responses and enable the swift distribution of information about arising security threats.

Implementing globally accepted standards of conduct is an essential aspect of strengthening international cooperation. These requirements ought to encompass particular responsibilities like preserving critical facilities, prohibiting the development and use of malicious codes, and safeguarding against inappropriate use of AI in cyber security. They should not serve as merely broad recommendations. Governments, the business sector, institutions of higher learning, and civil society groups have to be engaged in the meticulous and resilient manner of establishing these minimum standards. A multi-stakeholder approach ensures an expanded spectrum of perspectives and allows the development of effective, generally accepted standards.

In addition, these regulations have to be followed. While international legislation seldom incorporates resilient ways to ensure implementation of legal compliance, the global community has made efforts to hinder and criminalise violations. Developing systems for monitoring and attributing cyber attacks, specifically outlining the consequences for infringements, and examining likely worldwide restrictions or legal frameworks might be beneficial to combat international online criminal activity. Similar to present-day global laws tackling various kinds of cross-border criminal activity, a multilateral convention on cybercrime could provide an invaluable constitutional basis for handling offences and encourage new forms of global collaboration in prosecution for these offences. There would be numerous benefits even though this approach would call for a lot of diplomatic effort to make sure that different countries with various legal frameworks and perspectives are on the same wavelength.

In the end, promoting an optimistic and trustworthy culture is vitally important. This demands open discussion, clarity regarding national cyber security regulations, and state-by-state commitment towards addressing state cyberspace behaviour issues. Establishing confidence is a process as it calls for work continually to show your sincerity and interest to collaborate with others. Regular talks, collaborative endeavours, and CBMs support a shared comprehension and reduce the likelihood of misunderstanding or escalated situations. These measures could include, for example, a collaboration of technical experts, group cyber security instruction courses, or the establishment of avenues for communication for swift crisis reactions that follow. Enhanced interaction allows promoting an inclusive culture, greater transparency, and a shared understanding of the obstacles and risks jeopardising national and organisational cyber systems in place.

The primary objective is to foster better global collaboration in this domain, which is an essential and crucial task. Building capacity, fostering trust, and developing and carrying out global regulations should be the most important objectives of this broad strategy, encompassing the UN, regional bodies, and various other international venues. The problems at hand are not just technical; rather, they indicate an important development in international diplomacy that requires forward-thinking and mutually beneficial strategies to effectively address obstacles in the age of technology. Future world safety will rely progressively more on the establishment of this global technological cooperation. To safely and effectively handle cyber incidents and situations of crisis, an expanded strategy that goes beyond technical understanding is necessary. It requires an advanced knowledge of global politics, diplomatic efforts, and the complicated nature of national interests and objectives. As they safeguard national interests and respect global standards, new diplomats have to navigate through the challenges of attribution, duty, and escalated matters.

Effective response to incidents has been rendered feasible by an effective national cyber security approach. In addition to addressing the technical elements of cyber attack scenarios such as strong defences, detection of events systems, etc., this requires taking into account the diplomatic and political aspects as well. A national response strategy that sets forth communication, escalation, and authority exercise techniques is indispensable. The following strategy will spell out the respective functions as well as obligations of different government departments, businesses, and partners from abroad. Regular drills and training sessions allow for assessing the plan s effectiveness and identify domains for growth and development, ensuring that response is not just coordinated effectively but also quick and effective. The US employs a national cyber strategy that sets out an all-encompassing strategy, which includes sharing offensive, defensive, and diplomatic abilities. Similarly comprehensive approaches, which take into consideration the safety of their setting as well as assets, should be imitated by nations around the world.

Especially when using sophisticated technical analysis, attribution of cyber attacks is widely challenging. The obstacles of deeply recognising those responsible frequently lead to international disputes and escalated situations. Future diplomats ought to become aware of the limitations to attribution and the possibilities of oversight. Although extensive technological research is essential, diplomatic attempts have to focus on establishing common ground and an opportunity for collaboration even without a precise method of attribution; indispensable characteristics are willingness and demonstrating ability. Functioning on ongoing initiatives like the Budapest Convention on Cybercrime, UN Cybercrime Convention as well as creating global structures for collaborative research will assist in building trust while avoiding issues with unilateral actions regarding cyber attacks.

Two important international agreements that not only strengthen cyber security are the UN Cybercrime Convention and the Budapest Convention. The aforementioned agreements provide a framework for international cooperation in the investigation and criminal prosecution of cybercrimes including fraud, online exploitation, and cybercrime. The Budapest Convention is known for being very targeted and specific in its approach, putting a heavy emphasis on rights protection and enforcement. Its reach and coverage of offences is limited however. By difference, and the UN Cybercrime

Convention offers a broader take, it also establishes avenues for international collaboration and support while also addressing evolve new cyberthreats in enter. While the fidelity of the UN Cybercrime Convention is acknowledged, it has been criticized for its deficiencies of transparency, prevention of human rights and risk of abuse (Refer to Annexure 3 for more details).

In 2024 the UN General Assembly adopted the UN Convention against Cybercrime, a landmark global accord intended to enhance cooperation among nations in the fight against cybercrime and protect societies from technological threats. The signing of the Hanoi Convention, set for mid-2025, will act as a solid turning point in international security measures, showcasing the increasing role of Vietnam within the global realm.

In the light of above, diplomats are thus essential to ensure that participating countries honor and uphold such agreements, given the shared involuntary nature of the commitments described above. Through diplomacy they assist countries to negotiate mutually agreeable terms and information exchange that cannot be given the opportunity with other means. As technology expands and cyberthreats continue to evolve, ambassadors will thus play a critical role in forming international cybersecurity partnerships that defend the online infrastructure and combat cybercrime on a global scale.

Furthermore, massive oversights of cyber incidents are a worldwide endeavour. That involves creating specific processes for sharing data, collaborating on undertakings and putting together responses. Agreements, both multilateral and bilateral, could provide an enormous amount of support for this type of cooperation. Effective drafting of these instruments ensures that they are consistent with national laws and independence. Trust between nations necessitates constitutional and technological ways to facilitate data sharing. This requires tackling present-day problems, which includes different levels of cyber security specialisation and different understanding of global legislation. Enhancing partnerships would commence with creating and carrying out mutually agreed responsibility and response guidelines and processes. These regulations could include calls for legal recommendations for addressing questions over accountability and the issue of attribution technological procedures for examining cyber attacks, and methods for distributing information about threats along with supporting documentation.

Only with global organisations such as the UN, with world actors at the heart of things, can we encourage partnerships and establish guidelines for conduct in cyberspace. While effective and important, the UNs present methods call for simplification when dealing with specific challenges brought about by cyber attacks. In order to effectively address a problem of cyber security, this might require either a wholesale growth in existing firms or the establishment of an entirely new agency. Such firms can be quite beneficial in addressing disputes, supporting research, and providing countries that are developing technological advances support. When eventual widespread cyber attacks do take place, this expanded oversight of the UN will be essential for ensuring an orderly and coordinated global response that hinders the worsening of the circumstances.

In addition to the UN, regional organisations like the EU or NATO can be quite beneficial in allowing integrated responses to cyber incidents happening in their respective domains. These organisations could promote the exchange of data, assist regional cyber security guidelines to evolve, and carry out collaborative missions. Additionally, greater collaboration between the UN and regional organisations will be needed to ensure an integrated worldwide approach to cyber-related incidents. The partnership might provide opportunities for joint exercises, professional exchanges that are available and the creation of mutually strengthening cyber security strategies.

In the digital age, both response to incidents and safeguarding are dependent strategically on the business community. Understanding the significance of the private sector, future diplomats will need to communicate with and counsel companies to establish incentives for minimum involvement and engagement in worldwide undertakings. Creating broad avenues for dialogue and supportive mechanisms with businesses from the private sector will be essential in order to more effectively restrain the disruption brought about by cyber attacks. This is particularly important for important facilities where the general public and private sectors frequently have competing objectives and responsibility.

Cyber events have ethical and legal repercussions that need to be given special attention. Diplomats have become aware that cyber attacks further contravene human rights, which includes liberty of expression and confidentiality. Therefore, they ought to stand ready to uphold global standards adhering to these fundamental principles and foster the safeguarding of human rights in the regulatory environment of technology and cyberspace. This demands a cautious mix between national interests and promoting international human rights norms. Diplomats must be well versed in cyber security technology and human rights regulations since they must have the capacity for balancing measures necessary to safeguard national security with the need to acknowledge rules of conduct.

To aggravate the situation, nations that are developing may not have the tools or understanding for effectively managing cyber issues. Future diplomats have the opportunity to close this gap by providing assistance with technology, building capacity, and training. The determination towards developing cyber security capacities across borders will fortify the global system. The transfer of technology, group training operations, and innovative sharing tasks might as well form part of building capacity. More political initiatives towards enhancing global partnerships originate from this, including efforts to help nations that are developing to establish an additional equitable and secure digital environment for all. Additionally, there is no actual equality without the inclusion of technology. The wealthy countries and international organisations can be extremely beneficial when assisting such efforts by means of specialised assistance and strengthening capacity projects financing. Responding to cyber incidents and problems requires proactive, comprehensive strategies. It calls for great diplomatic capacity, an ongoing commitment to productive global partnership, and a thorough understanding of international issues. The future generation of diplomats needs to be able to navigate the multifaceted nature of this ever increasingly important realm if they want to maintain a secure and equitable international cyberspace. Effective diplomatic engagement going forward is contingent strategically on the capacity to weave together technical knowledge, diplomacy, and international law and bridge the gaps between them at all times.

In the ever more complex arena of cyber diplomacy, one must possess an extensive understanding of associated concerns regarding ethics. The extremely broad reach of cyberspace and its innately anonymous nature, which, one after the other shows alien challenges, has questioned conventions of diplomacy. Future diplomats have to have a resilient legal expertise along with expertise in technology in order that they can gain insight to make choices and act more ethically in this age of technology.

One of the most pressing ethical issues involves assigning cyber attacks. The biggest challenge in recognising perpetrators is the fact that they cannot be identified with absolute certainty, leading to allegations and counter-accusations that sow animosity between nation-states finally turning into a confrontation. One has to combat the urge to make rapid choices on what is not sufficient or inconsistent proof. On the contrary, thorough and comprehensive study including diplomatic interaction alongside technical evaluation is necessary. More specifically when domestically driven pressure from politics or a drive towards quick reprisal drives it to condemn responsibility, incidents still in progress can significantly sour global ties and hinder attempts at cooperation as well as coordination. For instance, although the attack on the Stuxnet of 2010 demonstrated the participation of the US and Israel, it initially caused anxiety and distrust among numerous individuals, emphasizing the risks of relying unverified allegations on such acts.

Future diplomatic officials have to be prepared to handle these scenarios with sensitivity, highlighting the importance of establishing the basis of conclusive evidence while preventing impulsive generalisations with profound repercussions. Employing offensive cyber capabilities provides a crucial ethical intervention point in time. While such types of powers could be observed as necessary for the efficient operation of national security systems, their establishment as well as implementation brings significant moral concerns regarding the principle of proportionality discrimination, and the possibility of adverse consequences. The strategies under debate are pre-emptively defensive in intent and behaviour; nevertheless their mere presence ignites assertions of conflict by simply the fact that the lines dividing offensive from defensive cyber operations have become gradually unclear. This also shows the uncertainty of moral problems, made even more complex by the lack of clear international regulations or standards for managing adverse cyber operations.

These difficulties will compel future diplomats to contribute to the development of exact global regulations articulating suitable applications of cyber warfare capabilities while keeping no less understanding of the vital importance of transparency and limited quantities. Powerful oversight and accountability structures have to be constructed in order to prevent improper utilisation of such legitimacy. Creating universal standards of actions equivalent to what determines the employment of conventional weapons might serve to bring about increased predictability and reduce the probability of inadvertent escalated situations.

The problem at hand pertains very closely to acts of provocation in cyber security and the protection of human rights. Cyber attacks could impact basic human rights such as those pertaining to data access, confidentiality, and the right to free speech. Targeting media professionals, non-profit groups, political dissidents, cyber espionage, security breaches, and disinformation campaigns undermines fundamental freedoms and constitutional processes. Considering this, future diplomats will have to deal with these problems and advocate online defence of fundamental liberties. In the regulatory environment of cyber diplomacy, this kind of expertise calls for not only expertise in technology but also expertise in human rights laws around the world and an active commitment to maintaining and protecting these fundamental principles. While those infringing fundamental liberties in cyberspace ought to be brought to justice, compliance to human rights in cyberspace demands the establishment of strong legal frameworks and redressal systems ensuring adequate damages for persecuted people in general.

Data privacy unveils yet another difficult ethical puzzle. In an era when data is becoming more and more important for the advancement of world relations, that is, collecting intelligence and counter-terrorism, there is an imperative for an appropriate compromise between national security goals and the safeguarding of ones privacy. More specifically, when comprehensive legal safeguards or surveillance mechanisms fail to exist, the collection and dissemination of sensitive information across national boundaries demands profound ethical concerns. Future diplomats have to push for globally recognised standards around the security and confidentiality of data to ensure data gathering and dissemination actions are ethically open, and in accordance with global human rights law. One has to continue forward, regardless of the obstacles presented. More formidable global agreements or the adoption of standard procedures maintaining the rights of individuals and ensuring accountable data handling used in those forming technologies might constitute part of this representation.

With the technological divide, ethical problems additionally encompass their own shortcomings. The plan of action predominantly discusses inequitable opportunities for technological advances and the shortage of digital skills as the primary root cause of the differing ability among countries to participate in the world of technology. Many developing nations lack the resources and expertise needed for dealing with cyber security threats and attacks. This could exacerbate existing disparities while encouraging the exclusion of communities that are disadvantaged. In order to bridge this digital gap, future ambassadors are expected to champion worldwide cooperation and capacity-building initiatives. This looks for an enthusiasm to provide assistance with technology, which promotes involvement and efficient procedures in the effective operation of cyberspace. Guaranteeing that the positive benefits of cyberspace are evenly distributed will contribute to avoiding technological exclusion for any particular country and ensure that each country has an equal opportunity to take action in the information age.

Using AI in cyber security raises concerns about ethics. Although machines with intelligence may enhance cyberspace, there are additional risks that include prejudice, discrimination, and autonomous weaponry. Future diplomats should rapidly communicate about the moral quandaries caused by the deployment of new war methods in ways that involve communication for an ethical development and application of AI in cyber security. With an eye on openness, responsibility, and oversight by humans, it involves pushing international collaboration in order to establish ethical guidelines and norms for the development and use of AI-powered advances in technology. In the end, the constantly shifting characteristic of cyberspace implies that moral standards and structures for governance have to be constantly reviewed. As technological advances expand, there are undoubtedly greater ethical difficulties. Future diplomats ought to strive to embrace an understanding of a lifelong pursuit of knowledge and critical thought so that they are potentially equipped to discuss these changes. This involves financing instructional and educational campaigns that offer diplomats the instruments they require to reach an agreement of the rapidly altering ethical landscape of cyber diplomacy.

In a nutshell, establishing the moral problems of cyber diplomacy will require an integrated approach. Future diplomats have to function in an ethically committed manner, accountable and open, deeply rooted in international law and respect for human rights and ethically severe. In basic terms, one may progress towards a secure and equitable technological future by tackling these challenges immediately and fostering global collaboration. Building a more equitable, thus more secure cyberspace will depend on discovering equilibrium between the need for national security and the upholding of human rights and promoting the development of global collaboration. In addition to just adhering to the letter of current rules, it will require an approach of evolving adaptation, partnership, and dedication in order to establish an ethical and upright digital age for everyone.

ANNEXURES

Annexure One

Draft United Nations Convention against Cybercrime

Strengthening international cooperation for combating certain crimes committed by means of information and communications technology systems and for the sharing of evidence in electronic form of serious crimes

New York, 29 July–9 August 2024

Preamble

The States Parties to the present Convention,

Bearing in mind the purposes and principles of the Charter of the United Nations, [*agreed ad referendum*]

Noting that information and communications technologies, while having enormous potential for the development of societies, create new opportunities for perpetrators, may contribute to the increase in the rate and diversity of criminal activities, and may have an adverse impact on States, enterprises and the well-being of individuals and society as a whole, [*agreed ad referendum*]

Concerned that the use of information and communications technology systems can have a considerable impact on the scale, speed and scope of criminal offences, including offences related to terrorism and transnational organized crime, such as trafficking in persons, the smuggling of migrants, the illicit manufacturing of and trafficking in firearms, their parts, components and ammunition, drug trafficking and trafficking in cultural property,

Convinced of the need to pursue, as a matter of priority, a global criminal justice policy aimed at the protection of society against cybercrime by, inter alia, adopting appropriate legislation, establishing common offences and procedural powers and fostering international cooperation to prevent and combat such activities more effectively at the national, regional and international levels,

Determined to deny safe havens to those who engage in cybercrime by prosecuting these crimes wherever they occur, [*agreed ad referendum*]

Stressing the need to enhance coordination and cooperation among States by, inter alia, providing technical assistance and capacity-building, including the transfer of technology on mutually agreed terms, to countries, in particular developing countries, upon their request, to improve national legislation and frameworks and enhance the capacity of national authorities to deal with cybercrime in all its forms, including its prevention, detection, investigation and prosecution, and emphasizing in this context the role that the United Nations plays,

Recognizing the increasing number of victims of cybercrime, the importance of obtaining justice for those victims and the necessity to address the needs of persons in vulnerable situations in measures taken to prevent and combat the offences covered by this Convention, [*agreed ad referendum*]

Determined to prevent, detect and suppress more effectively international transfers of property obtained as a result of cybercrime and to strengthen international cooperation in the recovery and return of proceeds of the crimes established in accordance with this Convention,

Bearing in mind that preventing and combating cybercrime is a responsibility of all States and that they must cooperate with one another, with the support and involvement of relevant international and regional organizations, as well as nongovernmental organizations, civil society organizations, academic institutions and private sector entities, if their efforts in this area are to be effective,

Recognizing the importance of mainstreaming a gender perspective in all relevant efforts to prevent and combat the offences covered by this Convention, in accordance with domestic law,

Mindful of the need to achieve law enforcement objectives and to ensure respect for human rights and fundamental freedoms as enshrined in applicable international and regional instruments,

Acknowledging the right to protection against arbitrary or unlawful interference with ones privacy, and the importance of protecting personal data,

Commending the work of the United Nations Office on Drugs and Crime and other international and regional organizations in preventing and combating cybercrime, [*agreed ad referendum*]

Recalling General Assembly resolutions 74/247 of 27 December 2019 and 75/282 of 26 May 2021,

Taking into account the existing international and regional conventions and treaties on cooperation in criminal matters, as well as similar treaties that exist between Member States of the United Nations, [*agreed ad referendum*]

Have agreed as follows:

Chapter I
General Provisions

Article 1: Statement of purpose

The purposes of this Convention are to:

(a) Promote and strengthen measures to prevent and combat cybercrime more efficiently and effectively; [*agreed ad referendum*]

(b) Promote, facilitate and strengthen international cooperation in preventing and combating cybercrime; and [*agreed ad referendum*]

(c) Promote, facilitate and support technical assistance and capacity-building to prevent and combat cybercrime, in particular for the benefit of developing countries.

Article 2: Use of terms

For the purposes of this Convention:

(a) Information and communications technology system shall mean any device or group of interconnected or related devices, one or more of which, pursuant to a program, gathers, stores and performs automatic processing of electronic data; [*agreed ad referendum*]

(b) Electronic data shall mean any representation of facts, information or concepts in a form suitable for processing in an information and communications technology system, including a program suitable to cause an information and communications technology system to perform a function; [*agreed ad referendum*]

(c) Traffic data shall mean any electronic data relating to a communication by means of an information and communications technology system, generated by an information and communications technology system that formed a part in the chain of communication, indicating the communications origin, destination, route, time, date, size, duration or type of underlying service; [*agreed ad referendum*]

(d) Content data shall mean any electronic data, other than subscriber information or traffic data, relating to the substance of the data transferred by an information and communications technology system, including, but not limited to, images, text messages, voice messages, audio recordings and video recordings; [*agreed ad referendum*]

(e) Service provider shall mean any public or private entity that:

(i) Provides to users of its service the ability to communicate by means of an information and communications technology system; or

(ii) Processes or stores electronic data on behalf of such a communications service or users of such a service;

(f) Subscriber information shall mean any information that is held by a service provider, relating to subscribers of its services other than traffic or content data and by which can be established:

(i) The type of communications service used, the technical provisions related thereto and the period of service;

(ii) The subscribers identity, postal or geographical address, telephone or other access number, billing or payment information, available on the basis of the service agreement or arrangement;

(iii) Any other information on the site of the installation of communications equipment, available on the basis of the service agreement or arrangement;

[*agreed ad referendum*]

(g) Personal data shall mean any information relating to an identified or identifiable natural person; [*agreed ad referendum*]

(h) Serious crime shall mean conduct constituting an offence punishable by a maximum deprivation of liberty of at least four years or a more serious penalty;

(i) Property shall mean assets of every kind, whether corporeal or incorporeal, movable or immovable, tangible or intangible, including virtual assets, and legal documents or instruments evidencing title to, or interest in, such assets; [*agreed ad referendum*]

(j) Proceeds of crime shall mean any property derived from or obtained, directly or indirectly, through the commission of an offence; [*agreed ad referendum*]

(k) Freezing or seizure shall mean temporarily prohibiting the transfer, conversion, disposition or movement of property or temporarily assuming custody or control of property on the basis of an order issued by a court or other competent authority; [*agreed ad referendum*]

(l) Confiscation, which includes forfeiture where applicable, shall mean the permanent deprivation of property by order of a court or other competent authority; [*agreed ad referendum*]

(m) Predicate offence shall mean any offence as a result of which proceeds have been generated that may become the subject of an offence as defined in article 17 of this Convention; [*agreed ad referendum*]

(n) Regional economic integration organization shall mean an organization constituted by sovereign States of a given region to which its member States have transferred competence in respect of matters governed by this Convention and which has been duly authorized, in accordance with its internal procedures, to sign, ratify, accept, approve or accede to it; references to States Parties under this Convention shall apply to such organizations within the limits of their competence;

(o) Emergency shall mean a situation in which there is a significant and imminent risk to the life or safety of any natural person.

Article 3: Scope of application

This Convention shall apply, except as otherwise stated herein, to:

(a) The prevention, investigation and prosecution of the criminal offences established in accordance with this Convention, including the freezing, seizure, confiscation and return of the proceeds from such offences;

(b) The collecting, obtaining, preserving and sharing of evidence in electronic form for the purpose of criminal investigations or proceedings, as provided for in articles 23 and 35 of this Convention.

Article 4: Offences established in accordance with other United Nations conventions and protocols

1. In giving effect to other applicable United Nations conventions and protocols to which they are Parties, States Parties shall ensure that criminal offences established in accordance with such conventions and protocols are also considered criminal offences under domestic law when committed through the use of information and communications technology systems.
2. Nothing in this article shall be interpreted as establishing criminal offences in accordance with this Convention.

Article 5: Protection of sovereignty [agreed ad referendum]

1. States Parties shall carry out their obligations under this Convention in a manner consistent with the principles of sovereign equality and territorial integrity of States and that of non-intervention in the domestic affairs of other States.
2. Nothing in this Convention shall entitle a State Party to undertake in the territory of another State the exercise of jurisdiction and performance of functions that are reserved exclusively for the authorities of that other State by its domestic law.

Article 6: Respect for human rights

1. States Parties shall ensure that the implementation of their obligations under this Convention is consistent with their obligations under international human rights law.
2. Nothing in this Convention shall be interpreted as permitting suppression of human rights or fundamental freedoms, including the rights related to the freedoms of expression, conscience, opinion, religion or belief, peaceful assembly and association, in accordance and in a manner consistent with applicable international human rights law.

Chapter II
Criminalization

Article 7: Illegal access

1. Each State Party shall adopt such legislative and other measures as may be necessary to establish as a criminal offence under its domestic law, when committed intentionally, the access to the whole or any part of an information and communications technology system without right. [*agreed ad referendum*]
2. A State Party may require that the offence be committed by infringing security measures, with the intent of obtaining electronic data or other dishonest or criminal intent or in relation to an information and communications technology system that is connected to another information and communications technology system.

Article 8: Illegal interception
[agreed ad referendum]

1. Each State Party shall adopt such legislative and other measures as may be necessary to establish as criminal offences under its domestic law, when committed intentionally and without right, the interception, made by technical means, of non-public transmissions of electronic

data to, from or within an information and communications technology system, including electromagnetic emissions from an information and communications technology system carrying such electronic data.

2. A State Party may require that the offence be committed with dishonest or criminal intent, or in relation to an information and communications technology system that is connected to another information and communications technology system.

Article 9: Interference with electronic data

1. Each State Party shall adopt such legislative and other measures as may be necessary to establish as criminal offences under its domestic law, when committed intentionally and without right, the damaging, deletion, deterioration, alteration or suppression of electronic data. [*agreed in informals*]
2. A State Party may require that the conduct described in paragraph 1 of this article result in serious harm. [*agreed ad referendum*]

Article 10: Interference with an information and communications technology system [agreed ad referendum]

Each State Party shall adopt such legislative and other measures as may be necessary to establish as criminal offences under its domestic law, when committed intentionally and without right, the serious hindering of the functioning of an information and communications technology system by inputting, transmitting, damaging, deleting, deteriorating, altering or suppressing electronic data.

Article 11: Misuse of devices [agreed ad referendum]

1. Each State Party shall adopt such legislative and other measures as may be necessary to establish as criminal offences under its domestic law, when committed intentionally and without right:
   (a) The obtaining, production, sale, procurement for use, import, distribution or otherwise making available of:
      (i) A device, including a program, designed or adapted primarily for the purpose of committing any of the offences established in accordance with articles 7 to 10 of this Convention; or
      (ii) A password, access credentials, electronic signature or similar data by which the whole or any part of an information and communications technology system is capable of being accessed;

   with the intent that the device, including a program, or the password, access credentials, electronic signature or similar data be used for the purpose of committing any of the offences established in accordance with articles 7 to 10 of this Convention; and

(b) The possession of an item referred to in paragraph 1 (a) (i) or (ii) of this article, with intent that it be used for the purpose of committing any of the offences established in accordance with articles 7 to 10 of this Convention.

2. This article shall not be interpreted as imposing criminal liability where the obtaining, production, sale, procurement for use, import, distribution or otherwise making available, or the possession referred to in paragraph 1 of this article is not for the purpose of committing an offence established in accordance with articles 7 to 10 of this Convention, such as for the authorized testing or protection of an information and communications technology system.
3. Each State Party may reserve the right not to apply paragraph 1 of this article, provided that the reservation does not concern the sale, distribution or otherwise making available of the items referred to in paragraph 1 (a) (ii) of this article.

Article 12: Information and communications technology system-related forgery

1. Each State Party shall adopt such legislative and other measures as may be necessary to establish as criminal offences under its domestic law, when committed intentionally and without right, the input, alteration, deletion or suppression of electronic data resulting in inauthentic data with the intent that they be considered or acted upon for legal purposes as if they were authentic, regardless of whether or not the data are directly readable and intelligible. [*agreed ad referendum*]
2. A State Party may require an intent to defraud, or a similar dishonest or criminal intent, before criminal liability attaches.

Article 13: Information and communications technology system-related theft or fraud

Each State Party shall adopt such legislative and other measures as may be necessary to establish as a criminal offence under its domestic law, when committed intentionally and without right, the causing of a loss of property to another person by means of: [*agreed ad referendum*]

(a) Any input, alteration, deletion or suppression of electronic data; [*agreed in informals*]

(b) Any interference with the functioning of an information and communications technology system; [*agreed ad referendum*]

(c) Any deception as to factual circumstances made through an information and communications technology system that causes a person to do or omit to do anything which that person would not otherwise do or omit to do; [*agreed ad referendum*]

with the fraudulent or dishonest intent of procuring for oneself or for another person, without right, a gain in money or other property.

Article 14: Offences related to online child sexual abuse or child sexual exploitation material

1. Each State Party shall adopt such legislative and other measures as may be necessary to establish as criminal offences under its domestic law, when committed intentionally and without right, the following conduct:
   (a) Producing, offering, selling, distributing, transmitting, broadcasting, displaying, publishing or otherwise making available child sexual abuse or child sexual exploitation material through an information and communications technology system;
   (b) Soliciting, procuring or accessing child sexual abuse or child sexual exploitation material through an information and communications technology system;
   (c) Possessing or controlling child sexual abuse or child sexual exploitation material stored in an information and communications technology system or another storage medium;
   (d) Financing the offences established in accordance with subparagraphs (a) to (c) of this paragraph, which States Parties may establish as a separate offence.
2. For the purposes of this article, the term child sexual abuse or child sexual exploitation material shall include visual material, and may include written or audio content, that depicts, describes or represents any person under 18 years of age:
   (a) Engaging in real or simulated sexual activity;
   (b) In the presence of a person engaging in any sexual activity;
   (c) Whose sexual parts are displayed for primarily sexual purposes; or
   (d) Subjected to torture or cruel, inhumane or degrading treatment or punishment and such material is sexual in nature.
3. A State Party may require that the material identified in paragraph 2 of this article be limited to material that:
   (a) Depicts, describes or represents an existing person; or
   (b) Visually depicts child sexual abuse or child sexual exploitation.

4. In accordance with their domestic law and consistent with applicable international obligations, States Parties may take steps to exclude the criminalization of:
   (a) Conduct by children for self-generated material depicting them; or
   (b) The consensual production, transmission, or possession of material described in paragraph 2 (a) to (c) of this article, where the underlying conduct depicted is legal as determined by domestic law, and where such material is maintained exclusively for the private and consensual use of the persons involved.
5. Nothing in this Convention shall affect any international obligations which are more conducive to the realization of the rights of the child.

Article 15: Solicitation or grooming for the purpose of committing a sexual offence against a child [agreed ad referendum]

1. Each State Party shall adopt such legislative and other measures as may be necessary to establish as criminal offences under its domestic law the act of intentionally communicating, soliciting, grooming, or making any arrangement through an information and communications technology system for the purpose of committing a sexual offence against a child, as defined in domestic law, including for the commission of any of the offences established in accordance with article 14 of this Convention.
2. A State Party may require an act in furtherance of the conduct described in paragraph 1 of this article.
3. A State Party may consider extending criminalization in accordance with paragraph 1 of this article in relation to a person believed to be a child.
4. States Parties may take steps to exclude the criminalization of conduct as described in paragraph 1 of this article when committed by children.

Article 16: Non-consensual dissemination of intimate images

1. Each State Party shall adopt such legislative and other measures as may be necessary to establish as criminal offences under its domestic law, when committed intentionally and without right, the selling, distributing, transmitting, publishing or otherwise making available of an intimate image of a person by means of an information and communications technology system, without the consent of the person depicted in the image.
2. For the purpose of paragraph 1 of this article, intimate image shall

mean a visual recording of a person over the age of 18 years made by any means, including a photograph or video recording, that is sexual in nature, in which the persons sexual parts are exposed or the person is engaged in sexual activity, which was private at the time of the recording, and in respect of which the person or persons depicted maintained a reasonable expectation of privacy at the time of the offence.

3. A State Party may extend the definition of intimate images, as appropriate, to depictions of persons who are under the age of 18 years if they are of legal age to engage in sexual activity under domestic law and the image does not depict child abuse or exploitation.
4. For the purposes of this article, a person who is under the age of 18 years and depicted in an intimate image cannot consent to the dissemination of an intimate image that constitutes child sexual abuse or child sexual exploitation material under article 14 of this Convention.
5. A State Party may require the intent to cause harm before criminal liability attaches.
6. States Parties may take other measures concerning matters related to this article, in accordance with their domestic law and consistent with applicable international obligations.

Article 17: Laundering of proceeds of crime
[agreed ad referendum]

1. Each State Party shall adopt, in accordance with fundamental principles of its domestic law, such legislative and other measures as may be necessary to establish as criminal offences, when committed intentionally:
   (a) (i) The conversion or transfer of property, knowing that such property is the proceeds of crime, for the purpose of concealing or disguising the illicit origin of the property or of helping any person who is involved in the commission of the predicate offence to evade the legal consequences of that persons actions;
   (ii) The concealment or disguise of the true nature, source, location, disposition, movement or ownership of or rights with respect to property, knowing that such property is the proceeds of crime;
   (b) Subject to the basic concepts of its legal system:
   (i) The acquisition, possession or use of property, knowing, at the time of receipt, that such property is the proceeds of crime;
   (ii) Participation in, association with or conspiracy to commit, attempts to commit and aiding, abetting, facilitating and

counselling the commission of any of the offences established in accordance with this article.

2. For purposes of implementing or applying paragraph 1 of this article:
   (a) Each State Party shall establish as predicate offences relevant offences established in accordance with articles 7 to 16 of this Convention;
   (b) In the case of States Parties whose legislation sets out a list of specific predicate offences, they shall, at a minimum, include in that list a comprehensive range of offences established in accordance with articles 7 to 16 of this Convention;
   (c) For the purposes of subparagraph (b) of this paragraph, predicate offences shall include offences committed both within and outside the jurisdiction of the State Party in question. However, offences committed outside the jurisdiction of a State Party shall constitute predicate offences only when the relevant conduct is a criminal offence under the domestic law of the State where it is committed and would be a criminal offence under the domestic law of the State Party implementing or applying this article, had it been committed there;
   (d) Each State Party shall furnish copies of its laws that give effect to this article and of any subsequent changes to such laws or a description thereof to the Secretary-General of the United Nations;
   (e) If required by fundamental principles of the domestic law of a State Party, it may be provided that the offences set forth in paragraph 1 of this article do not apply to the persons who committed the predicate offence;
   (f) Knowledge, intent or purpose required as an element of an offence set forth in paragraph 1 of this article may be inferred from objective factual circumstances.

Article 18: Liability of legal persons
[agreed ad referendum]

1. Each State Party shall adopt such measures as may be necessary, consistent with its legal principles, to establish the liability of legal persons for participation in the offences established in accordance with this Convention.
2. Subject to the legal principles of the State Party, the liability of legal persons may be criminal, civil or administrative.
3. Such liability shall be without prejudice to the criminal liability of the natural persons who have committed the offences.

4. Each State Party shall, in particular, ensure that legal persons held liable in accordance with this article are subject to effective, proportionate and dissuasive criminal or non-criminal sanctions, including monetary sanctions.

Article 19: Participation and attempt
[agreed ad referendum]

1. Each State Party shall adopt such legislative and other measures as may be necessary to establish as a criminal offence, in accordance with its domestic law, when committed intentionally, the participation in any capacity, such as that of an accomplice, assistant or instigator, in an offence established in accordance with this Convention.
2. Each State Party may adopt the necessary legislative and other measures to establish as a criminal offence, in accordance with its domestic law, when committed intentionally, any attempt to commit an offence established in accordance with this Convention.
3. Each State Party may adopt the necessary legislative and other measures to establish as a criminal offence, in accordance with its domestic law, when committed intentionally, the preparation for an offence established in accordance with this Convention.

Article 20: Statute of limitations
[agreed ad referendum]

Each State Party shall, where appropriate, considering the gravity of the crime, establish under its domestic law a long statute of limitations period in which to commence proceedings for any offence established in accordance with this Convention and establish a longer statute of limitations period or provide for the suspension of the statute of limitations where the alleged offender has evaded the administration of justice.

Article 21: Prosecution, adjudication and sanctions
[agreed ad referendum]

1. Each State Party shall make the commission of an offence established in accordance with this Convention liable to effective, proportionate and dissuasive sanctions that take into account the gravity of the offence.
2. Each State Party may adopt, in accordance with its domestic law, such legislative and other measures as may be necessary to establish aggravating circumstances in relation to the offences established in accordance with this Convention, including circumstances that affect critical information infrastructures.

3. Each State Party shall endeavour to ensure that any discretionary legal powers under its domestic law relating to the prosecution of persons for offences established in accordance with this Convention are exercised in order to maximize the effectiveness of law enforcement measures in respect of those offences and with due regard to the need to deter the commission of such offences.
4. Each State Party shall ensure that any person prosecuted for offences established in accordance with this Convention enjoys all rights and guarantees in conformity with domestic law and consistent with the applicable international obligations of the State Party, including the right to a fair trial and the rights of the defence.
5. In the case of offences established in accordance with this Convention, each State Party shall take appropriate measures, in accordance with its domestic law and with due regard to the rights of the defence, to seek to ensure that conditions imposed in connection with decisions on release pending trial or appeal take into consideration the need to ensure the presence of the defendant at subsequent criminal proceedings.
6. Each State Party shall take into account the gravity of the offences concerned when considering the eventuality of early release or parole of persons convicted of such offences.
7. States Parties shall ensure that appropriate measures are in place under domestic law to protect children who are accused of offences established in accordance with this Convention, consistent with the obligations under the Convention on the Rights of the Child and the applicable Protocols thereto, as well as other applicable international or regional instruments.
8. Nothing contained in this Convention shall affect the principle that the description of the offences established in accordance with this Convention and of the applicable legal defences or other legal principles controlling the lawfulness of conduct is reserved to the domestic law of a State Party and that such offences shall be prosecuted and punished in accordance with that law.

Chapter III
Jurisdiction

Article 22: Jurisdiction
[agreed ad referendum]

1. Each State Party shall adopt such measures as may be necessary to establish its jurisdiction over the offences established in accordance with this Convention when:

(a) The offence is committed in the territory of that State Party; or

(b) The offence is committed on board a vessel that is flying the flag of that State Party or an aircraft that is registered under the laws of that State Party at the time when the offence is committed.

2. Subject to article 5 of this Convention, a State Party may also establish its jurisdiction over any such offence when:

(a) The offence is committed against a national of that State Party; or

(b) The offence is committed by a national of that State Party or a stateless person with habitual residence in its territory; or

(c) The offence is one of those established in accordance with article 17, paragraph 1 (b) (ii), of this Convention and is committed outside its territory with a view to the commission of an offence established in accordance with article 17, paragraph 1 (a) (i) or (ii) or (b) (i), of this Convention within its territory; or

(d) The offence is committed against the State Party.

3. For the purposes of article 37, paragraph 11, of this Convention, each State Party shall take such measures as may be necessary to establish its jurisdiction over the offences established in accordance with this Convention when the alleged offender is present in its territory and it does not extradite such person solely on the ground that the person is one of its nationals.

4. Each State Party may also adopt such measures as may be necessary to establish its jurisdiction over the offences established in accordance with this Convention when the alleged offender is present in its territory and it does not extradite the person.

5. If a State Party exercising its jurisdiction under paragraph 1 or 2 of this article has been notified, or has otherwise learned, that any other States Parties are conducting an investigation, prosecution or judicial proceeding in respect of the same conduct, the competent authorities of those States Parties shall, as appropriate, consult one another with a view to coordinating their actions.

6. Without prejudice to norms of general international law, this Convention shall not exclude the exercise of any criminal jurisdiction established by a State Party in accordance with its domestic law.

Chapter IV
Procedural measures and law enforcement

Article 23: Scope of procedural measures

1. Each State Party shall adopt such legislative and other measures as may be necessary to establish the powers and procedures provided for

in this chapter for the purpose of specific criminal investigations or proceedings.

2. Except as provided otherwise in this Convention, each State Party shall apply the powers and procedures referred to in paragraph 1 of this article to:
   (a) The criminal offences established in accordance with this Convention;
   (b) Other criminal offences committed by means of an information and communications technology system; and
   (c) The collection of evidence in electronic form of any criminal offence.
3. (a) Each State Party may reserve the right to apply the measures referred to in article 29 of this Convention only to offences or categories of offences specified in the reservation, provided that the range of such offences or categories of offences is not more restricted than the range of offences to which it applies the measures referred to in article 30 of this Convention. Each State Party shall consider restricting such a reservation to enable the broadest application of the measures referred to in article 29;
   (b) Where a State Party, owing to limitations in its legislation in force at the time of the adoption of this Convention, is not able to apply the measures referred to in articles 29 and 30 of this Convention to communications being transmitted within an information and communications technology system of a service provider which:
      (i) Is being operated for the benefit of a closed group of users; and
      (ii) Does not employ public communications networks and is not connected with another information and communications technology system, whether public or private;

   that State Party may reserve the right not to apply these measures to such communications. Each State Party shall consider restricting such a reservation to enable the broadest application of the measures referred to in articles 29 and 30 of this Convention.

Article 24: Conditions and safeguards

1. Each State Party shall ensure that the establishment, implementation and application of the powers and procedures provided for in this chapter are subject to conditions and safeguards provided for under its domestic law, which shall provide for the protection of human rights, in accordance with its obligations under international human rights law, and which shall incorporate the principle of proportionality.
2. In accordance with and pursuant to the domestic law of each State

Party, such conditions and safeguards shall, as appropriate in view of the nature of the procedure or power concerned, include, inter alia, judicial or other independent review, the right to an effective remedy, grounds justifying application, and limitation of the scope and the duration of such power or procedure.

3. To the extent that it is consistent with the public interest, in particular the proper administration of justice, each State Party shall consider the impact of the powers and procedures in this chapter upon the rights, responsibilities and legitimate interests of third parties.
4. The conditions and safeguards established in accordance with this article shall apply at the domestic level to the powers and procedures set forth in this chapter, both for the purpose of domestic criminal investigations and proceedings and for the purpose of rendering international cooperation by the requested State Party.
5. References to judicial or other independent review in paragraph 2 of this article are references to such review at the domestic level.

Article 25: Expedited preservation of stored electronic data
[agreed ad referendum]

1. Each State Party shall adopt such legislative and other measures as may be necessary to enable its competent authorities to order or similarly obtain the expeditious preservation of specified electronic data, including traffic data, content data and subscriber information, that have been stored by means of an information and communications technology system, in particular where there are grounds to believe that the electronic data are particularly vulnerable to loss or modification.
2. Where a State Party gives effect to paragraph 1 of this article by means of an order to a person to preserve specified stored electronic data in the persons possession or control, the State Party shall adopt such legislative and other measures as may be necessary to oblige that person to preserve and maintain the integrity of those electronic data for a period of time as long as necessary, up to a maximum of 90 days, to enable the competent authorities to seek their disclosure. A State Party may provide for such an order to be subsequently renewed.
3. Each State Party shall adopt such legislative and other measures as may be necessary to oblige the custodian or other person who is to preserve the electronic data to keep confidential the undertaking of such procedures for the period of time provided for in its domestic legislation.

Article 26: Expedited preservation and partial disclosure of traffic data [agreed ad referendum]

Each State Party shall adopt, in respect of traffic data that are to be preserved under the provisions of article 25 of this Convention, such legislative and other measures as may be necessary to:

(a) Ensure that such expeditious preservation of traffic data is available regardless of whether one or more service providers were involved in the transmission of a communication; and

(b) Ensure the expeditious disclosure to the State Partys competent authority, or a person designated by that authority, of a sufficient amount of traffic data to enable the State Party to identify the service providers and the path through which the communication or indicated information was transmitted.

Article 27: Production order [agreed ad referendum]

Each State Party shall adopt such legislative and other measures as may be necessary to empower its competent authorities to order:

(a) A person in its territory to submit specified electronic data in that persons possession or control that are stored in an information and communications technology system or an electronic data storage medium; and

(b) A service provider offering its services in the territory of the State Party to submit subscriber information relating to such services in that service providers possession or control.

Article 28: Search and seizure of stored electronic data [agreed ad referendum]

1. Each State Party shall adopt such legislative and other measures as may be necessary to empower its competent authorities to search or similarly access:
   (a) An information and communications technology system, part of it, and electronic data stored therein; and
   (b) An electronic data storage medium in which the electronic data sought may be stored; in the territory of that State Party.
2. Each State Party shall adopt such legislative and other measures as may be necessary to ensure that, where its authorities search or similarly access a specific information and communications technology system or part of it, pursuant to paragraph 1 (a) of this article, and have grounds to believe that the electronic data sought are stored in another

information and communications technology system or part of it in its territory, and such data are lawfully accessible from or available to the initial system, such authorities shall be able to expeditiously conduct the search to obtain access to that other information and communications technology system.

3. Each State Party shall adopt such legislative and other measures as may be necessary to empower its competent authorities to seize or similarly secure electronic data in its territory accessed in accordance with paragraph 1 or 2 of this article. These measures shall include the power to:
   (a) Seize or similarly secure an information and communications technology system or part of it, or an electronic data storage medium;
   (b) Make and retain copies of those electronic data in electronic form;
   (c) Maintain the integrity of the relevant stored electronic data;
   (d) Render inaccessible or remove those electronic data in the accessed information and communications technology system.
4. Each State Party shall adopt such legislative and other measures as may be necessary to empower its competent authorities to order any person who has knowledge about the functioning of the information and communications technology system in question, the information and telecommunications network, or their component parts, or measures applied to protect the electronic data therein, to provide, as is reasonable, the necessary information to enable the undertaking of the measures referred to in paragraphs 1 to 3 of this article.

Article 29: Real-time collection of traffic data
[agreed ad referendum]

1. Each State Party shall adopt such legislative and other measures as may be necessary to empower its competent authorities to:
   (a) Collect or record, through the application of technical means in the territory of that State Party; and
   (b) Compel a service provider, within its existing technical capability:
      (i) To collect or record, through the application of technical means in the territory of that State Party; or
      (ii) To cooperate and assist the competent authorities in the collection or recording of;

   traffic data, in real time, associated with specified communications in its territory transmitted by means of an information and communications technology system.

2. Where a State Party, owing to the principles of its domestic legal system, cannot adopt the measures referred to in paragraph 1 (a) of this article, it may instead adopt such legislative and other measures as may be necessary to ensure the real-time collection or recording of traffic data associated with specified communications transmitted in its territory, through the application of technical means in that territory.
3. Each State Party shall adopt such legislative and other measures as may be necessary to oblige a service provider to keep confidential the fact of the execution of any power provided for in this article and any information relating to it.

Article 30: Interception of content data [agreed ad referendum]

1. Each State Party shall adopt such legislative and other measures as may be necessary, in relation to a range of serious criminal offences to be determined by domestic law, to empower its competent authorities to:
   (a) Collect or record, through the application of technical means in the territory of that State Party; and
   (b) Compel a service provider, within its existing technical capability:
      (i) To collect or record, through the application of technical means in the territory of that State Party; or
      (ii) To cooperate and assist the competent authorities in the collection or recording of;

   content data, in real time, of specified communications in its territory transmitted by means of an information and communications technology system.
2. Where a State Party, owing to the principles of its domestic legal system, cannot adopt the measures referred to in paragraph 1 (a) of this article, it may instead adopt such legislative and other measures as may be necessary to ensure the real-time collection or recording of content data on specified communications in its territory, through the application of technical means in that territory.
3. Each State Party shall adopt such legislative and other measures as may be necessary to oblige a service provider to keep confidential the fact of the execution of any power provided for in this article and any information relating to it.

Article 31: Freezing, seizure and confiscation of the proceeds of crime [agreed ad referendum]

1. Each State Party shall adopt, to the greatest extent possible within its domestic legal system, such measures as may be necessary to enable the confiscation of:

(a) Proceeds of crime derived from offences established in accordance with this Convention or property the value of which corresponds to that of such proceeds;

(b) Property, equipment or other instrumentalities used in or destined for use in offences established in accordance with this Convention.

2. Each State Party shall adopt such measures as may be necessary to enable the identification, tracing, freezing or seizure of any item referred to in paragraph 1 of this article for the purpose of eventual confiscation.
3. Each State Party shall adopt, in accordance with its domestic law, such legislative and other measures as may be necessary to regulate the administration by the competent authorities of frozen, seized or confiscated property covered in paragraphs 1 and 2 of this article.
4. If proceeds of crime have been transformed or converted, in part or in full, into other property, such property shall be liable to the measures referred to in this article instead of the proceeds.
5. If proceeds of crime have been intermingled with property acquired from legitimate sources, such property shall, without prejudice to any powers relating to freezing or seizure, be liable to confiscation up to the assessed value of the intermingled proceeds.
6. Income or other benefits derived from proceeds of crime, from property into which proceeds of crime have been transformed or converted or from property with which proceeds of crime have been intermingled, shall also be liable to the measures referred to in this article, in the same manner and to the same extent as proceeds of crime.
7. For the purposes of this article and article 50 of this Convention, each State Party shall empower its courts or other competent authorities to order that bank, financial or commercial records be made available or be seized. A State Party shall not decline to act under the provisions of this paragraph on the ground of bank secrecy.
8. Each State Party may consider the possibility of requiring that an offender demonstrate the lawful origin of alleged proceeds of crime or other property liable to confiscation, to the extent that such a requirement is consistent with the principles of their domestic law and with the nature of the judicial and other proceedings.
9. The provisions of this article shall not be construed as prejudicing the rights of bona fide third parties.
10. Nothing contained in this article shall affect the principle that the measures to which it refers shall be defined and implemented in accordance with the provisions of the domestic law of a State Party.

Article 32: Establishment of criminal record
[agreed ad referendum]

Each State Party may adopt such legislative or other measures as may be necessary to take into consideration, under such terms as, and for the purpose that, it deems appropriate, any previous conviction in another State of an alleged offender for the purpose of using such information in criminal proceedings relating to an offence established in accordance with this Convention.

Article 33: Protection of witnesses
[agreed ad referendum]

1. Each State Party shall take appropriate measures, in accordance with its domestic law and within its means, to provide effective protection from potential retaliation or intimidation for witnesses who give testimony or, in good faith and on reasonable grounds, provide information concerning offences established in accordance with this Convention or otherwise cooperate with investigative or judicial authorities and, as appropriate, for their relatives and other persons close to them.
2. The measures envisaged in paragraph 1 of this article may include, inter alia, without prejudice to the rights of the defendant, including the right to due process:
   (a) Establishing procedures for the physical protection of such persons, such as, to the extent necessary and feasible, relocating them and permitting, where appropriate, non-disclosure or limitations on the disclosure of information concerning the identity and whereabouts of such persons;
   (b) Providing evidentiary rules to permit witness testimony to be given in a manner that ensures the safety of the witness, such as permitting testimony to be given through the use of communications technology such as video links or other adequate means.
3. States Parties shall consider entering into agreements or arrangements with other States for the relocation of persons referred to in paragraph 1 of this article.
4. The provisions of this article shall also apply to victims insofar as they are witnesses.

Article 34: Assistance to and protection of victims
[agreed ad referendum]

1. Each State Party shall take appropriate measures within its means to provide assistance and protection to victims of offences established in

accordance with this Convention, in particular in cases of threat of retaliation or intimidation.

2. Each State Party shall, subject to its domestic law, establish appropriate procedures to provide access to compensation and restitution for victims of offences established in accordance with this Convention.
3. Each State Party shall, subject to its domestic law, enable views and concerns of victims to be presented and considered at appropriate stages of criminal proceedings against offenders in a manner not prejudicial to the rights of the defence.
4. With respect to the offences established in accordance with articles 14 to 16 of this Convention, each State Party shall, subject to its domestic law, take measures to provide assistance to victims of such offences, including for their physical and psychological recovery, in cooperation with relevant international organizations, non-governmental organizations, and other elements of civil society.
5. In applying the provisions of paragraphs 2 to 4 of this article, each State Party shall take into account the age, gender and the particular circumstances and needs of victims, including the particular circumstances and needs of children.
6. Each State Party shall, to the extent consistent with its domestic legal framework, take effective steps to ensure compliance with requests to remove or render inaccessible the content described in articles 14 and 16 of this Convention.

Chapter V
International cooperation

Article 35: General principles of international cooperation

1. States Parties shall cooperate with each other in accordance with the provisions of this Convention, as well as other applicable international instruments on international cooperation in criminal matters, and domestic laws, for the purpose of:
   (a) The investigation and prosecution of, and judicial proceedings in relation to, the criminal offences established in accordance with this Convention, including the freezing, seizure, confiscation and return of the proceeds from such offences;
   (b) The collecting, obtaining, preserving and sharing of evidence in electronic form of criminal offences established in accordance with this Convention;
   (c) The collecting, obtaining, preserving and sharing of evidence in electronic form of any serious crime, including serious crimes

established in accordance with other applicable United Nations conventions and protocols in force at the time of the adoption of this Convention.

2. For the purpose of the collecting, obtaining, preserving and sharing of evidence in electronic form of offences as provided for in paragraph 1 (b) and (c) of this article, the relevant paragraphs of article 40, and articles 41 to 46 of this Convention shall apply.
3. In matters of international cooperation, whenever dual criminality is considered a requirement, it shall be deemed fulfilled irrespective of whether the laws of the requested State Party place the offence within the same category of offence or denominate the offence by the same terminology as the requesting State Party, if the conduct underlying the offence for which assistance is sought is a criminal offence under the laws of both States Parties.

Article 36: Protection of personal data
[agreed ad referendum]

1. (a) A State Party transferring personal data pursuant to this Convention shall do so in accordance with its domestic law and any obligations the transferring Party may have under applicable international law. States Parties shall not be required to transfer personal data in accordance with this Convention if the data cannot be provided in compliance with their applicable laws concerning the protection of personal data;
   (b) Where the transfer of personal data would not be compliant with paragraph 1 (a) of this article, States Parties may seek to impose appropriate conditions, in accordance with such applicable laws, to achieve compliance in order to respond to a request for personal data;
   (c) States Parties are encouraged to establish bilateral or multilateral arrangements to facilitate the transfer of personal data.
2. For personal data transferred in accordance with this Convention, States Parties shall ensure that the personal data received are subject to effective and appropriate safeguards in the respective legal frameworks of the States Parties.
3. In order to transfer personal data obtained in accordance with this Convention to a third country or an international organization, a State Party shall notify the original transferring State Party of its intention and request its authorization. The State Party shall transfer such personal data only with the authorization of the original transferring

State Party, which may require that the authorization be provided in written form.

Article 37: Extradition
[agreed ad referendum]

1. This article shall apply to the criminal offences established in accordance with this Convention where the person who is the subject of the request for extradition is present in the territory of the requested State Party, provided that the offence for which extradition is sought is punishable under the domestic law of both the requesting State Party and the requested State Party. When the extradition is sought for the purpose of serving a final sentence of imprisonment or another form of detention imposed in respect of an extraditable offence, the requested State Party may grant the extradition in accordance with domestic law.
2. Notwithstanding paragraph 1 of this article, a State Party whose law so permits may grant the extradition of a person for any of the criminal offences established in accordance with this Convention that are not punishable under its own domestic law.
3. If the request for extradition includes several separate criminal offences, at least one of which is extraditable under this article and some of which are not extraditable by reason of their period of imprisonment but are related to offences established in accordance with this Convention, the requested State Party may apply this article also in respect of those offences.
4. Each of the offences to which this article applies shall be deemed to be included as an extraditable offence in any extradition treaty existing between States Parties. States Parties undertake to include such offences as extraditable offences in every extradition treaty to be concluded between them.
5. If a State Party that makes extradition conditional on the existence of a treaty receives a request for extradition from another State Party with which it has no extradition treaty, it may consider this Convention the legal basis for extradition in respect of any offence to which this article applies.
6. States Parties that make extradition conditional on the existence of a treaty shall:
   (a) At the time of deposit of their instruments of ratification, acceptance or approval of or accession to this Convention, inform the Secretary-General of the United Nations whether they will take this Convention as the legal basis for cooperation in extradition with other States Parties to this Convention; and

(b) If they do not take this Convention as the legal basis for cooperation in extradition, seek, where appropriate, to conclude treaties on extradition with other States Parties to this Convention in order to implement this article.

7. States Parties that do not make extradition conditional on the existence of a treaty shall recognize offences to which this article applies as extraditable offences between themselves.
8. Extradition shall be subject to the conditions provided for by the domestic law of the requested State Party or by applicable extradition treaties, including, inter alia, conditions in relation to the minimum penalty requirement for extradition and the grounds upon which the requested State Party may refuse extradition.
9. States Parties shall, subject to their domestic law, endeavour to expedite extradition procedures and to simplify evidentiary requirements relating thereto in respect of any offence to which this article applies.
10. Subject to the provisions of its domestic law and its extradition treaties, the requested State Party may, upon being satisfied that the circumstances so warrant and are urgent, and at the request of the requesting State Party, including when the request is transmitted through existing channels of the International Criminal Police Organization, take a person whose extradition is sought and who is present in its territory into custody or take other appropriate measures to ensure the persons presence at extradition proceedings.
11. A State Party in whose territory an alleged offender is found, if it does not extradite such person in respect of an offence to which this article applies solely on the ground that the person is one of its nationals, shall, at the request of the State Party seeking extradition, be obliged to submit the case without undue delay to its competent authorities for the purpose of prosecution. Those authorities shall take their decisions and conduct their proceedings in the same manner as in the case of any other offence of a comparable nature under the domestic law of that State Party. The States Parties concerned shall cooperate with each other, in particular on procedural and evidentiary aspects, to ensure the efficiency of such prosecution.
12. Whenever a State Party is permitted under its domestic law to extradite or otherwise surrender one of its nationals only upon the condition that the person will be returned to that State Party to serve the sentence imposed as a result of the trial or proceedings for which the extradition or surrender of the person was sought and that State Party and the State Party seeking the extradition of the person agree with this option and other terms that they may deem appropriate, such conditional

extradition or surrender shall be sufficient to discharge the obligation set forth in paragraph 11 of this article.

13. If extradition, sought for purposes of enforcing a sentence, is refused because the person sought is a national of the requested State Party, the requested State Party shall, if its domestic law so permits and in conformity with the requirements of such law, upon application of the requesting State Party, consider the enforcement of the sentence imposed under the domestic law of the requesting State Party or the remainder thereof.
14. Any person regarding whom proceedings are being carried out in connection with any of the offences to which this article applies shall be guaranteed fair treatment at all stages of the proceedings, including enjoyment of all the rights and guarantees provided by the domestic law of the State Party in the territory of which that person is present.
15. Nothing in this Convention shall be interpreted as imposing an obligation to extradite if the requested State Party has substantial grounds for believing that the request has been made for the purpose of prosecuting or punishing a person on account of that persons sex, race, language, religion, nationality, ethnic origin or political opinions, or that compliance with the request would cause prejudice to that persons position for any one of these reasons.
16. States Parties may not refuse a request for extradition on the sole ground that the offence is also considered to involve fiscal matters.
17. Before refusing extradition, the requested State Party shall, where appropriate, consult with the requesting State Party to provide it with ample opportunity to present its opinions and to provide information relevant to its allegation.
18. The requested State Party shall inform the requesting State Party of its decision with regard to the extradition. The requested State Party shall inform the requesting State Party of any reason for refusal of extradition unless the requested State Party is prevented from doing so by its domestic law or its international legal obligations.
19. Each State Party shall, at the time of signature or when depositing its instrument of ratification, acceptance, approval or accession, communicate to the Secretary-General of the United Nations the name and address of an authority responsible for making or receiving requests for extradition or provisional arrest. The Secretary-General shall set up and keep updated a register of authorities so designated by the States Parties. Each State Party shall ensure that the details held in the register are correct at all times.

20. States Parties shall seek to conclude bilateral and multilateral agreements or arrangements to carry out or to enhance the effectiveness of extradition.

Article 38: Transfer of sentenced persons
[agreed ad referendum]

States Parties may, taking into consideration the rights of sentenced persons, consider entering into bilateral or multilateral agreements or arrangements on the transfer to their territory of persons sentenced to imprisonment or other forms of deprivation of liberty for offences established in accordance with this Convention, in order that they may complete their sentences there. States Parties may also take into account issues relating to consent, rehabilitation and reintegration.

Article 39: Transfer of criminal proceedings
[agreed ad referendum]

1. States Parties shall consider the possibility of transferring to one another proceedings for the criminal prosecution of an offence established in accordance with this Convention where such a transfer is deemed to be in the interests of the proper administration of justice, particularly in cases where several jurisdictions are involved, with a view to concentrating the prosecution.
2. If a State Party that makes the transfer of criminal proceedings conditional on the existence of a treaty receives a request for transfer from another State Party with which it has no treaty in this matter, it may consider this Convention as the legal basis for the transfer of criminal proceedings in respect of any offence to which this article applies.

Article 40: General principles and procedures relating
to mutual legal assistance

1. States Parties shall afford one another the widest measure of mutual legal assistance in investigations, prosecutions and judicial proceedings in relation to the offences established in accordance with this Convention, and for the purposes of the collection of evidence in electronic form of offences established in accordance with this Convention, as well as of serious crimes. [*agreed ad referendum*]
2. Mutual legal assistance shall be afforded to the fullest extent possible under relevant laws, treaties, agreements and arrangements of the requested State Party with respect to investigations, prosecutions and judicial proceedings in relation to the offences for which a legal person

may be held liable in accordance with article 18 of this Convention in the requesting State Party. [*agreed ad referendum*]

3. Mutual legal assistance to be afforded in accordance with this article may be requested for any of the following purposes:
   (a) Taking evidence or statements from persons;
   (b) Effecting service of judicial documents;
   (c) Executing searches and seizures, and freezing;
   (d) Searching or similarly accessing, seizing or similarly securing, and disclosing electronic data stored by means of an information and communications technology system pursuant to article 44 of this Convention;
   (e) Collecting traffic data in real time pursuant to article 45 of this Convention;
   (f) Intercepting content data pursuant to article 46 of this Convention;
   (g) Examining objects and sites;
   (h) Providing information, evidence and expert evaluations; [*agreed ad referendum*]
   (i) Providing originals or certified copies of relevant documents and records, including government, bank, financial, corporate or business records;
   (j) Identifying or tracing proceeds of crime, property, instrumentalities or other things for evidentiary purposes;
   (k) Facilitating the voluntary appearance of persons in the requesting State Party;
   (l) Recovering proceeds of crime; [*agreed ad referendum*]
   (m) Any other type of assistance that is not contrary to the domestic law of the requested State Party. [*agreed ad referendum*]
4. Without prejudice to domestic law, the competent authorities of a State Party may, without prior request, transmit information relating to criminal matters to a competent authority in another State Party where they believe that such information could assist the authority in undertaking or successfully concluding inquiries and criminal proceedings or could result in a request formulated by the latter State Party pursuant to this Convention. [*agreed ad referendum*]
5. The transmission of information pursuant to paragraph 4 of this article shall be without prejudice to inquiries and criminal proceedings in the State of the competent authorities providing the information. The competent authorities receiving the information shall comply with a request that said information remain confidential, even temporarily, or with restrictions on its use. However, this shall not prevent the

receiving State Party from disclosing in its proceedings information that is exculpatory to an accused person. In such a case, the receiving State Party shall notify the transmitting State Party prior to the disclosure and, if so requested, consult with the transmitting State Party. If, in an exceptional case, advance notice is not possible, the receiving State Party shall inform the transmitting State Party of the disclosure without delay. [*agreed ad referendum*]

6. The provisions of this article shall not affect obligations under any other treaty, bilateral or multilateral, that governs or will govern, in whole or in part, mutual legal assistance. [*agreed ad referendum*]
7. Paragraphs 8 to 31 of this article shall apply to requests made pursuant to this article if the States Parties in question are not bound by a treaty on mutual legal assistance. If those States Parties are bound by such a treaty, the corresponding provisions of that treaty shall apply unless the States Parties agree to apply paragraphs 8 to 31 of this article in lieu thereof. States Parties are strongly encouraged to apply the provisions of those paragraphs if they facilitate cooperation. [*agreed ad referendum*]
8. States Parties may decline to render assistance pursuant to this article on the ground of absence of dual criminality. However, the requested State Party may, when it deems appropriate, provide assistance, to the extent it decides at its discretion, irrespective of whether the conduct would constitute an offence under the domestic law of the requested State Party. Assistance may be refused when requests involve matters of a *de minimis* nature or matters for which the cooperation or assistance sought is available under other provisions of this Convention. [*agreed ad referendum*]
9. A person who is being detained or is serving a sentence in the territory of one State Party and whose presence in another State Party is requested for purposes of identification, testimony or otherwise providing assistance in obtaining evidence for investigations, prosecutions or judicial proceedings in relation to offences established in accordance with this Convention may be transferred if the following conditions are met:
   (a) The person freely gives informed consent;
   (b) The competent authorities of both States Parties agree, subject to such conditions as those States Parties may deem appropriate.

   [*agreed ad referendum*]
10. For the purposes of paragraph 9 of this article:
   (a) The State Party to which the person is transferred shall have the authority and obligation to keep the person transferred in custody,

unless otherwise requested or authorized by the State Party from which the person was transferred;

(b) The State Party to which the person is transferred shall, without delay, implement its obligation to return the person to the custody of the State Party from which the person was transferred as agreed beforehand, or as otherwise agreed, by the competent authorities of both States Parties;

(c) The State Party to which the person is transferred shall not require the State Party from which the person was transferred to initiate extradition proceedings for the return of the person;

(d) The person transferred shall receive credit for service of the sentence being served in the State from which the person was transferred for time spent in the custody of the State Party to which the person was transferred.

[*agreed ad referendum*]

11. Unless the State Party from which a person is to be transferred in accordance with paragraphs 9 and 10 of this article so agrees, that person, regardless of the persons nationality, shall not be prosecuted, detained, punished or subjected to any other restriction of liberty in the territory of the State to which that person is transferred in respect of acts, omissions or convictions prior to the persons departure from the territory of the State from which the person was transferred. [*agreed ad referendum*]

12. (a) Each State Party shall designate a central authority or authorities that shall have the responsibility and power to receive requests for mutual legal assistance and either to execute them or to transmit them to the competent authorities for execution. Where a State Party has a special region or territory with a separate system of mutual legal assistance, it may designate a distinct central authority that shall have the same function for that region or territory;

(b) Central authorities shall ensure the speedy and proper execution or transmission of the requests received. Where the central authority transmits the request to a competent authority for execution, it shall encourage the speedy and proper execution of the request by the competent authority;

(c) The Secretary-General of the United Nations shall be notified of the central authority designated for this purpose at the time each State Party deposits its instrument of ratification, acceptance or approval of or accession to this Convention, and shall set up and keep updated a register of central authorities designated by the

States Parties. Each State Party shall ensure that the details held in the register are correct at all times;

(d) Requests for mutual legal assistance and any communication related thereto shall be transmitted to the central authorities designated by the States Parties. This requirement shall be without prejudice to the right of a State Party to require that such requests and communications be addressed to it through diplomatic channels and, in urgent circumstances, where the States Parties agree, through the International Criminal Police Organization, if possible.

[*agreed ad referendum*]

13. Requests shall be made in writing or, where possible, by any means capable of producing a written record, in a language acceptable to the requested State Party, under conditions allowing that State Party to establish authenticity. The Secretary-General of the United Nations shall be notified of the language or languages acceptable to each State Party at the time it deposits its instrument of ratification, acceptance or approval of or accession to this Convention. In urgent circumstances and where agreed by the States Parties, requests may be made orally, but shall be confirmed in writing forthwith. [*agreed ad referendum*]

14. Where not prohibited by their respective laws, central authorities of States Parties are encouraged to transmit and receive requests for mutual legal assistance, and communications related thereto, as well as evidence, in electronic form under conditions allowing the requested State Party to establish authenticity and ensuring the security of communications. [*agreed ad referendum*]

15. A request for mutual legal assistance shall contain:

(a) The identity of the authority making the request;

(b) The subject matter and nature of the investigation, prosecution or judicial proceeding to which the request relates and the name and functions of the authority conducting the investigation, prosecution or judicial proceeding;

(c) A summary of the relevant facts, except in relation to requests for the purpose of service of judicial documents;

(d) A description of the assistance sought and details of any particular procedure that the requesting State Party wishes to be followed;

(e) Where possible and appropriate, the identity, location and nationality of any person concerned, as well as the country of origin, description and location of any item or accounts concerned;

(f) Where applicable, the time period for which the evidence, information or other assistance is sought; and

(g) The purpose for which the evidence, information or other assistance is sought.

[*agreed ad referendum*]

16. The requested State Party may request additional information when it appears necessary for the execution of the request in accordance with its domestic law or when it can facilitate such execution. [*agreed ad referendum*]

17. A request shall be executed in accordance with the domestic law of the requested State Party and, to the extent not contrary to the domestic law of the requested State Party and where possible, in accordance with the procedures specified in the request.

[*agreed ad referendum*]

18. Wherever possible and consistent with fundamental principles of domestic law, when an individual is in the territory of a State Party and has to be heard as a witness, victim or expert by the judicial authorities of another State Party, the first State Party may, at the request of the other, permit the hearing to take place by videoconference if it is not possible or desirable for the individual in question to appear in person in the territory of the requesting State Party. States Parties may agree that the hearing shall be conducted by a judicial authority of the requesting State Party and attended by a judicial authority of the requested State Party. If the requested State Party does not have access to the technical means necessary for holding a videoconference, such means may be provided by the requesting State Party, upon mutual agreement. [*agreed ad referendum*]

19. The requesting State Party shall not transmit or use information or evidence furnished by the requested State Party for investigations, prosecutions or judicial proceedings other than those stated in the request without the prior consent of the requested State Party. Nothing in this paragraph shall prevent the requesting State Party from disclosing in its proceedings information or evidence that is exculpatory to an accused person. In the latter case, the requesting State Party shall notify the requested State Party prior to the disclosure and, if so requested, consult with the requested State Party. If, in an exceptional case, advance notice is not possible, the requesting State Party shall inform the requested State Party of the disclosure without delay. [*agreed ad referendum*]

20. The requesting State Party may require that the requested State Party keep confidential the fact and substance of the request, except to the extent necessary to execute the request. If the requested State Party

cannot comply with the requirement of confidentiality, it shall promptly inform the requesting State Party. [*agreed ad referendum*]

21. Mutual legal assistance may be refused:
    (a) If the request is not made in conformity with the provisions of this article;
    (b) If the requested State Party considers that execution of the request is likely to prejudice its sovereignty, security, *ordre public* or other essential interests;
    (c) If the authorities of the requested State Party would be prohibited by its domestic law from carrying out the action requested with regard to any similar offence, had it been subject to investigation, prosecution or judicial proceedings under their own jurisdiction;
    (d) If it would be contrary to the legal system of the requested State Party relating to mutual legal assistance for the request to be granted.
22. Nothing in this Convention shall be interpreted as imposing an obligation to afford mutual legal assistance if the requested State Party has substantial grounds for believing that the request has been made for the purpose of prosecuting or punishing a person on account of that persons sex, race, language, religion, nationality, ethnic origin or political opinions, or that compliance with the request would cause prejudice to that persons position for any one of these reasons.
23. States Parties may not refuse a request for mutual legal assistance on the sole ground that the offence is also considered to involve fiscal matters. [*agreed ad referendum*]
24. States Parties shall not decline to render mutual legal assistance pursuant to this article on the ground of bank secrecy. [*agreed ad referendum*]
25. Reasons shall be given for any refusal of mutual legal assistance. [*agreed ad referendum*]
26. The requested State Party shall execute the request for mutual legal assistance as soon as possible and shall take as full account as possible of any deadlines suggested by the requesting State Party and for which reasons are given, preferably in the request. The requested State Party shall respond to reasonable requests by the requesting State Party on the status, and progress in its handling, of the request. The requesting State Party shall promptly inform the requested State Party when the assistance sought is no longer required. [*agreed ad referendum*]
27. Mutual legal assistance may be postponed by the requested State Party on the ground that it interferes with an ongoing investigation, prosecution or judicial proceeding. [*agreed ad referendum*]

28. Before refusing a request pursuant to paragraph 21 of this article or postponing its execution pursuant to paragraph 27 of this article, the requested State Party shall consult with the requesting State Party to consider whether assistance may be granted subject to such terms and conditions as it deems necessary. If the requesting State Party accepts assistance subject to those conditions, it shall comply with the conditions. [*agreed ad referendum*]
29. Without prejudice to the application of paragraph 11 of this article, a witness, expert or other person who, at the request of the requesting State Party, consents to give evidence in a proceeding or to assist in an investigation, prosecution or judicial proceeding in the territory of the requesting State Party shall not be prosecuted, detained, punished or subjected to any other restriction of the persons liberty in that territory in respect of acts, omissions or convictions prior to the persons departure from the territory of the requested State Party. Such safe conduct shall cease when the witness, expert or other person having had, for a period of 15 consecutive days or for any period agreed upon by the States Parties from the date on which the person has been officially informed that the presence of the person is no longer required by the judicial authorities, an opportunity of leaving, has nevertheless remained voluntarily in the territory of the requesting State Party or, having left it, has returned of the persons own free will. [*agreed ad referendum*]
30. The ordinary costs of executing a request shall be borne by the requested State Party, unless otherwise agreed by the States Parties concerned. If expenses of a substantial or extraordinary nature are or will be required to fulfil the request, the States Parties shall consult to determine the terms and conditions under which the request will be executed, as well as the manner in which the costs shall be borne. [*agreed ad referendum*]
31. The requested State Party:
    (a) Shall provide to the requesting State Party copies of government records, documents or information in its possession that under its domestic law are available to the general public;
    (b) May, at its discretion, provide to the requesting State Party, in whole, in part or subject to such conditions as it deems appropriate, copies of any government records, documents or information in its possession that under its domestic law are not available to the general public.

    [*agreed ad referendum*]
32. States Parties shall consider, as may be necessary, the possibility of concluding bilateral or multilateral agreements or arrangements that

would serve the purposes of, give practical effect to or enhance the provisions of this article. [*agreed ad referendum*]

Article 41: 24/7 network

1. Each State Party shall designate a point of contact available 24 hours a day, 7 days a week, in order to ensure the provision of immediate assistance for the purpose of specific criminal investigations, prosecutions or judicial proceedings concerning offences established in accordance with this Convention, or for the collection, obtaining and preservation of evidence in electronic form for the purposes of paragraph 3 of this article and in relation to the offences established in accordance with this Convention, as well as to serious crime.
2. The Secretary-General of the United Nations shall be notified of such point of contact and keep an updated register of points of contact designated for the purposes of this article and shall annually circulate to the States Parties the updated list of contact points. [*agreed ad referendum*]
3. Such assistance shall include facilitating or, if permitted by the domestic law and practice of the requested State Party, directly carrying out the following measures:
   (a) The provision of technical advice;
   (b) The preservation of stored electronic data pursuant to articles 42 and 43 of this Convention, including, as appropriate, information about the location of the service provider, if known to the requested State Party, to assist the requesting State Party in making a request;
   (c) The collection of evidence and the provision of legal information;
   (d) The locating of suspects; or
   (e) The provision of electronic data to avert an emergency.

   [*agreed ad referendum*]
4. A State Partys point of contact shall have the capacity to carry out communications with the point of contact of another State Party on an expedited basis. If the point of contact designated by a State Party is not part of that State Partys authority or authorities responsible for mutual legal assistance or extradition, the point of contact shall ensure that it is able to coordinate with that authority or those authorities on an expedited basis. [*agreed ad referendum*]
5. Each State Party shall ensure that trained and equipped personnel are available to ensure the operation of the 24/7 network. [*agreed ad referendum*]
6. States Parties may also use and strengthen existing authorized networks

of points of contact, where applicable, and within the limits of their domestic laws, including the 24/7 networks for computer-related crime of the International Criminal Police Organization for prompt police-to-police cooperation and other methods of information exchange cooperation. [*agreed ad referendum*]

Article 42: International cooperation for the purpose of expedited preservation of stored electronic data

1. A State Party may request another State Party to order or otherwise obtain, in accordance with article 25 of this Convention, the expeditious preservation of electronic data stored by means of an information and communications technology system located within the territory of that other State Party, and in respect of which the requesting State Party intends to submit a request for mutual legal assistance in the search or similar access, seizure or similar securing, or disclosure of the electronic data. [*agreed ad referendum*]
2. The requesting State Party may use the 24/7 network provided for in article 41 of this Convention to seek information concerning the location of the electronic data stored by means of an information and communications technology system and, as appropriate, information about the location of the service provider. [*agreed ad referendum*]
3. A request for preservation made under paragraph 1 of this article shall specify:
   (a) The authority seeking the preservation;
   (b) The offence that is the subject of a criminal investigation, prosecution or judicial proceeding and a brief summary of the related facts;
   (c) The stored electronic data to be preserved and their relationship to the offence;
   (d) Any available information identifying the custodian of the stored electronic data or the location of the information and communications technology system;
   (e) The necessity of the preservation;
   (f) That the requesting State Party intends to submit a request for mutual legal assistance in the search or similar access, seizure or similar securing, or disclosure of the stored electronic data;

   (g) As appropriate, the need to keep the request for preservation confidential and not to notify the user.

   [*agreed ad referendum*]
4. Upon receiving the request from another State Party, the requested

State Party shall take all appropriate measures to preserve expeditiously the specified electronic data in accordance with its domestic law. For the purposes of responding to a request, dual criminality shall not be required as a condition for providing such preservation. [*agreed ad referendum*]

5. A State Party that requires dual criminality as a condition for responding to a request for mutual legal assistance in the search or similar access, seizure or similar securing, or disclosure of stored electronic data may, in respect of offences other than those established in accordance with this Convention, reserve the right to refuse the request for preservation under this article in cases where it has reasons to believe that, at the time of disclosure, the condition of dual criminality could not be fulfilled. [*agreed ad referendum*]
6. In addition, a request for preservation may be refused only on the basis of the grounds contained in article 40, paragraph 21 (b) and (c) and paragraph 22, of this Convention.
7. Where the requested State Party believes that preservation will not ensure the future availability of the data or will threaten the confidentiality of or otherwise prejudice the requesting State Partys investigation, it shall promptly so inform the requesting State Party, which shall then determine whether the request should nevertheless be executed. [*agreed ad referendum*]
8. Any preservation effected in response to a request made pursuant to paragraph 1 of this article shall be for a period of not less than 60 days, in order to enable the requesting State Party to submit a request for the search or similar access, seizure or similar securing, or disclosure of the data. Following the receipt of such a request, the data shall continue to be preserved pending a decision on that request. [*agreed ad referendum*]
9. Before the expiry of the preservation period in paragraph 8 of this article, the requesting State Party may request an extension of the period of preservation. [*agreed ad referendum*]

Article 43: International cooperation for the purpose of expedited disclosure of preserved traffic data

1. Where, in the course of the execution of a request made pursuant to article 42 of this Convention to preserve traffic data concerning a specific communication, the requested State Party discovers that a service provider in another State Party was involved in the transmission of the communication, the requested State Party shall expeditiously disclose to the requesting State Party a sufficient amount of traffic data to identify that service provider and the path through which the communication was transmitted. [*agreed ad referendum*]

2. Disclosure of traffic data under paragraph 1 of this article may be refused only on the basis of the grounds contained in article 40, paragraph 21 (b) and (c) and paragraph 22, of this Convention.

Article 44: Mutual legal assistance in accessing stored electronic data [agreed ad referendum]

1. A State Party may request another State Party to search or similarly access, seize or similarly secure, and disclose electronic data stored by means of an information and communications technology system located within the territory of the requested State Party, including electronic data that have been preserved pursuant to article 42 of this Convention.
2. The requested State Party shall respond to the request through the application of relevant international instruments and laws referred to in article 35 of this Convention, and in accordance with other relevant provisions of this chapter.
3. The request shall be responded to on an expedited basis where:
   (a) There are grounds to believe that the relevant data are particularly vulnerable to loss or modification; or
   (b) The instruments and laws referred to in paragraph 2 of this article otherwise provide for expedited cooperation.

Article 45: Mutual legal assistance in the real-time collection of traffic data [agreed ad referendum]

1. States Parties shall endeavour to provide mutual legal assistance to each other in the real-time collection of traffic data associated with specified communications in their territory transmitted by means of an information and communications technology system. Subject to the provisions of paragraph 2 of this article, such assistance shall be governed by the conditions and procedures provided for under domestic law.
2. Each State Party shall endeavour to provide such assistance at least with respect to criminal offences for which the real-time collection of traffic data would be available in a similar domestic case.
3. A request made in accordance with paragraph 1 of this article shall specify:
   (a) The name of the requesting authority;
   (b) A summary of the main facts and the nature of the investigation, prosecution or judicial proceeding to which the request relates;
   (c) The electronic data in relation to which the collection of the traffic data is required and their relationship to the offence;

(d) Any available data that identify the owner or user of the data or the location of the information and communications technology system;

(e) Justification for the need to collect the traffic data;

(f) The period for which traffic data are to be collected and a corresponding justification of its duration.

Article 46: Mutual legal assistance in the interception of content data [agreed ad referendum]

States Parties shall endeavour to provide mutual legal assistance to each other in the real-time collection or recording of content data of specified communications transmitted by means of an information and communications technology system, to the extent permitted under treaties applicable to them or under their domestic laws.

Article 47: Law enforcement cooperation [agreed ad referendum]

1. States Parties shall cooperate closely with one another, consistent with their respective domestic legal and administrative systems, to enhance the effectiveness of law enforcement action to combat the offences established in accordance with this Convention. States Parties shall, in particular, take effective measures:
   (a) To enhance and, where necessary, to establish channels of communication between their competent authorities, agencies and services, taking into account existing channels, including those of the International Criminal Police Organization, in order to facilitate the secure and rapid exchange of information concerning all aspects of the offences established in accordance with this Convention, including, if the States Parties concerned deem it appropriate, links with other criminal activities;
   (b) To cooperate with other States Parties in conducting inquiries with respect to offences established in accordance with this Convention concerning:
      (i) The identity, whereabouts and activities of persons suspected of involvement in such offences or the location of other persons concerned;
      (ii) The movement of proceeds of crime or property derived from the commission of such offences;
      (iii) The movement of property, equipment or other instrumentalities used or intended for use in the commission of such offences;

(c) To provide, where appropriate, necessary items or data for analytical or investigative purposes;

(d) To exchange, where appropriate, information with other States Parties concerning specific means and methods used to commit the offences established in accordance with this Convention, including the use of false identities, forged, altered or false documents and other means of concealing activities, as well as cybercrime tactics, techniques and procedures;

(e) To facilitate effective coordination between their competent authorities, agencies and services and to promote the exchange of personnel and other experts, including, subject to bilateral agreements or arrangements between the States Parties concerned, the posting of liaison officers;

(f) To exchange information and coordinate administrative and other measures taken, as appropriate, for the purpose of early identification of the offences established in accordance with this Convention.

2. With a view to giving effect to this Convention, States Parties shall consider entering into bilateral or multilateral agreements or arrangements on direct cooperation between their law enforcement agencies and, where such agreements or arrangements already exist, amending them. In the absence of such agreements or arrangements between the States Parties concerned, the States Parties may consider this Convention to be the basis for mutual law enforcement cooperation in respect of the offences established in accordance with this Convention. Whenever appropriate, States Parties shall make full use of agreements or arrangements, including international or regional organizations, to enhance the cooperation between their law enforcement agencies.

Article 48: Joint investigations
[agreed ad referendum]

States Parties shall consider concluding bilateral or multilateral agreements or arrangements whereby, in relation to offences established in accordance with this Convention that are the subject of criminal investigations, prosecutions or judicial proceedings in one or more States, the competent authorities concerned may establish joint investigative bodies. In the absence of such agreements or arrangements, joint investigations may be undertaken by agreement on a case-by-case basis. The States Parties involved shall ensure that the sovereignty of the State Party in whose territory such investigations are to take place is fully respected.

Article 49: Mechanisms for the recovery of property through international cooperation in confiscation [agreed ad referendum]

1. Each State Party, in order to provide mutual legal assistance pursuant to article 50 of this Convention with respect to property acquired through or involved in the commission of an offence established in accordance with this Convention, shall, in accordance with its domestic law:
   (a) Take such measures as may be necessary to permit its competent authorities to give effect to an order of confiscation issued by a court of another State Party;
   (b) Take such measures as may be necessary to permit its competent authorities, where they have jurisdiction, to order the confiscation of such property of foreign origin by adjudication of an offence of money-laundering or such other offence as may be within its jurisdiction or by other procedures authorized under its domestic law; and
   (c) Consider taking such measures as may be necessary to allow confiscation of such property without a criminal conviction in cases in which the offender cannot be prosecuted by reason of death, flight or absence or in other appropriate cases.
2. Each State Party, in order to provide mutual legal assistance upon a request made pursuant to article 50, paragraph 2, of this Convention, shall, in accordance with its domestic law:
   (a) Take such measures as may be necessary to permit its competent authorities to freeze or seize property upon a freezing or seizure order issued by a court or competent authority of a requesting State Party that provides a reasonable basis for the requested State Party to believe that there are sufficient grounds for taking such actions and that the property would eventually be subject to an order of confiscation for the purposes of paragraph 1 (a) of this article;
   (b) Take such measures as may be necessary to permit its competent authorities to freeze or seize property upon a request that provides a reasonable basis for the requested State Party to believe that there are sufficient grounds for taking such actions and that the property would eventually be subject to an order of confiscation for the purposes of paragraph 1 (a) of this article; and
   (c) Consider taking additional measures to permit its competent authorities to preserve property for confiscation, such as on the basis of a foreign arrest or criminal charge related to the acquisition of such property.

Article 50: International cooperation for the purposes of confiscation [agreed ad referendum]

1. A State Party that has received a request from another State Party having jurisdiction over an offence established in accordance with this Convention for the confiscation of proceeds of crime, property, equipment or other instrumentalities referred to in article 31, paragraph 1, of this Convention situated in its territory shall, to the greatest extent possible within its domestic legal system:
   (a) Submit the request to its competent authorities for the purpose of obtaining an order of confiscation and, if such an order is granted, give effect to it; or
   (b) Submit to its competent authorities, with a view to giving effect to it to the extent requested, an order of confiscation issued by a court in the territory of the requesting State Party in accordance with article 31, paragraph 1, of this Convention insofar as it relates to proceeds of crime, property, equipment or other instrumentalities situated in the territory of the requested State Party.
2. Following a request made by another State Party having jurisdiction over an offence established in accordance with this Convention, the requested State Party shall take measures to identify, trace and freeze or seize proceeds of crime, property, equipment or other instrumentalities referred to in article 31, paragraph 1, of this Convention for the purpose of eventual confiscation to be ordered either by the requesting State Party or, pursuant to a request under paragraph 1 of this article, by the requested State Party.
3. The provisions of article 40 of this Convention are applicable, mutatis mutandis, to this article. In addition to the information specified in article 40, paragraph 15, of this Convention, requests made pursuant to this article shall contain:
   (a) In the case of a request pertaining to paragraph 1 (a) of this article, a description of the property to be confiscated, including, to the extent possible, the location, and where relevant, the estimated value of the property and a statement of the facts relied upon by the requesting State Party sufficient to enable the requested State Party to seek the order under its domestic law;
   (b) In the case of a request pertaining to paragraph 1 (b) of this article, a legally admissible copy of an order of confiscation upon which the request is based issued by the requesting State Party, a statement of the facts and information as to the extent to which execution of the order is requested, a statement specifying the measures taken by the requesting State Party to provide adequate notification to

bona fide third parties and to ensure due process, and a statement that the confiscation order is final;

(c) In the case of a request pertaining to paragraph 2 of this article, a statement of the facts relied upon by the requesting State Party and a description of the actions requested and, where available, a legally admissible copy of an order on which the request is based.

4. The decisions or actions provided for in paragraphs 1 and 2 of this article shall be taken by the requested State Party in accordance with and subject to the provisions of its domestic law and its procedural rules or any bilateral or multilateral treaty, agreement or arrangement to which it may be bound in relation to the requesting State Party.
5. Each State Party shall furnish copies of its laws and regulations that give effect to this article and of any subsequent changes to such laws and regulations or a description thereof to the Secretary-General of the United Nations.
6. If a State Party elects to make the taking of the measures referred to in paragraphs 1 and 2 of this article conditional on the existence of a relevant treaty, that State Party shall consider this Convention the necessary and sufficient treaty basis.
7. Cooperation under this article may also be refused or provisional measures may be lifted if the requested State Party does not receive sufficient and timely evidence or if the property is of a *de minimis* value.
8. Before lifting any provisional measure taken pursuant to this article, the requested State Party shall, wherever possible, give the requesting State Party an opportunity to present its reasons in favour of continuing the measure.
9. The provisions of this article shall not be construed as prejudicing the rights of bona fide third parties.
10. States Parties shall consider concluding bilateral or multilateral treaties, agreements or arrangements to enhance the effectiveness of international cooperation undertaken pursuant to this article.

Article 51: Special cooperation [agreed ad referendum]

Without prejudice to its domestic law, each State Party shall endeavour to take measures to permit it to forward, without prejudice to its own criminal investigations, prosecutions or judicial proceedings, information on proceeds of offences established in accordance with this Convention to another State Party without prior request, when it considers that the disclosure of such information might assist the receiving State Party in initiating or carrying out criminal investigations, prosecutions or judicial proceedings or might lead to a request by that State Party under article 50 of this Convention.

Article 52: Return and disposal of confiscated proceeds of crime or property [agreed ad referendum]

1. Proceeds of crime or property confiscated by a State Party pursuant to article 31 or 50 of this Convention shall be disposed of by that State Party in accordance with its domestic law and administrative procedures.
2. When acting on a request made by another State Party in accordance with article 50 of this Convention, States Parties shall, to the extent permitted by domestic law and if so requested, give priority consideration to returning the confiscated proceeds of crime or property to the requesting State Party so that it can give compensation to the victims of the crime or return such proceeds of crime or property to their prior legitimate owners.
3. When acting on a request made by another State Party in accordance with articles 31 and 50 of this Convention, a State Party may, after due consideration has been given to compensation of victims, give special consideration to concluding agreements or arrangements on:
   (a) Contributing the value of such proceeds of crime or property or funds derived from the sale of such proceeds of crime or property or a part thereof to the account designated in accordance with article 56, paragraph 2 (c), of this Convention, and to intergovernmental bodies specializing in the fight against cybercrime;
   (b) Sharing with other States Parties, on a regular or case-by-case basis, such proceeds of crime or property, or funds derived from the sale of such proceeds of crime or property, in accordance with its domestic law or administrative procedures.
4. Where appropriate, unless States Parties decide otherwise, the requested State Party may deduct reasonable expenses incurred in investigations, prosecutions or judicial proceedings leading to the return or disposition of confiscated property pursuant to this article.

Chapter VI
Preventive measures

Article 53: Preventive measures

1. Each State Party shall endeavour, in accordance with fundamental principles of its legal system, to develop and implement or maintain effective and coordinated policies and best practices to reduce existing

or future opportunities for cybercrime through appropriate legislative, administrative or other measures. [*agreed ad referendum*]

2. Each State Party shall take appropriate measures, within its means and in accordance with fundamental principles of its domestic law, to promote the active participation of relevant individuals and entities outside the public sector, such as non-governmental organizations, civil society organizations, academic institutions and private sector entities, as well as the general public, in the relevant aspects of prevention of the offences established in accordance with this Convention. [*agreed ad referendum*]
3. Preventive measures may include:
   (a) Strengthening cooperation between law enforcement agencies or prosecutors and relevant individuals and entities outside the public sector, such as non-governmental organizations, civil society organizations, academic institutions and private sector entities for the purpose of addressing relevant aspects of preventing and combating the offences established in accordance with this Convention; [*agreed ad referendum*]
   (b) Promoting public awareness regarding the existence, causes and gravity of the threat posed by the offences established in accordance with this Convention through public information activities, public education, media and information literacy programmes and curricula that promote public participation in preventing and combating such offences; [*agreed ad referendum*]
   (c) Building and making efforts to increase the capacity of domestic criminal justice systems, including training and developing expertise among criminal justice practitioners, as part of national prevention strategies against the offences established in accordance with this Convention; [*agreed ad referendum*]
   (d) Encouraging service providers to take effective measures, where feasible in the light of national circumstances and to the extent permitted by domestic law, to strengthen the security of the service providers products, services and customers;
   (e) Recognizing the contributions of the legitimate activities of security researchers when intended solely, and to the extent permitted and subject to the conditions prescribed by domestic law, to strengthen and improve the security of service providers products, services and customers located within the territory of the State Party; [*agreed ad referendum*]
   (f) Developing, facilitating and promoting programmes and activities in order to discourage those at risk of engaging in cybercrime from

becoming offenders and to develop their skills in a lawful manner; [*agreed ad referendum*]

(g) Endeavouring to promote the reintegration into society of persons convicted of offences established in accordance with this Convention; [*agreed ad referendum*]

(h) Developing strategies and policies, in accordance with domestic law, to prevent and eradicate gender-based violence that occurs through the use of an information and communications technology system, as well as taking into consideration the special circumstances and needs of persons in vulnerable situations in developing preventive measures;

(i) Undertaking specific and tailored efforts to keep children safe online, including through education and training on and raising public awareness of child sexual abuse or child sexual exploitation online and through revising domestic legal frameworks and enhancing international cooperation aimed at its prevention, as well as making efforts to ensure the swift removal of child sexual abuse and child sexual exploitation material; [*agreed ad referendum*]

(j) Enhancing the transparency of and promoting the contribution of the public to decision-making processes and ensuring that the public has adequate access to information; [*agreed ad referendum*]

(k) Respecting, promoting and protecting the freedom to seek, receive and impart public information concerning cybercrime; [*agreed ad referendum*]

(l) Developing or strengthening support programmes for victims of the offences established in accordance with this Convention; [*agreed ad referendum*]

(m) Preventing and detecting transfers of proceeds of crime and property related to the offences established in accordance with this Convention. [*agreed ad referendum*]

4. Each State Party shall take appropriate measures to ensure that the relevant competent authority or authorities responsible for preventing and combating cybercrime are known and accessible to the public, where appropriate, for the reporting, including anonymously, of any incident that may be considered a criminal offence established in accordance with this Convention. [*agreed ad referendum*]

5. States Parties shall endeavour to periodically evaluate existing relevant national legal frameworks and administrative practices with a view to identifying gaps and vulnerabilities and ensuring their relevance in the face of changing threats posed by the offences established in accordance with this Convention. [*agreed ad referendum*]

6. States Parties may collaborate with each other and with relevant international and regional organizations in promoting and developing the measures referred to in this article. This includes participation in international projects aimed at the prevention of cybercrime. [*agreed ad referendum*]
7. Each State Party shall inform the Secretary-General of the United Nations of the name and address of the authority or authorities that may assist other States Parties in developing and implementing specific measures to prevent cybercrime. [*agreed ad referendum*]

Chapter VII
Technical assistance and information exchange

Article 54: Technical assistance and capacity-building

1. States Parties shall, according to their capacity, consider affording one another the widest measure of technical assistance and capacity-building, including training and other forms of assistance, the mutual exchange of relevant experience and specialized knowledge and the transfer of technology on mutually agreed terms, taking into particular consideration the interests and needs of developing States Parties, with a view to facilitating the prevention, detection, investigation and prosecution of the offences covered by this Convention.
2. States Parties shall, to the extent necessary, initiate, develop, implement or improve specific training programmes for their personnel responsible for the prevention, detection, investigation and prosecution of the offences covered by this Convention. [*agreed ad referendum*]
3. Activities referred to in paragraphs 1 and 2 of this article may deal, to the extent permitted by domestic law, with the following: [*agreed ad referendum*]
   (a) Methods and techniques used in the prevention, detection, investigation and prosecution of the offences covered by this Convention; [*agreed ad referendum*]
   (b) Building capacity in the development and planning of strategic policies and legislation to prevent and combat cybercrime; [*agreed ad referendum*]
   (c) Building capacity in the collection, preservation and sharing of evidence, in particular in electronic form, including the maintenance of the chain of custody and forensic analysis; [*agreed ad referendum*]
   (d) Modern law enforcement equipment and the use thereof; [*agreed ad referendum*]

(e) Training of competent authorities in the preparation of requests for mutual legal assistance and other means of cooperation that meet the requirements of this Convention, especially for the collection, preservation and sharing of evidence in electronic form; [*agreed ad referendum*]

(f) Prevention, detection and monitoring of the movements of proceeds deriving from the commission of the offences covered by this Convention, property, equipment or other instrumentalities and methods used for the transfer, concealment or disguise of such proceeds, property, equipment or other instrumentalities; [*agreed ad referendum*]

(g) Appropriate and efficient legal and administrative mechanisms and methods for facilitating the seizure, confiscation and return of proceeds of offences covered by this Convention; [*agreed ad referendum*]

(h) Methods used in the protection of victims and witnesses who cooperate with judicial authorities; [*agreed ad referendum*]

(i) Training in relevant substantive and procedural law, and law enforcement investigation powers, as well as in national and international regulations and in languages. [*agreed ad referendum*]

4. States Parties shall, subject to their domestic law, endeavour to leverage the expertise of and cooperate closely with other States Parties and relevant international and regional organizations, non-governmental organizations, civil society organizations, academic institutions and private sector entities, with a view to enhancing the effective implementation of this Convention. [*agreed ad referendum*]

5. States Parties shall assist one another in planning and implementing research and training programmes designed to share expertise in the areas referred to in paragraph 3 of this article, and to that end shall also, when appropriate, use regional and international conferences and seminars to promote cooperation and to stimulate discussion on problems of mutual concern. [*agreed ad referendum*]

6. States Parties shall consider assisting one another, upon request, in conducting evaluations, studies and research relating to the types, causes and effects of offences covered by this Convention committed in their respective territories, with a view to developing, with the participation of the competent authorities and relevant nongovernmental organizations, civil society organizations, academic institutions and private sector entities, strategies and action plans to prevent and combat cybercrime.

7. States Parties shall promote training and technical assistance that

facilitates timely extradition and mutual legal assistance. Such training and technical assistance may include language training, assistance with the drafting and handling of mutual legal assistance requests, and secondments and exchanges between personnel in central authorities or agencies with relevant responsibilities. [*agreed ad referendum*]

8. States Parties shall strengthen, to the extent necessary, efforts to maximize the effectiveness of technical assistance and capacity-building in international and regional organizations and in the framework of relevant bilateral and multilateral agreements or arrangements. [*agreed ad referendum*]
9. States Parties shall consider establishing voluntary mechanisms with a view to contributing financially to the efforts of developing countries to implement this Convention through technical assistance programmes and capacity-building projects. [*agreed ad referendum*]
10. Each State Party shall endeavour to make voluntary contributions to the United Nations Office on Drugs and Crime for the purpose of fostering, through the Office, programmes and projects with a view to implementing this Convention through technical assistance and capacity-building. [*agreed ad referendum*]

Article 55: Exchange of information
[agreed ad referendum]

1. Each State Party shall consider analysing, as appropriate, in consultation with relevant experts, including from non-governmental organizations, civil society organizations, academic institutions and private sector entities, trends in its territory with respect to offences covered by this Convention, as well as the circumstances in which such offences are committed.
2. States Parties shall consider developing and sharing with each other and through international and regional organizations statistics, analytical expertise and information concerning cybercrime, with a view to developing, insofar as possible, common definitions, standards and methodologies, as well as best practices, to prevent and combat such crime.
3. Each State Party shall consider monitoring its policies and practical measures to prevent and combat offences covered by this Convention and making assessments of their effectiveness and efficiency.
4. States Parties shall consider exchanging information on legal, policy and technological developments related to cybercrime and the collection of evidence in electronic form.

Article 56: Implementation of the Convention through economic development and technical assistance [agreed ad referendum]

1. States Parties shall take measures conducive to the optimal implementation of this Convention to the extent possible, through international cooperation, taking into account the negative effects of the offences covered by this Convention on society in general and, in particular, on sustainable development.
2. States Parties are strongly encouraged to make concrete efforts, to the extent possible and in coordination with each other, as well as with international and regional organizations:
   (a) To enhance their cooperation at various levels with other States Parties, in particular developing countries, with a view to strengthening their capacity to prevent and combat the offences covered by this Convention;
   (b) To enhance financial and material assistance to support the efforts of other States Parties, in particular developing countries, in effectively preventing and combating the offences covered by this Convention and to help them to implement this Convention;
   (c) To provide technical assistance to other States Parties, in particular developing countries, in support of meeting their needs regarding the implementation of this Convention. To that end, States Parties shall endeavour to make adequate and regular voluntary contributions to an account specifically designated for that purpose in a United Nations funding mechanism;
   (d) To encourage, as appropriate, non-governmental organizations, civil society organizations, academic institutions and private sector entities, as well as financial institutions, to contribute to the efforts of States Parties, including in accordance with this article, in particular by providing more training programmes and modern equipment to developing countries in order to assist them in achieving the objectives of this Convention;
   (e) To exchange best practices and information with regard to activities undertaken, with a view to improving transparency, avoiding duplication of effort and making best use of any lessons learned.
3. States Parties shall also consider using existing subregional, regional and international programmes, including conferences and seminars, to promote cooperation and technical assistance and to stimulate discussion on problems of mutual concern, including the special problems and needs of developing countries.

4. To the extent possible, States Parties shall ensure that resources and efforts are distributed and directed to support the harmonization of standards, skills, capacity, expertise and technical capabilities with the aim of establishing common minimum standards among States Parties to eradicate safe havens for the offences covered by this Convention and strengthen the fight against cybercrime.
5. To the extent possible, the measures taken under this article shall be without prejudice to existing foreign assistance commitments or to other financial cooperation arrangements at the bilateral, regional or international levels.
6. States Parties may conclude bilateral, regional or multilateral agreements or arrangements on material and logistical assistance, taking into consideration the financial arrangements necessary for the means of international cooperation provided for by this Convention to be effective and for the prevention, detection, investigation and prosecution of the offences covered by this Convention.

Chapter VIII
Mechanism of implementation

Article 57: Conference of the States Parties to the Convention

1. A Conference of the States Parties to the Convention is hereby established to improve the capacity of and cooperation between States Parties to achieve the objectives set forth in this Convention and to promote and review its implementation. [*agreed ad referendum*]
2. The Secretary-General of the United Nations shall convene the Conference of the States Parties not later than one year following the entry into force of this Convention. Thereafter, regular meetings of the Conference shall be held in accordance with the rules of procedure adopted by the Conference. [*agreed ad referendum*]
3. The Conference of the States Parties shall adopt rules of procedure and rules governing the activities set forth in this article, including rules concerning the admission and participation of observers, and the payment of expenses incurred in carrying out those activities. Such rules and related activities shall take into account principles such as effectiveness, inclusivity, transparency, efficiency and national ownership.
4. In establishing its regular meetings, the Conference of the States Parties shall take into account the time and location of the meetings of other relevant international and regional organizations and mechanisms in similar matters, including their subsidiary treaty bodies, consistent with the principles identified in paragraph 3 of this article.

5. The Conference of the States Parties shall agree upon activities, procedures and methods of work to achieve the objectives set forth in paragraph 1 of this article, including:
   (a) Facilitating the effective use and implementation of this Convention, the identification of any problems thereof, as well as the activities carried out by States Parties under this Convention, including encouraging the mobilization of voluntary contributions;
   (b) Facilitating the exchange of information on legal, policy and technological developments pertaining to the offences established in accordance with this Convention and the collection of evidence in electronic form among States Parties and relevant international and regional organizations, as well as non-governmental organizations, civil society organizations, academic institutions and private sector entities, in accordance with domestic law, as well as on patterns and trends in cybercrime and on successful practices for preventing and combating such offences;
   (c) Cooperating with relevant international and regional organizations, as well as non-governmental organizations, civil society organizations, academic institutions and private sector entities;
   (d) Making appropriate use of relevant information produced by other international and regional organizations and mechanisms for preventing and combating the offences established in accordance with this Convention, in order to avoid unnecessary duplication of work;
   (e) Reviewing periodically the implementation of this Convention by its States Parties;
   (f) Making recommendations to improve this Convention and its implementation as well as considering possible supplementation or amendment of the Convention;
   (g) Elaborating and adopting supplementary protocols to this Convention on the basis of articles 61 and 62 of this Convention;
   (h) Taking note of the technical assistance and capacity-building requirements of States Parties regarding the implementation of this Convention and recommending any action it may deem necessary in that respect.

   [*agreed ad referendum*]

6. Each State Party shall provide the Conference of the States Parties with information on legislative, administrative and other measures, as well as on its programmes, plans and practices, to implement this Convention, as required by the Conference. The Conference shall examine the most effective way of receiving and acting upon

information, including, inter alia, information received from States Parties and from competent international and regional organizations. Inputs received from representatives of relevant non-governmental organizations, civil society organizations, academic institutions and private sector entities, duly accredited in accordance with procedures to be decided upon by the Conference, may also be considered.

7. For the purpose of paragraph 5 of this article, the Conference of the States Parties may establish and administer such review mechanisms as it considers necessary.
8. Pursuant to paragraphs 5 to 7 of this article, the Conference of the States Parties shall establish, if it deems necessary, any appropriate mechanisms or subsidiary bodies to assist in the effective implementation of the Convention. [*agreed ad referendum*]

Article 58: Secretariat
[agreed ad referendum]

1. The Secretary-General of the United Nations shall provide the necessary secretariat services to the Conference of the States Parties to the Convention.
2. The secretariat shall:
   (a) Assist the Conference of the States Parties in carrying out the activities set forth in this Convention and make arrangements and provide the necessary services for the sessions of the Conference as they pertain to this Convention;
   (b) Upon request, assist States Parties in providing information to the Conference of the States Parties, as envisaged in this Convention; and
   (c) Ensure the necessary coordination with the secretariats of relevant international and regional organizations.

Chapter IX
Final provisions

Article 59: Implementation of the Convention
[agreed ad referendum]

1. Each State Party shall take the necessary measures, including legislative and administrative measures, in accordance with fundamental principles of its domestic law, to ensure the implementation of its obligations under this Convention.
2. Each State Party may adopt more strict or severe measures than those provided for by this Convention for preventing and combating the offences established in accordance with this Convention.

Article 60: Effects of the Convention

1. If two or more States Parties have already concluded an agreement or treaty on the matters dealt with in this Convention or have otherwise established their relations on such matters, or should they in future do so, they shall also be entitled to apply that agreement or treaty or to regulate those relations accordingly.
2. Nothing in this Convention shall affect other rights, restrictions, obligations and responsibilities of a State Party under international law. [*agreed ad referendum*]

Article 61: Relation with protocols *[agreed ad referendum]*

1. This Convention may be supplemented by one or more protocols.
2. In order to become a Party to a protocol, a State or a regional economic integration organization must also be a Party to this Convention.
3. A State Party to this Convention is not bound by a protocol unless it becomes a Party to the protocol in accordance with the provisions thereof.
4. Any protocol to this Convention shall be interpreted together with this Convention, taking into account the purpose of that protocol.

Article 62: Adoption of supplementary protocols

1. At least 60 States Parties shall be required before any supplementary protocol is considered for adoption by the Conference of the States Parties. The Conference shall make every effort to achieve consensus on any supplementary protocol. If all efforts at consensus have been exhausted and no agreement has been reached, the supplementary protocol shall, as a last resort, require for its adoption at least a two-thirds majority vote of the States Parties present and voting at the meeting of the Conference.
2. Regional economic integration organizations, in matters within their competence, shall exercise their right to vote under this article with a number of votes equal to the number of their member States that are Parties to this Convention. Such organizations shall not exercise their right to vote if their member States exercise theirs and vice versa.

Article 63: Settlement of disputes *[agreed ad referendum]*

1. States Parties shall endeavour to settle disputes concerning the interpretation or application of this Convention through negotiation or any other peaceful means of their own choice.

2. Any dispute between two or more States Parties concerning the interpretation or application of this Convention that cannot be settled through negotiation or other peaceful means within a reasonable time shall, at the request of one of those States Parties, be submitted to arbitration. If, six months after the date of the request for arbitration, those States Parties are unable to agree on the organization of the arbitration, any one of those States Parties may refer the dispute to the International Court of Justice by request in accordance with the Statute of the Court.
3. Each State Party may, at the time of signature, ratification, acceptance or approval of or accession to this Convention, declare that it does not consider itself bound by paragraph 2 of this article. The other States Parties shall not be bound by paragraph 2 of this article with respect to any State Party that has made such a reservation.
4. Any State Party that has made a reservation in accordance with paragraph 3 of this article may at any time withdraw that reservation by notification to the Secretary-General of the United Nations.

Article 64: Signature, ratification, acceptance, approval and accession [agreed ad referendum]

1. This Convention shall be open to all States for signature at United Nations Headquarters in New York until 31 December 2026.
2. This Convention shall also be open for signature by regional economic integration organizations, provided that at least one member State of such an organization has signed this Convention in accordance with paragraph 1 of this article.
3. This Convention is subject to ratification, acceptance or approval. Instruments of ratification, acceptance or approval shall be deposited with the Secretary-General of the United Nations. A regional economic integration organization may deposit its instrument of ratification, acceptance or approval if at least one of its member States has done likewise. In that instrument of ratification, acceptance or approval, such organization shall declare the extent of its competence with respect to the matters governed by this Convention. Such organization shall also inform the depositary of any relevant modification in the extent of its competence.
4. This Convention is open for accession by any State or any regional economic integration organization of which at least one member State is a Party to this Convention. Instruments of accession shall be deposited with the Secretary-General of the United Nations. At the time of its accession, a regional economic integration organization shall declare

the extent of its competence with respect to matters governed by this Convention. Such organization shall also inform the depositary of any relevant modification in the extent of its competence.

Article 65: Entry into force

1. This Convention shall enter into force on the ninetieth day after the date of deposit of the fortieth instrument of ratification, acceptance, approval or accession. For the purpose of this paragraph, any instrument deposited by a regional economic integration organization shall not be counted as additional to those deposited by member States of that organization.
2. For each State or regional economic integration organization ratifying, accepting, approving or acceding to this Convention after the deposit of the fortieth instrument of such action, this Convention shall enter into force on the thirtieth day after the date of deposit by such State or organization of the relevant instrument or on the date on which this Convention enters into force pursuant to paragraph 1 of this article, whichever is later.

Article 66: Amendment

1. After the expiry of five years from the entry into force of this Convention, a State Party may propose an amendment and transmit it to the Secretary-General of the United Nations, who shall thereupon communicate the proposed amendment to the States Parties and to the Conference of the States Parties to the Convention for the purpose of considering and deciding on the proposal. The Conference shall make every effort to achieve consensus on each amendment. If all efforts at consensus have been exhausted and no agreement has been reached, the amendment shall, as a last resort, require for its adoption a two-thirds majority vote of the States Parties present and voting at the meeting of the Conference.
2. Regional economic integration organizations, in matters within their competence, shall exercise their right to vote under this article with a number of votes equal to the number of their member States that are Parties to this Convention. Such organizations shall not exercise their right to vote if their member States exercise theirs and vice versa. [*agreed ad referendum*]
3. An amendment adopted in accordance with paragraph 1 of this article is subject to ratification, acceptance or approval by States Parties. [*agreed ad referendum*]
4. An amendment adopted in accordance with paragraph 1 of this article

shall enter into force in respect of a State Party 90 days after the date of the deposit with the Secretary-General of the United Nations of an instrument of ratification, acceptance or approval of such amendment. [*agreed ad referendum*]

5. When an amendment enters into force, it shall be binding on those States Parties that have expressed their consent to be bound by it. Other States Parties shall still be bound by the provisions of this Convention and any earlier amendments that they have ratified, accepted or approved. [*agreed ad referendum*]

Article 67: Denunciation
[agreed ad referendum]

1. A State Party may denounce this Convention by written notification to the Secretary-General of the United Nations. Such denunciation shall become effective one year after the date of receipt of the notification by the Secretary-General.
2. A regional economic integration organization shall cease to be a Party to this Convention when all of its member States have denounced it.
3. Denunciation of this Convention in accordance with paragraph 1 of this article shall entail the denunciation of any protocols thereto.

Article 68: Depositary and languages
[agreed ad referendum]

1. The Secretary-General of the United Nations is designated depositary of this Convention.
2. The original of this Convention, of which the Arabic, Chinese, English, French, Russian and Spanish texts are equally authentic, shall be deposited with the Secretary-General of the United Nations.

IN WITNESS WHEREOF, the undersigned plenipotentiaries, being duly authorized thereto by their respective Governments, have signed this Convention.[1] [*agreed ad referendum*]

---

1 It is noted that interpretative notes on articles 2, 17, 23 and 35 of this Convention were approved by the Ad Hoc Committee to Elaborate a Comprehensive International Convention on Countering the Use of Information and Communications Technologies for Criminal Purposes and annexed to the report on its reconvened concluding session, held from 29 July to 9 August 2024 in New York.

Annexure Two

Convention on Cybercrime

European Treaty Series No. 185
Council of Europe

Budapest, 23-11-2001

Preamble

The member States of the Council of Europe and the other States signatory hereto,

Considering that the aim of the Council of Europe is to achieve a greater unity between its members;

Recognising the value of fostering co-operation with the other States parties to this Convention;

Convinced of the need to pursue, as a matter of priority, a common criminal policy aimed at the protection of society against cybercrime, *inter alia*, by adopting appropriate legislation and fostering international co-operation;

Conscious of the profound changes brought about by the digitalisation, convergence and continuing globalisation of computer networks;

Concerned by the risk that computer networks and electronic information may also be used for committing criminal offences and that evidence relating to such offences may be stored and transferred by these networks;

Recognising the need for co-operation between States and private industry in combating cybercrime and the need to protect legitimate interests in the use and development of information technologies;

Believing that an effective fight against cybercrime requires increased, rapid and wellfunctioning international co-operation in criminal matters;

Convinced that the present Convention is necessary to deter action directed against the confidentiality, integrity and availability of computer systems, networks and computer data as well as the misuse of such systems, networks and data by providing for the criminalisation of such conduct, as described in this Convention, and the adoption of powers sufficient for effectively combating such criminal offences, by facilitating their detection, investigation and prosecution at both the domestic and international levels and by providing arrangements for fast and reliable international co-operation;

Mindful of the need to ensure a proper balance between the interests of law enforcement and respect for fundamental human rights as enshrined in the 1950 Council of Europe Convention for the Protection of Human Rights and Fundamental Freedoms, the 1966 United Nations International Covenant on Civil and Political Rights and other applicable international human rights treaties, which reaffirm the right of everyone to hold opinions without interference, as well as the right to freedom of expression, including the freedom to seek, receive, and impart information and ideas of all kinds, regardless of frontiers, and the rights concerning the respect for privacy;

Mindful also of the right to the protection of personal data, as conferred, for example, by the 1981 Council of Europe Convention for the Protection of Individuals with regard to Automatic Processing of Personal Data;

Considering the 1989 United Nations Convention on the Rights of the Child and the 1999 International Labour Organization Worst Forms of Child Labour Convention;

Taking into account the existing Council of Europe conventions on co-operation in the penal field, as well as similar treaties which exist between Council of Europe member States and other States, and stressing that the present Convention is intended to supplement those conventions in order to make criminal investigations and proceedings concerning criminal offences related to computer systems and data more effective and to enable the collection of evidence in electronic form of a criminal offence;

Welcoming recent developments which further advance international understanding and cooperation in combating cybercrime, including action taken by the United Nations, the OECD, the European Union and the G8;

Recalling Committee of Ministers Recommendations No. R (85) 10 concerning the practical application of the European Convention on Mutual Assistance in Criminal Matters in respect of letters rogatory for the interception of telecommunications, No. R (88) 2 on piracy in the field of copyright and neighbouring rights, No. R (87) 15 regulating the use of personal data in the police sector, No. R (95) 4 on the protection of personal data in the area of telecommunication services, with particular reference to telephone services, as well as No. R (89) 9 on computer-related crime providing guidelines for national legislatures concerning the definition of certain computer crimes and No. R (95) 13 concerning problems of criminal procedural law connected with information technology;

Having regard to Resolution No. 1 adopted by the European Ministers of Justice at their 21st Conference (Prague, 10 and 11 June 1997), which recommended that the Committee of Ministers support the work on cybercrime carried out by the European Committee on Crime Problems (CDPC) in order to bring domestic criminal law provisions closer to each other and enable the use of effective means of investigation into such offences, as well as to Resolution No. 3 adopted at the 23rd Conference of the European Ministers of Justice (London, 8 and 9 June 2000), which encouraged the negotiating parties to pursue their efforts with a view to finding appropriate solutions to enable the largest possible number of States to become parties to the Convention and acknowledged the need for a swift and efficient system of international co-operation, which duly takes into account the specific requirements of the fight against cybercrime;

Having also regard to the Action Plan adopted by the Heads of State and Government of the Council of Europe on the occasion of their Second Summit (Strasbourg, 10 and 11 October 1997), to seek common responses to the development of the new information technologies based on the standards and values of the Council of Europe;

Have agreed as follows:

Chapter I
Use of terms

Article 1: Definitions

For the purposes of this Convention:

(a) computer system means any device or a group of interconnected or related devices, one or more of which, pursuant to a program, performs automatic processing of data;

(b) computer data means any representation of facts, information or concepts in a form suitable for processing in a computer system, including a program suitable to cause a computer system to perform a function;

(c) service provider means:

(i) any public or private entity that provides to users of its service the ability to communicate by means of a computer system, and

(ii) any other entity that processes or stores computer data on behalf of such communication service or users of such service.

(d) traffic data means any computer data relating to a communication by means of a computer system, generated by a computer system that formed a part in the chain of communication, indicating the communications origin, destination, route, time, date, size, duration, or type of underlying service.

Chapter II
Measures to be taken at the national level

Section 1: Substantive criminal law

Title 1: Offences against the confidentiality, integrity and availability of computer data and systems

Article 2: Illegal access

Each Party shall adopt such legislative and other measures as may be necessary to establish as criminal offences under its domestic law, when committed intentionally, the access to the whole or any part of a computer system without right. A Party may require that the offence be committed by infringing security measures, with the intent of obtaining computer data or other dishonest intent, or in relation to a computer system that is connected to another computer system.

Article 3: Illegal interception

Each Party shall adopt such legislative and other measures as may be necessary to establish as criminal offences under its domestic law, when committed intentionally, the interception without right, made by technical means, of non-public transmissions of computer data to, from or within a computer system, including electromagnetic emissions from a computer system carrying such computer data. A Party may require that the offence be committed with dishonest intent, or in relation to a computer system that is connected to another computer system.

Article 4: Data interference

1. Each Party shall adopt such legislative and other measures as may be necessary to establish as criminal offences under its domestic law, when

committed intentionally, the damaging, deletion, deterioration, alteration or suppression of computer data without right.

2. A Party may reserve the right to require that the conduct described in paragraph 1 result in serious harm.

Article 5: System interference

Each Party shall adopt such legislative and other measures as may be necessary to establish as criminal offences under its domestic law, when committed intentionally, the serious hindering without right of the functioning of a computer system by inputting, transmitting, damaging, deleting, deteriorating, altering or suppressing computer data.

Article 6: Misuse of devices

1. Each Party shall adopt such legislative and other measures as may be necessary to establish as criminal offences under its domestic law, when committed intentionally and without right:
   (a) the production, sale, procurement for use, import, distribution or otherwise making available of:
      (i) a device, including a computer program, designed or adapted primarily for the purpose of committing any of the offences established in accordance with Articles 2 through 5;
      (ii) a computer password, access code, or similar data by which the whole or any part of a computer system is capable of being accessed,

   with intent that it be used for the purpose of committing any of the offences established in Articles 2 through 5; and
   (b) the possession of an item referred to in paragraphs a.i or ii above, with intent that it be used for the purpose of committing any of the offences established in Articles 2 through 5. A Party may require by law that a number of such items be possessed before criminal liability attaches.
2. This article shall not be interpreted as imposing criminal liability where the production, sale, procurement for use, import, distribution or otherwise making available or possession referred to in paragraph 1 of this article is not for the purpose of committing an offence established in accordance with Articles 2 through 5 of this Convention, such as for the authorised testing or protection of a computer system.
3. Each Party may reserve the right not to apply paragraph 1 of this article, provided that the reservation does not concern the sale, distribution or otherwise making available of the items referred to in paragraph 1 a.ii of this article.

Title 2: Computer-related offences

Article 7: Computer-related forgery

Each Party shall adopt such legislative and other measures as may be necessary to establish as criminal offences under its domestic law, when committed intentionally and without right, the input, alteration, deletion, or suppression of computer data, resulting in inauthentic data with the intent that it be considered or acted upon for legal purposes as if it were authentic, regardless whether or not the data is directly readable and intelligible. A Party may require an intent to defraud, or similar dishonest intent, before criminal liability attaches.

Article 8: Computer-related fraud

Each Party shall adopt such legislative and other measures as may be necessary to establish as criminal offences under its domestic law, when committed intentionally and without right, the causing of a loss of property to another person by:

(a) any input, alteration, deletion or suppression of computer data,

(b) any interference with the functioning of a computer system,

with fraudulent or dishonest intent of procuring, without right, an economic benefit for oneself or for another person.

Title 3: Content-related offences

Article 9: Offences related to child pornography

1. Each Party shall adopt such legislative and other measures as may be necessary to establish as criminal offences under its domestic law, when committed intentionally and without right, the following conduct:
   (a) producing child pornography for the purpose of its distribution through a computer system;
   (b) offering or making available child pornography through a computer system;
   (c) distributing or transmitting child pornography through a computer system;
   (d) procuring child pornography through a computer system for oneself or for another person;
   (e) possessing child pornography in a computer system or on a computer-data storage medium.
2. For the purpose of paragraph 1 above, the term child pornography shall include pornographic material that visually depicts:

(a) a minor engaged in sexually explicit conduct;
(b) a person appearing to be a minor engaged in sexually explicit conduct;
(c) realistic images representing a minor engaged in sexually explicit conduct.

3. For the purpose of paragraph 2 above, the term minor shall include all persons under 18 years of age. A Party may, however, require a lower age-limit, which shall be not less than 16 years.
4. Each Party may reserve the right not to apply, in whole or in part, paragraphs 1, subparagraphs d and e, and 2, sub-paragraphs b and c.

Title 4: Offences related to infringements of copyright and related rights

Article 10: Offences related to infringements of copyright and related rights

1. Each Party shall adopt such legislative and other measures as may be necessary to establish as criminal offences under its domestic law the infringement of copyright, as defined under the law of that Party, pursuant to the obligations it has undertaken under the Paris Act of 24 July 1971 revising the Bern Convention for the Protection of Literary and Artistic Works, the Agreement on Trade-Related Aspects of Intellectual Property Rights and the WIPO Copyright Treaty, with the exception of any moral rights conferred by such conventions, where such acts are committed wilfully, on a commercial scale and by means of a computer system.
2. Each Party shall adopt such legislative and other measures as may be necessary to establish as criminal offences under its domestic law the infringement of related rights, as defined under the law of that Party, pursuant to the obligations it has undertaken under the International Convention for the Protection of Performers, Producers of Phonograms and Broadcasting Organisations (Rome Convention), the Agreement on Trade-Related Aspects of Intellectual Property Rights and the WIPO Performances and Phonograms Treaty, with the exception of any moral rights conferred by such conventions, where such acts are committed wilfully, on a commercial scale and by means of a computer system.
3. A Party may reserve the right not to impose criminal liability under paragraphs 1 and 2 of this article in limited circumstances, provided that other effective remedies are available and that such reservation does not derogate from the Partys international obligations set forth

in the international instruments referred to in paragraphs 1 and 2 of this article.

Title 5: Ancillary liability and sanctions

Article 11: Attempt and aiding or abetting

1. Each Party shall adopt such legislative and other measures as may be necessary to establish as criminal offences under its domestic law, when committed intentionally, aiding or abetting the commission of any of the offences established in accordance with Articles 2 through 10 of the present Convention with intent that such offence be committed.
2. Each Party shall adopt such legislative and other measures as may be necessary to establish as criminal offences under its domestic law, when committed intentionally, an attempt to commit any of the offences established in accordance with Articles 3 through 5, 7, 8, and 9.1.a and c of this Convention.
3. Each Party may reserve the right not to apply, in whole or in part, paragraph 2 of this article.

Article 12: Corporate liability

1. Each Party shall adopt such legislative and other measures as may be necessary to ensure that legal persons can be held liable for a criminal offence established in accordance with this Convention, committed for their benefit by any natural person, acting either individually or as part of an organ of the legal person, who has a leading position within it, based on:
   (a) a power of representation of the legal person;
   (b) an authority to take decisions on behalf of the legal person;
   (c) an authority to exercise control within the legal person.
2. In addition to the cases already provided for in paragraph 1 of this article, each Party shall take the measures necessary to ensure that a legal person can be held liable where the lack of supervision or control by a natural person referred to in paragraph 1 has made possible the commission of a criminal offence established in accordance with this Convention for the benefit of that legal person by a natural person acting under its authority.
3. Subject to the legal principles of the Party, the liability of a legal person may be criminal, civil or administrative.
4. Such liability shall be without prejudice to the criminal liability of the natural persons who have committed the offence.

Article 13: Sanctions and measures

1. Each Party shall adopt such legislative and other measures as may be necessary to ensure that the criminal offences established in accordance with Articles 2 through 11 are punishable by effective, proportionate and dissuasive sanctions, which include deprivation of liberty.
2. Each Party shall ensure that legal persons held liable in accordance with Article 12 shall be subject to effective, proportionate and dissuasive criminal or non-criminal sanctions or measures, including monetary sanctions.

Section 2: Procedural law

Title 1: Common provisions

Article 14: Scope of procedural provisions

1. Each Party shall adopt such legislative and other measures as may be necessary to establish the powers and procedures provided for in this section for the purpose of specific criminal investigations or proceedings.
2. Except as specifically provided otherwise in Article 21, each Party shall apply the powers and procedures referred to in paragraph 1 of this article to:
   (a) the criminal offences established in accordance with Articles 2 through 11 of this Convention;
   (b) other criminal offences committed by means of a computer system; and
   (c) the collection of evidence in electronic form of a criminal offence.
3. (a) Each Party may reserve the right to apply the measures referred to in Article 20 only to offences or categories of offences specified in the reservation, provided that the range of such offences or categories of offences is not more restricted than the range of offences to which it applies the measures referred to in Article 21. Each Party shall consider restricting such a reservation to enable the broadest application of the measure referred to in Article 20.
   (b) Where a Party, due to limitations in its legislation in force at the time of the adoption of the present Convention, is not able to apply the measures referred to in Articles 20 and 21 to communications being transmitted within a computer system of a service provider, which system:
      (i) is being operated for the benefit of a closed group of users, and

(ii) does not employ public communications networks and is not connected with another computer system, whether public or private,

that Party may reserve the right not to apply these measures to such communications. Each Party shall consider restricting such a reservation to enable the broadest application of the measures referred to in Articles 20 and 21.

Article 15: Conditions and safeguards

1. Each Party shall ensure that the establishment, implementation and application of the powers and procedures provided for in this Section are subject to conditions and safeguards provided for under its domestic law, which shall provide for the adequate protection of human rights and liberties, including rights arising pursuant to obligations it has undertaken under the 1950 Council of Europe Convention for the Protection of Human Rights and Fundamental Freedoms, the 1966 United Nations International Covenant on Civil and Political Rights, and other applicable international human rights instruments, and which shall incorporate the principle of proportionality.
2. Such conditions and safeguards shall, as appropriate in view of the nature of the procedure or power concerned, *inter alia*, include judicial or other independent supervision, grounds justifying application, and limitation of the scope and the duration of such power or procedure.
3. To the extent that it is consistent with the public interest, in particular the sound administration of justice, each Party shall consider the impact of the powers and procedures in this section upon the rights, responsibilities and legitimate interests of third parties.

Title 2: Expedited preservation of stored computer data

Article 16: Expedited preservation of stored computer data

1. Each Party shall adopt such legislative and other measures as may be necessary to enable its competent authorities to order or similarly obtain the expeditious preservation of specified computer data, including traffic data, that has been stored by means of a computer system, in particular where there are grounds to believe that the computer data is particularly vulnerable to loss or modification.
2. Where a Party gives effect to paragraph 1 above by means of an order to a person to preserve specified stored computer data in the persons possession or control, the Party shall adopt such legislative and other measures as may be necessary to oblige that person to preserve and

maintain the integrity of that computer data for a period of time as long as necessary, up to a maximum of ninety days, to enable the competent authorities to seek its disclosure. A Party may provide for such an order to be subsequently renewed.

3. Each Party shall adopt such legislative and other measures as may be necessary to oblige the custodian or other person who is to preserve the computer data to keep confidential the undertaking of such procedures for the period of time provided for by its domestic law.
4. The powers and procedures referred to in this article shall be subject to Articles 14 and 15.

Article 17: Expedited preservation and partial disclosure of traffic data

1. Each Party shall adopt, in respect of traffic data that is to be preserved under Article 16, such legislative and other measures as may be necessary to:
   (a) ensure that such expeditious preservation of traffic data is available regardless of whether one or more service providers were involved in the transmission of that communication; and
   (b) ensure the expeditious disclosure to the Partys competent authority, or a person designated by that authority, of a sufficient amount of traffic data to enable the Party to identify the service providers and the path through which the communication was transmitted.
2 The powers and procedures referred to in this article shall be subject to Articles 14 and 15.

Title 3: Production order

Article 18: Production order

1. Each Party shall adopt such legislative and other measures as may be necessary to empower its competent authorities to order:
   (a) a person in its territory to submit specified computer data in that persons possession or control, which is stored in a computer system or a computer-data storage medium; and
   (b) a service provider offering its services in the territory of the Party to submit subscriber information relating to such services in that service providers possession or control.
2. The powers and procedures referred to in this article shall be subject to Articles 14 and 15.
3. For the purpose of this article, the term subscriber information means any information contained in the form of computer data or any other

form that is held by a service provider, relating to subscribers of its services other than traffic or content data and by which can be established:

(a) the type of communication service used, the technical provisions taken thereto and the period of service;
(b) the subscribers identity, postal or geographic address, telephone and other access number, billing and payment information, available on the basis of the service agreement or arrangement;
(c) any other information on the site of the installation of communication equipment, available on the basis of the service agreement or arrangement.

Title 4: Search and seizure of stored computer data

Article 19: Search and seizure of stored computer data

1. Each Party shall adopt such legislative and other measures as may be necessary to empower its competent authorities to search or similarly access:
   (a) a computer system or part of it and computer data stored therein; and
   (b) a computer-data storage medium in which computer data may be stored

   in its territory.
2. Each Party shall adopt such legislative and other measures as may be necessary to ensure that where its authorities search or similarly access a specific computer system or part of it, pursuant to paragraph 1.a, and have grounds to believe that the data sought is stored in another computer system or part of it in its territory, and such data is lawfully accessible from or available to the initial system, the authorities shall be able to expeditiously extend the search or similar accessing to the other system.
3. Each Party shall adopt such legislative and other measures as may be necessary to empower its competent authorities to seize or similarly secure computer data accessed according to paragraphs 1 or 2. These measures shall include the power to:
   (a) seize or similarly secure a computer system or part of it or a computer-data storage medium;
   (b) make and retain a copy of those computer data;
   (c) maintain the integrity of the relevant stored computer data;
   (d) render inaccessible or remove those computer data in the accessed computer system.

4. Each Party shall adopt such legislative and other measures as may be necessary to empower its competent authorities to order any person who has knowledge about the functioning of the computer system or measures applied to protect the computer data therein to provide, as is reasonable, the necessary information, to enable the undertaking of the measures referred to in paragraphs 1 and 2.
5. The powers and procedures referred to in this article shall be subject to Articles 14 and 15.

Title 5: Real-time collection of computer data

Article 20: Real-time collection of traffic data

1. Each Party shall adopt such legislative and other measures as may be necessary to empower its competent authorities to:
   (a) collect or record through the application of technical means on the territory of that Party, and
   (b) compel a service provider, within its existing technical capability:
      (i) to collect or record through the application of technical means on the territory of that Party; or
      (ii) to co-operate and assist the competent authorities in the collection or recording of,

   traffic data, in real-time, associated with specified communications in its territory transmitted by means of a computer system.
2. Where a Party, due to the established principles of its domestic legal system, cannot adopt the measures referred to in paragraph 1.a, it may instead adopt legislative and other measures as may be necessary to ensure the real-time collection or recording of traffic data associated with specified communications transmitted in its territory, through the application of technical means on that territory.
3. Each Party shall adopt such legislative and other measures as may be necessary to oblige a service provider to keep confidential the fact of the execution of any power provided for in this article and any information relating to it.
4. The powers and procedures referred to in this article shall be subject to Articles 14 and 15.

Article 21: Interception of content data

1. Each Party shall adopt such legislative and other measures as may be necessary, in relation to a range of serious offences to be determined by domestic law, to empower its competent authorities to:

(a) collect or record through the application of technical means on the territory of that Party, and

(b) compel a service provider, within its existing technical capability:

  (i) to collect or record through the application of technical means on the territory of that Party, or

  (ii) to co-operate and assist the competent authorities in the collection or recording of,

content data, in real-time, of specified communications in its territory transmitted by means of a computer system.

2. Where a Party, due to the established principles of its domestic legal system, cannot adopt the measures referred to in paragraph 1.a, it may instead adopt legislative and other measures as may be necessary to ensure the real-time collection or recording of content data on specified communications in its territory through the application of technical means on that territory.
3. Each Party shall adopt such legislative and other measures as may be necessary to oblige a service provider to keep confidential the fact of the execution of any power provided for in this article and any information relating to it.
4. The powers and procedures referred to in this article shall be subject to Articles 14 and 15.

Section 3: Jurisdiction

Article 22: Jurisdiction

1. Each Party shall adopt such legislative and other measures as may be necessary to establish jurisdiction over any offence established in accordance with Articles 2 through 11 of this Convention, when the offence is committed:
   (a) in its territory; or
   (b) on board a ship flying the flag of that Party; or
   (c) on board an aircraft registered under the laws of that Party; or
   (d) by one of its nationals, if the offence is punishable under criminal law where it was committed or if the offence is committed outside the territorial jurisdiction of any State.
2. Each Party may reserve the right not to apply or to apply only in specific cases or conditions the jurisdiction rules laid down in paragraphs 1.b through 1.d of this article or any part thereof.
3. Each Party shall adopt such measures as may be necessary to establish jurisdiction over the offences referred to in Article 24, paragraph 1, of

this Convention, in cases where an alleged offender is present in its territory and it does not extradite him or her to another Party, solely on the basis of his or her nationality, after a request for extradition.

4. This Convention does not exclude any criminal jurisdiction exercised by a Party in accordance with its domestic law.
5. When more than one Party claims jurisdiction over an alleged offence established in accordance with this Convention, the Parties involved shall, where appropriate, consult with a view to determining the most appropriate jurisdiction for prosecution.

Chapter III: International co-operation
Section 1: General principles

Title 1: General principles relating to international co-operation

Article 23: General principles relating to international co-operation

The Parties shall co-operate with each other, in accordance with the provisions of this chapter, and through the application of relevant international instruments on international cooperation in criminal matters, arrangements agreed on the basis of uniform or reciprocal legislation, and domestic laws, to the widest extent possible for the purposes of investigations or proceedings concerning criminal offences related to computer systems and data, or for the collection of evidence in electronic form of a criminal offence.

Title 2: Principles relating to extradition

Article 24: Extradition

1. (a) This article applies to extradition between Parties for the criminal offences established in accordance with Articles 2 through 11 of this Convention, provided that they are punishable under the laws of both Parties concerned by deprivation of liberty for a maximum period of at least one year, or by a more severe penalty.
   (b) Where a different minimum penalty is to be applied under an arrangement agreed on the basis of uniform or reciprocal legislation or an extradition treaty, including the European Convention on Extradition (ETS No. 24), applicable between two or more parties, the minimum penalty provided for under such arrangement or treaty shall apply.
2. The criminal offences described in paragraph 1 of this article shall be deemed to be included as extraditable offences in any extradition treaty

existing between or among the Parties. The Parties undertake to include such offences as extraditable offences in any extradition treaty to be concluded between or among them.

3. If a Party that makes extradition conditional on the existence of a treaty receives a request for extradition from another Party with which it does not have an extradition treaty, it may consider this Convention as the legal basis for extradition with respect to any criminal offence referred to in paragraph 1 of this article.
4. Parties that do not make extradition conditional on the existence of a treaty shall recognise the criminal offences referred to in paragraph 1 of this article as extraditable offences between themselves.
5. Extradition shall be subject to the conditions provided for by the law of the requested Party or by applicable extradition treaties, including the grounds on which the requested Party may refuse extradition.
6. If extradition for a criminal offence referred to in paragraph 1 of this article is refused solely on the basis of the nationality of the person sought, or because the requested Party deems that it has jurisdiction over the offence, the requested Party shall submit the case at the request of the requesting Party to its competent authorities for the purpose of prosecution and shall report the final outcome to the requesting Party in due course. Those authorities shall take their decision and conduct their investigations and proceedings in the same manner as for any other offence of a comparable nature under the law of that Party.
7. (a) Each Party shall, at the time of signature or when depositing its instrument of ratification, acceptance, approval or accession, communicate to the Secretary General of the Council of Europe the name and address of each authority responsible for making or receiving requests for extradition or provisional arrest in the absence of a treaty.
   (b) The Secretary General of the Council of Europe shall set up and keep updated a register of authorities so designated by the Parties. Each Party shall ensure that the details held on the register are correct at all times.

Title 3: General principles relating to mutual assistance

Article 25: General principles relating to mutual assistance

1. The Parties shall afford one another mutual assistance to the widest extent possible for the purpose of investigations or proceedings concerning criminal offences related to computer systems and data, or for the collection of evidence in electronic form of a criminal offence.

2. Each Party shall also adopt such legislative and other measures as may be necessary to carry out the obligations set forth in Articles 27 through 35.
3. Each Party may, in urgent circumstances, make requests for mutual assistance or communications related thereto by expedited means of communication, including fax or email, to the extent that such means provide appropriate levels of security and authentication (including the use of encryption, where necessary), with formal confirmation to follow, where required by the requested Party. The requested Party shall accept and respond to the request by any such expedited means of communication.
4. Except as otherwise specifically provided in articles in this chapter, mutual assistance shall be subject to the conditions provided for by the law of the requested Party or by applicable mutual assistance treaties, including the grounds on which the requested Party may refuse co-operation. The requested Party shall not exercise the right to refuse mutual assistance in relation to the offences referred to in Articles 2 through 11 solely on the ground that the request concerns an offence which it considers a fiscal offence.
5. Where, in accordance with the provisions of this chapter, the requested Party is permitted to make mutual assistance conditional upon the existence of dual criminality, that condition shall be deemed fulfilled, irrespective of whether its laws place the offence within the same category of offence or denominate the offence by the same terminology as the requesting Party, if the conduct underlying the offence for which assistance is sought is a criminal offence under its laws.

Article 26: Spontaneous information

1. A Party may, within the limits of its domestic law and without prior request, forward to another Party information obtained within the framework of its own investigations when it considers that the disclosure of such information might assist the receiving Party in initiating or carrying out investigations or proceedings concerning criminal offences established in accordance with this Convention or might lead to a request for co-operation by that Party under this chapter.
2. Prior to providing such information, the providing Party may request that it be kept confidential or only used subject to conditions. If the receiving Party cannot comply with such request, it shall notify the providing Party, which shall then determine whether the information should nevertheless be provided. If the receiving Party accepts the information subject to the conditions, it shall be bound by them.

Title 4: Procedures pertaining to mutual assistance requests in the absence of applicable international agreements

Article 27: Procedures pertaining to mutual assistance requests in the absence of applicable international agreements

1. Where there is no mutual assistance treaty or arrangement on the basis of uniform or reciprocal legislation in force between the requesting and requested Parties, the provisions of paragraphs 2 through 9 of this article shall apply. The provisions of this article shall not apply where such treaty, arrangement or legislation exists, unless the Parties concerned agree to apply any or all of the remainder of this article in lieu thereof.
2. (a) Each Party shall designate a central authority or authorities responsible for sending and answering requests for mutual assistance, the execution of such requests or their transmission to the authorities competent for their execution.
   (b) The central authorities shall communicate directly with each other;
   (c) Each Party shall, at the time of signature or when depositing its instrument of ratification, acceptance, approval or accession, communicate to the Secretary General of the Council of Europe the names and addresses of the authorities designated in pursuance of this paragraph;
   (d) The Secretary General of the Council of Europe shall set up and keep updated a register of central authorities designated by the Parties. Each Party shall ensure that the details held on the register are correct at all times.
3. Mutual assistance requests under this article shall be executed in accordance with the procedures specified by the requesting Party, except where incompatible with the law of the requested Party.
4. The requested Party may, in addition to the grounds for refusal established in Article 25, paragraph 4, refuse assistance if:
   (a) the request concerns an offence which the requested Party considers a political offence or an offence connected with a political offence, or
   (b) it considers that execution of the request is likely to prejudice its sovereignty, security, *ordre public* or other essential interests.
5. The requested Party may postpone action on a request if such action would prejudice criminal investigations or proceedings conducted by its authorities.
6. Before refusing or postponing assistance, the requested Party shall,

where appropriate after having consulted with the requesting Party, consider whether the request may be granted partially or subject to such conditions as it deems necessary.

7. The requested Party shall promptly inform the requesting Party of the outcome of the execution of a request for assistance. Reasons shall be given for any refusal or postponement of the request. The requested Party shall also inform the requesting Party of any reasons that render impossible the execution of the request or are likely to delay it significantly.
8. The requesting Party may request that the requested Party keep confidential the fact of any request made under this chapter as well as its subject, except to the extent necessary for its execution. If the requested Party cannot comply with the request for confidentiality, it shall promptly inform the requesting Party, which shall then determine whether the request should nevertheless be executed.
9. (a) In the event of urgency, requests for mutual assistance or communications related thereto may be sent directly by judicial authorities of the requesting Party to such authorities of the requested Party. In any such cases, a copy shall be sent at the same time to the central authority of the requested Party through the central authority of the requesting Party.
   (b) Any request or communication under this paragraph may be made through the International Criminal Police Organisation (Interpol).
   (c) Where a request is made pursuant to sub-paragraph a. of this article and the authority is not competent to deal with the request, it shall refer the request to the competent national authority and inform directly the requesting Party that it has done so.
   (d) Requests or communications made under this paragraph that do not involve coercive action may be directly transmitted by the competent authorities of the requesting Party to the competent authorities of the requested Party.
   (e) Each Party may, at the time of signature or when depositing its instrument of ratification, acceptance, approval or accession, inform the Secretary General of the Council of Europe that, for reasons of efficiency, requests made under this paragraph are to be addressed to its central authority.

Article 28: Confidentiality and limitation on use

1. When there is no mutual assistance treaty or arrangement on the basis of uniform or reciprocal legislation in force between the requesting and the requested Parties, the provisions of this article shall apply. The

provisions of this article shall not apply where such treaty, arrangement or legislation exists, unless the Parties concerned agree to apply any or all of the remainder of this article in lieu thereof.

2. The requested Party may make the supply of information or material in response to a request dependent on the condition that it is:
   (a) kept confidential where the request for mutual legal assistance could not be complied with in the absence of such condition, or
   (b) not used for investigations or proceedings other than those stated in the request.
3. If the requesting Party cannot comply with a condition referred to in paragraph 2, it shall promptly inform the other Party, which shall then determine whether the information should nevertheless be provided. When the requesting Party accepts the condition, it shall be bound by it.
4. Any Party that supplies information or material subject to a condition referred to in paragraph 2 may require the other Party to explain, in relation to that condition, the use made of such information or material.

Section 2: Specific provisions

Title 1: Mutual assistance regarding provisional measures

Article 29: Expedited preservation of stored computer data

1. A Party may request another Party to order or otherwise obtain the expeditious preservation of data stored by means of a computer system, located within the territory of that other Party and in respect of which the requesting Party intends to submit a request for mutual assistance for the search or similar access, seizure or similar securing, or disclosure of the data.
2. A request for preservation made under paragraph 1 shall specify:
   (a) the authority seeking the preservation;
   (b) the offence that is the subject of a criminal investigation or proceedings and a brief summary of the related facts;
   (c) the stored computer data to be preserved and its relationship to the offence;
   (d) any available information identifying the custodian of the stored computer data or the location of the computer system;
   (e) the necessity of the preservation; and
   (f) that the Party intends to submit a request for mutual assistance for the search or similar access, seizure or similar securing, or disclosure of the stored computer data.

3. Upon receiving the request from another Party, the requested Party shall take all appropriate measures to preserve expeditiously the specified data in accordance with its domestic law. For the purposes of responding to a request, dual criminality shall not be required as a condition to providing such preservation.
4. A Party that requires dual criminality as a condition for responding to a request for mutual assistance for the search or similar access, seizure or similar securing, or disclosure of stored data may, in respect of offences other than those established in accordance with Articles 2 through 11 of this Convention, reserve the right to refuse the request for preservation under this article in cases where it has reasons to believe that at the time of disclosure the condition of dual criminality cannot be fulfilled.
5. In addition, a request for preservation may only be refused if:
   (a) the request concerns an offence which the requested Party considers a political offence or an offence connected with a political offence, or
   (b) the requested Party considers that execution of the request is likely to prejudice its sovereignty, security, *ordre public* or other essential interests.
6. Where the requested Party believes that preservation will not ensure the future availability of the data or will threaten the confidentiality of or otherwise prejudice the requesting Partys investigation, it shall promptly so inform the requesting Party, which shall then determine whether the request should nevertheless be executed.
7. Any preservation effected in response to the request referred to in paragraph 1 shall be for a period not less than sixty days, in order to enable the requesting Party to submit a request for the search or similar access, seizure or similar securing, or disclosure of the data. Following the receipt of such a request, the data shall continue to be preserved pending a decision on that request.

Article 30: Expedited disclosure of preserved traffic data

1. Where, in the course of the execution of a request made pursuant to Article 29 to preserve traffic data concerning a specific communication, the requested Party discovers that a service provider in another State was involved in the transmission of the communication, the requested Party shall expeditiously disclose to the requesting Party a sufficient amount of traffic data to identify that service provider and the path through which the communication was transmitted.

2. Disclosure of traffic data under paragraph 1 may only be withheld if:
   (a) the request concerns an offence which the requested Party considers a political offence or an offence connected with a political offence; or
   (b) the requested Party considers that execution of the request is likely to prejudice its sovereignty, security, *ordre public* or other essential interests.

Title 2: Mutual assistance regarding investigative powers

Article 31: Mutual assistance regarding accessing of stored computer data

1. A Party may request another Party to search or similarly access, seize or similarly secure, and disclose data stored by means of a computer system located within the territory of the requested Party, including data that has been preserved pursuant to Article 29.
2. The requested Party shall respond to the request through the application of international instruments, arrangements and laws referred to in Article 23, and in accordance with other relevant provisions of this chapter.
3. The request shall be responded to on an expedited basis where:
   (a) there are grounds to believe that relevant data is particularly vulnerable to loss or modification; or
   (b) the instruments, arrangements and laws referred to in paragraph 2 otherwise provide for expedited co-operation.

Article 32: Trans-border access to stored computer data with consent or where publicly available

A Party may, without the authorisation of another Party:

(a) access publicly available (open source) stored computer data, regardless of where the data is located geographically; or

(b) access or receive, through a computer system in its territory, stored computer data located in another Party, if the Party obtains the lawful and voluntary consent of the person who has the lawful authority to disclose the data to the Party through that computer system.

Article 33: Mutual assistance regarding the real-time collection of traffic data

1. The Parties shall provide mutual assistance to each other in the real-time collection of traffic data associated with specified communications in their territory transmitted by means of a computer system. Subject

to the provisions of paragraph 2, this assistance shall be governed by the conditions and procedures provided for under domestic law.

2. Each Party shall provide such assistance at least with respect to criminal offences for which real-time collection of traffic data would be available in a similar domestic case.

Article 34: Mutual assistance regarding the interception of content data

The Parties shall provide mutual assistance to each other in the real-time collection or recording of content data of specified communications transmitted by means of a computer system to the extent permitted under their applicable treaties and domestic laws.

Title 3: 24 /7 Network

Article 35: 24/7 Network

1. Each Party shall designate a point of contact available on a twenty-four hour, seven-day-aweek basis, in order to ensure the provision of immediate assistance for the purpose of investigations or proceedings concerning criminal offences related to computer systems and data, or for the collection of evidence in electronic form of a criminal offence. Such assistance shall include facilitating, or, if permitted by its domestic law and practice, directly carrying out the following measures:
   (a) the provision of technical advice;
   (b) the preservation of data pursuant to Articles 29 and 30;
   (c) the collection of evidence, the provision of legal information, and locating of suspects.
2. (a) A Partys point of contact shall have the capacity to carry out communications with the point of contact of another Party on an expedited basis.
   (b) If the point of contact designated by a Party is not part of that Partys authority or authorities responsible for international mutual assistance or extradition, the point of contact shall ensure that it is able to co-ordinate with such authority or authorities on an expedited basis.
3. Each Party shall ensure that trained and equipped personnel are available, in order to facilitate the operation of the network.

Chapter IV: Final provisions

Article 36: Signature and entry into force

1. This Convention shall be open for signature by the member States of the Council of Europe and by non-member States which have participated in its elaboration.
2. This Convention is subject to ratification, acceptance or approval. Instruments of ratification, acceptance or approval shall be deposited with the Secretary General of the Council of Europe.
3. This Convention shall enter into force on the first day of the month following the expiration of a period of three months after the date on which five States, including at least three member States of the Council of Europe, have expressed their consent to be bound by the Convention in accordance with the provisions of paragraphs 1 and 2.
4. In respect of any signatory State which subsequently expresses its consent to be bound by it, the Convention shall enter into force on the first day of the month following the expiration of a period of three months after the date of the expression of its consent to be bound by the Convention in accordance with the provisions of paragraphs 1 and 2.

Article 37: Accession to the Convention

1. After the entry into force of this Convention, the Committee of Ministers of the Council of Europe, after consulting with and obtaining the unanimous consent of the Contracting States to the Convention, may invite any State which is not a member of the Council and which has not participated in its elaboration to accede to this Convention. The decision shall be taken by the majority provided for in Article 20.d. of the Statute of the Council of Europe and by the unanimous vote of the representatives of the Contracting States entitled to sit on the Committee of Ministers.
2. In respect of any State acceding to the Convention under paragraph 1 above, the Convention shall enter into force on the first day of the month following the expiration of a period of three months after the date of deposit of the instrument of accession with the Secretary General of the Council of Europe.

Article 38: Territorial application

1. Any State may, at the time of signature or when depositing its instrument of ratification, acceptance, approval or accession, specify the territory or territories to which this Convention shall apply.

2. Any State may, at any later date, by a declaration addressed to the Secretary General of the Council of Europe, extend the application of this Convention to any other territory specified in the declaration. In respect of such territory the Convention shall enter into force on the first day of the month following the expiration of a period of three months after the date of receipt of the declaration by the Secretary General.
3. Any declaration made under the two preceding paragraphs may, in respect of any territory specified in such declaration, be withdrawn by a notification addressed to the Secretary General of the Council of Europe. The withdrawal shall become effective on the first day of the month following the expiration of a period of three months after the date of receipt of such notification by the Secretary General.

Article 39: Effects of the Convention

1. The purpose of the present Convention is to supplement applicable multilateral or bilateral treaties or arrangements as between the Parties, including the provisions of:

    the European Convention on Extradition, opened for signature in Paris, on 13 December 1957 (ETS No. 24);

    the European Convention on Mutual Assistance in Criminal Matters, opened for signature in Strasbourg, on 20 April 1959 (ETS No. 30);

    the Additional Protocol to the European Convention on Mutual Assistance in Criminal Matters, opened for signature in Strasbourg, on 17 March 1978 (ETS No. 99).
2. If two or more Parties have already concluded an agreement or treaty on the matters dealt with in this Convention or have otherwise established their relations on such matters, or should they in future do so, they shall also be entitled to apply that agreement or treaty or to regulate those relations accordingly. However, where Parties establish their relations in respect of the matters dealt with in the present Convention other than as regulated therein, they shall do so in a manner that is not inconsistent with the Conventions objectives and principles.
3. Nothing in this Convention shall affect other rights, restrictions, obligations and responsibilities of a Party.

Article 40: Declarations

By a written notification addressed to the Secretary General of the Council of Europe, any State may, at the time of signature or when depositing its instrument of ratification, acceptance, approval or accession, declare that it avails itself of the possibility of requiring additional elements as provided for under Articles 2, 3, 6 paragraph 1.b, 7, 9 paragraph 3, and 27 , paragraph 9.e.

Article 41: Federal clause

1. A federal State may reserve the right to assume obligations under Chapter II of this Convention consistent with its fundamental principles governing the relationship between its central government and constituent States or other similar territorial entities provided that it is still able to co-operate under Chapter III.
2. When making a reservation under paragraph 1, a federal State may not apply the terms of such reservation to exclude or substantially diminish its obligations to provide for measures set forth in Chapter II. Overall, it shall provide for a broad and effective law enforcement capability with respect to those measures.
3. With regard to the provisions of this Convention, the application of which comes under the jurisdiction of constituent States or other similar territorial entities, that are not obliged by the constitutional system of the federation to take legislative measures, the federal government shall inform the competent authorities of such States of the said provisions with its favourable opinion, encouraging them to take appropriate action to give them effect.

Article 42: Reservations

By a written notification addressed to the Secretary General of the Council of Europe, any State may, at the time of signature or when depositing its instrument of ratification, acceptance, approval or accession, declare that it avails itself of the reservation(s) provided for in Article 4, paragraph 2, Article 6, paragraph 3, Article 9, paragraph 4, Article 10, paragraph 3, Article 11, paragraph 3, Article 14, paragraph 3, Article 22, paragraph 2, Article 29, paragraph 4, and Article 41, paragraph 1. No other reservation may be made.

Article 43: Status and withdrawal of reservations

1. A Party that has made a reservation in accordance with Article 42 may wholly or partially withdraw it by means of a notification addressed to the Secretary General of the Council of Europe. Such withdrawal shall take effect on the date of receipt of such notification by the Secretary General. If the notification states that the withdrawal of a reservation is to take effect on a date specified therein, and such date is

later than the date on which the notification is received by the Secretary General, the withdrawal shall take effect on such a later date.

2. A Party that has made a reservation as referred to in Article 42 shall withdraw such reservation, in whole or in part, as soon as circumstances so permit.
3. The Secretary General of the Council of Europe may periodically enquire with Parties that have made one or more reservations as referred to in Article 42 as to the prospects for withdrawing such reservation(s).

Article 44: Amendments

1. Amendments to this Convention may be proposed by any Party, and shall be communicated by the Secretary General of the Council of Europe to the member States of the Council of Europe, to the non-member States which have participated in the elaboration of this Convention as well as to any State which has acceded to, or has been invited to accede to, this Convention in accordance with the provisions of Article 37.
2. Any amendment proposed by a Party shall be communicated to the European Committee on Crime Problems (CDPC), which shall submit to the Committee of Ministers its opinion on that proposed amendment.
3. The Committee of Ministers shall consider the proposed amendment and the opinion submitted by the CDPC and, following consultation with the non-member States Parties to this Convention, may adopt the amendment.
4. The text of any amendment adopted by the Committee of Ministers in accordance with paragraph 3 of this article shall be forwarded to the Parties for acceptance.
5. Any amendment adopted in accordance with paragraph 3 of this article shall come into force on the thirtieth day after all Parties have informed the Secretary General of their acceptance thereof.

Article 45: Settlement of disputes

1. The European Committee on Crime Problems (CDPC) shall be kept informed regarding the interpretation and application of this Convention.
2. In case of a dispute between Parties as to the interpretation or application of this Convention, they shall seek a settlement of the dispute through negotiation or any other peaceful means of their choice, including submission of the dispute to the CDPC, to an arbitral tribunal

whose decisions shall be binding upon the Parties, or to the International Court of Justice, as agreed upon by the Parties concerned.

Article 46: Consultations of the Parties

1. The Parties shall, as appropriate, consult periodically with a view to facilitating:
   (a) the effective use and implementation of this Convention, including the identification of any problems thereof, as well as the effects of any declaration or reservation made under this Convention;
   (b) the exchange of information on significant legal, policy or technological developments pertaining to cybercrime and the collection of evidence in electronic form;
   (c) consideration of possible supplementation or amendment of the Convention.
2. The European Committee on Crime Problems (CDPC) shall be kept periodically informed regarding the result of consultations referred to in paragraph 1.
3. The CDPC shall, as appropriate, facilitate the consultations referred to in paragraph 1 and take the measures necessary to assist the Parties in their efforts to supplement or amend the Convention. At the latest three years after the present Convention enters into force, the European Committee on Crime Problems (CDPC) shall, in co-operation with the Parties, conduct a review of all of the Conventions provisions and, if necessary, recommend any appropriate amendments.
4. Except where assumed by the Council of Europe, expenses incurred in carrying out the provisions of paragraph 1 shall be borne by the Parties in the manner to be determined by them.
5. The Parties shall be assisted by the Secretariat of the Council of Europe in carrying out their functions pursuant to this article.

Article 47: Denunciation

1. Any Party may, at any time, denounce this Convention by means of a notification addressed to the Secretary General of the Council of Europe.
2. Such denunciation shall become effective on the first day of the month following the expiration of a period of three months after the date of receipt of the notification by the Secretary General.

Article 48: Notification

The Secretary General of the Council of Europe shall notify the member States of the Council of Europe, the non-member States which have participated in the elaboration of this Convention as well as any State which has acceded to, or has been invited to accede to, this Convention of:

(a) any signature;

(b) the deposit of any instrument of ratification, acceptance, approval or accession;

(c) any date of entry into force of this Convention in accordance with Articles 36 and 37;

(d) any declaration made under Article 40 or reservation made in accordance with Article 42;

(e) any other act, notification or communication relating to this Convention.

In witness whereof the undersigned, being duly authorised thereto, have signed this Convention.

Done at Budapest, this 23rd day of November 2001, in English and in French, both texts being equally authentic, in a single copy which shall be deposited in the archives of the Council of Europe. The Secretary General of the Council of Europe shall transmit certified copies to each member State of the Council of Europe, to the non-member States which have participated in the elaboration of this Convention, and to any State invited to accede to it.

Annexure Three

Crime Covered

Offense	**Budapest Convention**	**UN Convention**
Illegal Access	✓	✓
Illegal Interception	✓	✓
Data Interference	✓	✓
System Interference	✓	✓
Misuse of Devices	✓	✓
Computer-related Forgery	✓	✓
Computer-related Fraud	✓	✓
CSAM	✓	✓
Copyright and Related Rights	✓	✓
Identity Theft	✗	✓
Racism/Xenophobia	✓ (via protocol)	✓
Non-Consensual Dissemination of Intimate Images	✗	✓
Solicitation/Grooming of Children	✗	✓
Money Laundering	✗	✓

Annexure Four

Human Rights Assessment of the Draft United Nations Cybercrime Convention

Statement by the United Nations Special Rapporteur on the promotion and protection of human rights while countering terrorism, Ben Saul

25 July 2024

Introduction

1. The Special Rapporteur on the promotion and protection of human rights while countering terrorism is pleased to offer this brief assessment of selected human rights implications of the third revised draft United Nations Convention against Cybercrime,[1] with suggestions to improve its compatibility with international human rights law. Due to its subject matter and scope, the Convention poses distinctive human rights risks that require heightened scrutiny and safeguards. The Special Rapporteur broadly endorses the Submission of the Office of the United Nations High Commissioner for Human Rights dated 22 July 2024.

Offences Committed through the Use of an Information and Communications Technology System: Article 4

2. Article 4 requires states parties to criminalize offences under other applicable United Nations conventions and protocols when committed through the use of an information and communications technology system. The provision has the practical effect of extending ending the scope of the offences under other conventions to encompass cyber means, without formally amending each of those conventions. In principle there may be legitimate reasons for so extending some offences under some conventions, to update earlier conventions in the light of the potential for the criminal use of cyber technologies.

3. However, Article 4 is objectionable for two reasons. First, it is inherently vague and uncertain in scope because it does not identify the specific conventions or their offences. There are dozens of such instruments and many more offences within them. Each of the offences under those conventions was carefully negotiated with due legal scrutiny given to the particular elements of each substantive and inchoate offence under each convention. Article 4 requires the wholescale and indiscriminate potential extension of every offence under every convention, without close drafting scrutiny of whether it is appropriate, or even possible, to so extend each individual offence and of the human rights implications or other adverse consequences of doing so. Such haphazard extension of a wide range of criminal offences serving a variety of different purposes is not consistent with good practice in the drafting of criminal instruments and could result in inconsistencies with human rights law.
4. Secondly, the criminalization of offences committed *through the use of* an information and communications technology system is ambiguous and does not indicate with sufficient precision the circumstances in which cyber means should be unlawful. Commission through the use of information and communications technology could encompass a wide range of conduct and interactions with such systems, from intentional and direct deployment of cyber means through to inadvertent, unconscious, incidental, indirect or offline connections with an information and communications system. The indeterminacy of the conduct and fault elements is of concern for two reasons. First, it violates the fundamental principle in international human rights law of legal certainty, whereby offences must be sufficiently clearly defined so as to enable individuals to prospectively regulate their conduct. Secondly, it is likely to produce considerable variations in national implementation and fail to satisfy the double criminality rule in extradition and mutual assistance, thus weakening prospects for international cooperation.
5. **It is recommended** to delete Article 4, unless: (a) an assessment is made of each offence under each of the United Nations conventions and protocols to which Article 4 could apply, to determine the appropriateness of applying Article 4 to them; (b) the Convention specifically lists the specific offences under each United Nations convention and protocol to which Article 4 appropriately applies; and (c) the conduct and fault elements of the expression committed through the use of an information and communications technology system are clarified to limit the offences to only acts that intend to produce criminally harmful consequences.

Cybercrime Offences: Articles 7 to 12

6. Articles 7 to 12 of the Convention generally criminalize intentional conduct without right, while some of these offences offer states parties the option to qualify the fault element with more restrictive intent requirements (e.g. intent to obtain data; dishonest or criminal intent; or intent to defraud) and/or to include additional objective elements (e.g. infringing security measures; or a result of serious harm). The very existence of the optional elements recognizes that the offences are otherwise over-broad and capture conduct that not only may not be sufficiently serious or harmful to warrant criminalization, but that may be positively beneficial or in the public interest. Thus, the baseline offences risk criminalizing whistleblower disclosure of information to expose illegality or fraud;[2] action to prevent crime; the activities of ethical hackers, cybersecurity researchers, and pentesters who keep the digital ecosystem secure from genuinely criminal interferences;[3] or acts of protest that that constitute protected freedom of expression. The optional elements will also produce divergence in the offences between national laws, which in turn will increase cases where the double criminality rule cannot be satisfied in extradition and mutual assistance, thus weakening prospects for international cooperation.
7. **It is recommended** that the optional elements be made mandatory in order to ensure that the offences are confined to sufficiently serious and harmful conduct that warrants transnational criminalization and cooperation. An alternative would be to establish mandatory exceptions to the scope of otherwise over-broad offences, as is the position under Article 11(2) (carving out authorized testing or protection of an information and communications technology system).

Requiring an Explicit Intention for Inchoate Of fences

8. It is welcome that the fault element of intention is explicitly required for the offences of participation and attempt under Article 19. **It is recommended** that the inchoate offences that currently lack an express intention requirement under Article 17(1)(b)(ii) be amended to similarly include it, namely [p]articipation in, association with or conspiracy to commit, attempts to commit and aiding, abetting, facilitating and counselling the commission of any of the offences established in accordance with this article.

Scope of the Convention: Articles 3, 23, and 35

9. While the express purpose of the Convention is the prevention and combating of cybercrime (see Article 1), the Convention covers

collection and so forth of electronic evidence for criminal investigations and proceedings not only in relation to cybercrimes but also for any criminal offence (Article 23(2)(c)). It further provides for international cooperation on electronic evidence relating to any serious crime (Article 35(1)(c)).[4] These expansions beyond the original and core purpose of the Convention in combating cybercrimes proper are not desirable and **it is recommended** that they be deleted from the Convention. Article 23(c) enables the application of highly invasive measures in relation to data connected to even trivial or minor offences under national law, as well as to innocent or legitimate conduct that is abusively criminalized in particular jurisdictions, where such restrictions on rights would not be necessary or proportionate in pursuit of a legitimate law enforcement aim. Article 35(1)(c) limits international cooperation to serious crimes, defined as those punishable by a maximum of four years imprisonment or a more serious penalty (Article 2(h)). Even so, such offences may not be sufficiently serious to warrant transnational cooperation where they do not involve death or injury to persons or other grave harms,[5] given the wide divergence in criminal penalties between states and the excessive penalization of minor or legitimate conduct in states that misuse the criminal law.

Respect for Human Rights: Article 6

10. Article 6(1) commendably affirms that states parties must implement their obligations consistently with their international human rights law obligations, thus responding to the significant risks of rights violations when criminally regulating cyber activities.[6] Article 6(2) provides that the Convention is without prejudice to specified human rights. **It is recommended** to add to this list other rights particularly affected by the Convention, namely the rights to: (a) liberty and security of person; (b) fair trial; (c) privacy; (d) nondiscrimination; (e) participate in public affairs; (f) humane conditions of detention and freedom from torture or cruel, inhuman or degrading treatment or punishment; and (g) nonrefoulement. **It is also recommended** that Article 6(1) additionally refer to international refugee law and non-exhaustively highlight the International Covenant on Civil and Political Rights 1966 as a particularly relevant instrument.

Conditions and Safeguards: Article 24

11. Article 24(1) contains a welcome obligation on states parties to ensure that the procedural measures and law enforcement under Chapter IV of the Convention protect human rights, including the principle of

proportionality. [7] The selective reference to proportionality is, however, plainly under-inclusive of the range of core rights affected by Chapter IV. **It is recommended that** other fundamental principles related to the limitation or restriction of rights be explicitly mentioned, including lawful authority, legitimate aim, necessity and non-discrimination. **It is further recommended** that the list of specific human rights protections in Article 24(2)[8] be reformulated as binding reflecting their legal status under international law rather than being presented as subject to discretionary qualifications ([i]n accordance with and pursuant to the domestic law of each State Party, and as appropriate in view of the nature of the procedure or the power concerned). [9] These should also be strengthened to reflect their full scope under international law, such not only judicial review but prior judicial authorization of certain intrusive measures such as surveillance.

General Human Rights Safeguards in Chapters II, V , VI and VII

12. The inclusion of the human rights clause (Article 24(1)) in Chapter IV invites reflection on why similar clauses are not included in other relevant chapters, notwithstanding the applicability of the Article 4 human rights clause to the whole Convention. Other chapters each raise distinctive human rights risks, including Chapter II on criminalization, Chapter V on international cooperation, Chapter VI on preventive measures and Chapter VII on technical assistance and capacity building. Chapter V, for example, includes Article 35 on general principles of international cooperation but there is no mention of human rights. The inclusion of a safeguard clause in Chapter IV but not the other chapters may imply that human rights are less important in those chapters, despite the inclusion of specific human rights in particular articles of the chapters. The omission is heightened because some of these chapters make a state partys obligations subject to domestic law [10] or fundamental principles of its legal system, [11] but there is no comparable reference to international law. **It is accordingly recommended** that safeguards similar to those in Article 24(1), albeit strengthened as indicated earlier, be applied and tailored to these other chapters.

Prosecution, Adjudication and Sanctions: Article 21

13. **It is recommended** that:
   (a) In Article 21(4), the human rights safeguards in relation to prosecutions, including for fair trial and defence rights, be expanded to include other fundamental rights specially affected,

namely the right to liberty and security of person, humane conditions of detention, and freedom from torture or cruel, inhumane or degrading treatment.

(b) In Article 21(2), the discretion for states parties to take into account aggravating circumstances in relation to offences should be balanced with equal provision for states to consider mitigating factors (e.g. severity of the offence and harm caused, age, character, criminal history, personal circumstances, admission of guilt, cooperation with police, blameworthiness, detention as a last resort etc.), in accordance with general principles of criminal law and proportionality in sentencing

(c) In Article 21(3), the direction to exercise any prosecutorial discretion to maximize the effectiveness of law enforcement and deterrence should be balanced by the recognition of other equally relevant public interest factors (e.g. the seriousness/triviality of the offence, the passage of time, the degree of culpability, factors and characteristics personal to the accused and any victims, the interests of justice, other remedies, public confidence, fair trial and other human rights risks etc.).

Extradition and Mutual Assistance: Articles 37 and 40

14. **It is recommended** that:

(a) In Article 37(14), the guarantee of fair treatment in extradition should refer not only to rights under domestic law but also under international human rights law.

(b) In Article 37(15), the welcome inclusion of a savings clause for non-discrimination as a basis for refusing extradition should be strengthened and supplemented:

(i) Discrimination should be a mandatory ground of refusal under the Convention;

(ii) Other human rights-based grounds of mandatory refusal should be included, namely *non-refoulement* generally (i.e. not limited to discrimination), including protection against return to: arbitrary deprivation of life, including the death penalty where it is not consistent with international law; torture or cruel, inhuman or degrading treatment or punishment; persecution; flagrant denial of justice or unfair trial; or other serious violations of international law.

(iii) The political offence exception to an extradition request should also be expressly recognized as a permissible ground of refusal.

(c) In Article 40(21), the same considerations pertaining to the refusal of an extradition request in the preceding point of this Statement should apply to mutual assistance. In addition, lack of double criminality should be recognized as a ground of refusal, as it already is in relation to extradition (Article 37(1)).

Assistance to and Protection of V ictims: Article 34

15. **It is recommended** that the positive measures for victims of crime in Article 34 be strengthened by encouraging states parties to pay due regard to the United Nations Declaration of Basic Principles of Justice for Victims of Crime and Abuse of Power 1985.[12]

Personal Data Protection: Article 36

16. While Article 36 requires personal data sharing to be consistent with international law, implicitly including the right to privacy and other relevant human rights, **it is recommended** to include more explicit and detailed data protection safeguards. In this respect the Special Rapporteur endorses the substance of the drafting proposal of Privacy International.[13]

Preventive Measures: Chapter VI

17. Chapter VI contains numerous potentially positive measures of prevention from a human rights standpoint, including in relation to civil society participation, reintegration of offenders into society, addressing gender-based violence and child safety, enhancing transparency and public participation in decision making and public access to information, respecting freedom to seek, receive and impart public information, and supporting victims of crime. **It is recommended** that Chapter VI also include as a preventive measure the need to address the conditions conducive to cybercrime, which may include state violations of human rights committed whether committed by cyber or other means.

Technical Assistance and Capacity Building: Chapter VII

18. Chapter VI refers in detail to capacity building, training, exchange of information and best practices, technical assistance and technology transfer as means of facilitating the prevention and suppression of Convention offences. Strikingly, there is no reference at all to human rights in the context of any of these activities, including both the importance of mainstreaming human rights in all such activities where relevant and conducting human rights impact assessments in advance

of and after such activities. Given the well-recognized potential for abuse of law enforcement powers and data collection in relation to cybercrimes and other crimes covered by the Convention, **it is recommended** that human rights should be incorporated as a mandatory component of Chapter VII activities.

Mechanism of Implementation: Chapter VII

19. **It is recommended** that the periodic conferences of states parties to the Convention charged with reviewing its implementation (Articles 57(1) and (5)(e)) and making recommendations for its improvement (Article 57(5)(f)) be explicitly mandated to review the consistency of implementation with international human rights law and to recommend necessary improvements.

NOTES

1 United Nations Convention against Cybercrime (Crimes Committed through the Use of an Information and Communications Technology System), A/AC.291/22/Rev.3.

2 https://www.ohchr.org/sites/default/files/2024-05/Human-Rights-Draft-Cybercrime-Convention.pdf.

3 https://cyberpeaceinstitute.org/news/proposed-cybercrime-convention-risks-making-cyberspace-lesssecure/#4169daa5-7691-4a3b-8f52-44302bc0ea45-link.

4 See relatedly Article 3(b), indicating the scope of application of the Convention to [t]he collecting, obtaining, preserving and sharing of evidence in electronic form for the purpose of criminal investigations or proceedings, as provided for in articles 23 and 35 of this Convention.

5 OHCHR Submission dated 22 July 2024, p. 5.

6 See e.g. A/RES/76/174 (10 January 2022).

7 Article 24(2) further requires judicial or other independent review, the right to an effective remedy, grounds justifying application, and limitation of the scope and the duration of such power or procedure.

8 Namely, judicial or other independent review, the right to an effective remedy, grounds justifying application, and limitation of the scope and the duration of such power or procedure.

9 See also the drafting suggestion in the OHCHR Submission, p. 6.

10 Article 35 on international cooperation under Chapter V; Article 54(3) on technical assistance and capacity building under Chapter VII.

11 Article 53 regarding prevention under Chapter VI.

12 A/RES/40/34 (29 November 1985).

13 Privacy Internationals Comments on the Updated Draft Text of the UN Cybercrime Convention, May 2024.

Annexure Five

Article 19s analysis of the UN Convention Against Cybercrime

October 2024

ARTICLE 19 is seriously concerned about the Draft of the UN Convention on Cybercrime, which is pending formal adoption by the UN General Assembly later in 2024. While we agree that addressing cybercrime is important, we warn that the Draft Convention does little to actually prevent or deter transnational cybercrime. Instead, it retains several provisions that enable or legitimise the violation of international human rights law both through domestic legislation and international cooperation without the provision of adequate human rights safeguards. While several cyber enabled crimes were removed during the negotiation process, a broadly worded preamble clause combined with a future General Assembly Resolution could enable their reintroduction through the back door. Several provisions of the Draft Convention serve as barriers for legitimate security researchers and security research, thus undermining cybersecurity and privacy worldwide. The Draft Convention also enables sweeping legal assistance between countries without providing for adequate safeguards. The Draft Convention both enables intrusive surveillance of users and does away with transparency and accountability requirements for the governments of State Parties. Finally, it legitimises and encourages the establishment of jurisdiction through a range of sovereign controls that violate human rights.

ARTICLE 19 urges UN member states to not sign and ratify this Convention or use it as a template for designing domestic cybercrime legislation.

Cybercrime has emerged as a significant global threat, posing serious challenges to individuals, businesses, and governments worldwide. As digital technologies become increasingly integrated into peoples daily lives, the potential for malicious actors to exploit vulnerabilities in computer networks and systems has grown exponentially. While addressing cybercrime is crucial for protecting peoples rights and livelihoods, in ARTICLE 19s experience, cybercrime legislations often serve as instruments enabling the violation of international human rights law by states under the guise of furthering national security or ensuring public order.

After three years of negotiations, on 9 August 2024, the **UN *Ad Hoc* Committee** finalised the draft of the United Nations Convention against Cybercrime (the Draft Cybercrime Convention). The treaty negotiations were initiated by Russia and were legally enabled by a **2018 General Assembly Resolution** that set up an *Ad Hoc* Committee to carry out these negotiations. While the United States, the European Union and several other countries initially opposed the treaty and the negotiation process, they have since participated in the seven rounds of the negotiation process. The draft of the Cybercrime Convention is now to be submitted to the UN General Assembly for formal adoption later in 2024.

ARTICLE 19 has been actively participating in the negotiations process and issued comments on the earlier drafts. In this brief, we build on our earlier analysis and demonstrate why the Draft Cybercrime Convention is problematic from international human rights law perspective.

At the outset, ARTICLE 19 warns that the Draft Convention does little to actually prevent or deter transnational cybercrime or increase cyber security. Instead, it aims to reconfigure sovereign controls over a global and open internet and enable governments to use these controls to violate the rights of their citizens.

While several provisions of the treaty are worded using non-mandatory language such as may, we are concerned that the inclusion of such voluntary provisions serves as a model for several countries that have not yet adopted domestic cybercrime legislation. In essence, it allows the legitimisation and **export of rights-violating domestic legislative provisions**. At the same time, it enables and in certain cases obliges cross-border cooperation between countries that do not uphold the same international human rights standards domestically, thereby starting a race to the bottom.

ARTICLE 19's key concerns with the Draft Cybercrime Convention

1. Failure to incorporate effective and specific human rights safeguards

The Draft Cybercrime Convention fails to incorporate human rights safeguards for the broad range of cross-border procedural and law enforcement measures that it enables. We note that Article 6 is an all-encompassing human rights clause which states that nothing in this Convention shall be interpreted as permitting the suppression of human rights or fundamental freedoms. While this is an important safeguard in theory, the provision itself and the other provisions of the Draft Convention are not robust enough to ensure that the rights of individuals and users are protected for the following reasons:

Wording of human rights safeguards clause is inadequate Article 6(1) limits human rights safeguards in the Draft Convention to member states obligations under human rights law. Essentially, this means that states that have not signed or ratified other human rights conventions but are party to the Cybercrime Convention are not bound by international human rights law when acting in pursuance of the provisions of the Convention.

Article 6.2 rectifies this somewhat and identifies some core human rights including the rights to the freedom of expression, conscience, opinion, religion or belief, and peaceful assembly and association. However, the right to privacy and the right to equality and non-discrimination, both also core components of international human rights law, are not a part of this list. As we outline below, several provisions could negatively impact these rights as well.

There are no specific human rights safeguards across various provisions of the Draft Convention: Even if the flawed general safeguards clause was more robustly framed, we are concerned it would not be effective without the inclusion of specific human rights safeguards incorporated into various rights-infringing provisions of the treaty. We find that including specific safeguards is absolutely necessary to ensure the protection of human rights. Rights-violating conduct in pursuance of any of the treaty provisions would be undertaken by a law enforcement official of a certain State. Even if the victim of rights-violating conduct finds out about this and wants to challenge it, the only authority would be a domestic court of law or a regional human rights tribunal. While Article 6 and applicable international human rights law may be useful in that judicial context, they will not be able to prevent specific rights-infringing activity carried out in pursuance of the provisions of this Draft Cybercrime Convention in the first place. In this brief, we will further demonstrate the range of provisions where the absence of safeguards could turn them into rights-violating instruments.

2. *Broad scope of preamble and potential for introducing more "cyber enabled" crimes through the backdoor*

In the analysis of the previous versions of the Draft Cybercrime Convention, ARTICLE 19 raised concerns about numerous cyber enabled crimes. Cyber enabled crimes are crimes that can be committed without information and communications technology (ICT) but could be enabled through the use of ICT. Cyber dependent crimes on the other hand are crimes that cannot be committed without the use of ICT systems, such as illegal access to a computer system or illegal interception.

Although the number of cyber-enable crimes in the Draft Cybercrime Convention have been significantly reduced since previous versions, there is no clarity on the definition or threshold of the offences that may constitute a cybercrime. For example, paragraph 3 of the Preamble notes several cyber enabled crimes including terrorism, and transnational organised crime such as trafficking in persons, the smuggling of migrants, the illicit manufacturing of and trafficking in firearms, their parts and components and ammunition, drug trafficking and trafficking in cultural property.

Given that these crimes were removed from the operative clauses of the Draft Cybercrime Convention, their retention in the Preamble provides legitimacy for countries to criminalise them in domestic legislation or even through the Draft Convention through subsequent Protocols. In particular, the inclusion of terrorism as a crime in the Preamble is problematic given that there is no universal consensus on the definition of terrorism, and the amorphous idea of terrorism has been used to justify states abrogation of international human rights law in a range of contexts, in particular in combating **terrorism** and the **war on terrorism**.

Further, we also note with concern that Article 21 legitimises domestic legislation that adds aggravating circumstances in order to increase the sanctions associated with a particular offence. In particular, it adds the phrase including circumstances that affect critical information infrastructure. Given that the criminalisation of attacks against critical information infrastructure (CII) was removed as a crime in its own right over the course of the negotiations, we find it disappointing that it has been added as an aggravating circumstance through another provision. Elsewhere, we have already investigated and explained how domestic legislation dealing with critical information infrastructure could be used to stifle freedom of expression and the right to privacy of a range of business entities, including business entities and online platforms (e.g. in **Hong Kong**).

This enlargement of the scope of criminalisation is further enabled by a draft **General Assembly Resolution linked with the Draft Convention** This resolution mandates the Ad Hoc Committee to commence negotiations on a Supplementary Protocol in order to include additional criminal offences. This would include a number of other offences (terrorism, blasphemy) that do not have universal definitions and would represent an even greater threat to human rights around the world.

3. *Barriers for legitimate security research and security researchers*

ARTICLE 19 also warns that various provisions of the Draft Cybercrime Convention will have negative impacts on the legitimate work of security researchers. We would especially like to highlight the following issues:

> Articles 7 and Article 8 of the Draft call for the criminalisation of illegal access and illegal interception respectively. We find the phrase without right to be an extremely ambiguous and broad threshold for criminality. Apart from hindering good faith security research, this provision could **end up criminalising minor civil infractions** like violations of private terms of service (TOS) contracts. Articles 7(2) and 8(2) clarify that a State may require such offences with the intent of obtaining electronic data or other dishonest or criminal intent. Now, the establishment of *mens rea* or criminal intent is a mandatory requirement for any crime. Article 7 violates this fairly basic threshold as it ends up making criminal intent optional and enables states to bring within the ambit of criminality a far broader range of activities (including conduct categorised as civil violations) undertaken without right.
>
> Article 9 criminalises interference with electronic data. Again, Article 9(2) stipulates that a State may require serious harm to accrue in order for an offence to be constituted. Security researchers often simulate cyber-attacks through such interference to test computer systems an activity that could be criminalised through the Draft Cybercrime Convention.

Given the significant barriers to security research that the various provisions of this Draft Cybercrime Convention pose, the recognition of the contributions of security researchers and ethical hackers in Article 53 on preventive measures is meaningless as it does not outline any specific protection or incentives. Ultimately, this Draft Convention could have a chilling effect on security researchers looking to do legitimate cybersecurity work, and undermine overall cybersecurity as well as the rights of individual users.

4. *There is a lack of specific human rights safeguards in procedural and law enforcement measures enabled by the Draft Cybercrime Convention*

ARTICLE 19 is concerned about the absence of specific safeguards to preserve the rights to freedom of expression and privacy. We believe this omission will enable States to violate human rights law through domestic legislation enacted in furtherance of provisions of the Draft Convention. We are particularly concerned with the following provisions:

Article 24, which provides for conditions and safeguards for the Chapter on Procedural Measures, defers entirely to domestic law. Article 24(1) specifies that domestic law must provide for the protection of human rights in accordance with [the member states] obligations under international human rights law} and which shall incorporate the principle of proportionality. This safeguard is grossly inadequate as it provides an extremely broad margin of appreciation for states when enacting domestic policy and allows them to selectively comply only with those human rights treaties or conventions that it has already signed. Second, the provision only mentions the principle of proportionality as a safeguard and not the principles of legality and necessity, which are **legally mandated thresholds for restricting a right**.

We are also aware that Article 24(2) mentions due process mechanisms including judicial review, the right to an effective remedy, and limitation of the scope and duration. However, yet again, it leaves the application of these provisions discretionary and contingent on domestic law.

Article 28(4) of the Draft Convention enables legislative measures that empower competent authorities to order any person who has knowledge about the functioning of the information and communications technology system in question to provide this information to enable the search and seizure of electronic data. Notably, this provision does not include any specific safeguard protecting the right to privacy of the individual questioned. The ability to order any person who has knowledge about the functioning of a computer system pays scant regard to instances where the knowledge in question may be a trade secret, sensitive information or technical information on vulnerabilities that security researchers may be working with to conduct legitimate security research. We are also concerned, **alongside other experts**, that this provision may also be used to compel individuals or entities to turn over encrypted information.

Article 29 enables states to compel a service provider with existing technical capability to engage in the real time collection of traffic data, again without any international human rights safeguards. Therefore, this provision essentially enables states to compel service providers to enable global bulk surveillance without any considerations for the legal standards of legality, necessity or proportionality. Given the **acknowledged illegality of existing bulk surveillance programs** , we find this provision specifically concerning.

Article 30 of the Draft Convention enables even more intrusive surveillance. Article 30(b) enables domestic provisions that can compel any service provider to either collect and record themselves or cooperate and assist competent authorities to collect and record content data for specified communications within its territory. This provision does not mention checks and balances that could be provided by the judiciary such as the production of a warrant, which again provides government institutions carte blanche authority to conduct intrusive surveillance without guardrails.

Article 47(c) encourages law enforcement cooperation for necessary items or data for analytical or investigative purposes. We find that this amorphous phrase legitimises rights-violating law enforcement practices such as **predictive policing or emotional recognition. As we** and **other experts** warned, with the absence of privacy-protecting safeguards, it also sets the stage for sharing sensitive data and building biometric databases that could be used to disproportionately target and discriminate against marginalised communities.

5. *The Draft Cybercrime Convention provides for sweeping mutual legal assistance enabled without adequate safeguards*

ARTICLE 19 is concerned about the undermining of human rights through a framework for mutual legal assistance between countries that may not have compatible human rights frameworks domestically and may not be in consonance with international human rights law. In particular:

As we **warned earlier**, Article 40(3) of the Draft Convention provides for a broad array of purposes for which mutual legal assistance may be rendered without any human rights safeguards for the right to privacy or data protection, or safeguards specifically for vulnerable persons. These include a) taking evidence from person; b) effecting service of judicial documents; c) executing searches and seizures and freezing; d) searching or similarly accessing or similarly securing and disclosing electronic data; e) collecting traffic data in real time, f) intercepting content data, g) examining objects and sites; h) providing information, evidence and expert evaluations; i) providing originals or certified copies of business documents; j) identifying or tracing proceeds of crime; j) facilitating the voluntary production of persons in the Requesting State.

Furthermore, Article 40(8) essentially does away with the requirement of dual criminality. The provision stipulates that States may decline to render mutual legal assistance, which implies that they have an option to do away with dual criminality. The provision also explicitly enables the state to provide assistance to the extent it decides at its discretion irrespective of whether the conduct would be a crime within its own jurisdiction.

This provision has two impacts that negatively impact international human rights. First, if a state fails to pass domestic legislation declaring a certain offence a crime, it could still enable the harassment of individuals engaging in said conduct by rendering mutual legal assistance that enables a foreign state to prosecute that individual utilising provisions of the treaty. Second, the requesting state could exert external political or economic pressure on the requested state to render mutual legal assistance even if dual criminality is not established, thus arbitrarily enlarging the scope of criminalisation globally.

The grounds for refusal for mutual assistance provided for in Article 40(21), on the other hand, are excessively narrow. For example, Article 40 Clause 21(b) mentions sovereignty, security, *ordre public* or other essential interests of a state but conspicuously leaves out human rights concerns as grounds for a refusal. Further, Article 40 Clause 22 exempts obligations to render mutual legal assistance only if the member state has substantial grounds for believing that the request has been made for prosecuting a person based on a number of protected characteristics. The threshold of substantial grounds is legally undefined but a **dictionary definition of the word** substantial meaning large in size, value or importance indicates a relatively high threshold for a refusal. Further, the protected characteristics include a persons sex, race, language, religion, nationality, ethnicity, origin or political opinions. These grounds suffer from two lacunae. First, it leaves out sexual orientation as a protected category. Given the number of **potential member states who still criminalize LGBTQ+ communities** domestically, the Draft Convention could serve as an ideal instrument to obtain data from other countries to prosecute or harass LGBTQ+ individuals. Second, the Draft Convention protects political opinion, which is covered under the freedom of speech and expression but explicitly leaves out political offences.

6. *The Draft Cybercrime Convention fails to provide any transparency and accountability obligations on States*

While various provisions of the Draft Convention give intrusive surveillance provisions to the government, several provisions simultaneously protect governments by doing away with transparency and accountability requirements, which are cornerstones of international human rights law.

ARTICLE 19 warns that this lack of transparency will prevent users from challenging acts undertaken through the Draft Convention that violate international human rights law. These provisions include:

Article 29 (3), which enables legislative measures that oblige a service provider that is compelled to engage in bulk surveillance to keep the details of the surveillance confidential.

Article 40 (20), which deals with mutual legal assistance, allows the State requesting mutual legal assistance to require that the details of the request be kept confidential. If the State Party executing the mutual legal assistance request cannot maintain confidentiality, it needs to inform the requesting State Party. We warn that while the confidentiality requirement here is discretionary, it perpetuates a culture of secrecy when executing key provisions of the Draft Convention, which enables governments to evade accountability.

Article 42(3) provides that, as appropriate, a request for preservation of user data be kept confidential by the State Party executing the request without notifying the user.

7. *The Draft Cybercrime Convention legitimises and encourages the establishment of jurisdiction through sovereign controls over the internet*

ARTICLE 19 observes that Article 22 of the Cybercrime Convention encourages state parties to adopt such measures as may be necessary to establish jurisdiction over an offence in the Draft Convention. As we have already noted, states adopt a variety of strict technical and legal measures to exercise territorial control over various layers of the internet. These regimes include data localisation requirements, strict licensing requirements and local presence mandates for platforms, and blocking platforms that do not comply with local laws.

In essence, these measures attempt to circumvent the values of an open and global internet that enables the freedom of expression and aligns it instead with the interests of the territorial state.

Given the severe array of rights-infringing provisions in the Draft Convention itself as well as the potential use of these provisions in constructing rights-violating domestic legislation, ARTICLE 19 urges UN member states to not sign and ratify this Convention or use it as a template for designing domestic cybercrime legislation.

Annexure Six

Explanatory notes on the draft United Nations convention against cybercrime; strengthening international cooperation for combating certain crimes committed by means of information and communications technology systems and for the sharing of evidence in electronic form of serious crimes, its interpretative notes and related draft General Assembly resolution

3 September 2024

The present document contains explanations of the changes reflected in the draft United Nations convention against cybercrime; strengthening international cooperation for combating certain crimes committed by means of information and communications technology systems and for the sharing of evidence in electronic form of serious crimes[1] (A/AC.291/L.15) made to the Updated draft text of the convention (UDTC, A/AC.291/22/Rev.3), as well as explanations of the changes to the draft resolution for consideration by the General Assembly (A/AC.291/L.16). These explanations were prepared by the Chair of the Ad Hoc Committee to Elaborate a Comprehensive International Convention on Countering the Use of Information and Communications Technologies for Criminal Purposes, with the assistance of the secretariat. The document also provides context for the Interpretative notes on specific articles of the draft convention (A/AC.291/27/Rev.1).

Title: draft United Nations convention against cybercrime; strengthening international cooperation for combating certain crimes committed by means of information and communications technology systems and for the sharing of evidence in electronic form of serious crimes

The title United Nations convention against cybercrime; strengthening international cooperation for combating certain crimes committed by means of information and communications technology systems and for the sharing of evidence in electronic form of serious crimes reflects the preference of a large majority of Member States to include the term cybercrime in the title. The addition, separated by a semicolon, of strengthening international cooperation for combating certain crimes committed by means of information and communications technology systems and for the sharing of evidence in electronic form of serious crimes mirrors the main content and characteristics of the draft convention.

Preamble

In preambular paragraph (PP) 4, the expression crimes committed through the use of information and communications technology systems, established in accordance with this Convention has been deleted, to retain the word cybercrime only, following the change in the title.

In PP 6, the words where possible before the transfer of technology on mutually agreed terms have been deleted. This change reflects the large number of Member States that underlined the inherently voluntary nature of this provision as reflected in the caveat on mutually agreed terms. A similar amendment has been made in article 54, paragraph 1 of the draft convention.

In PP 10, the introductory term *Affirming*, as reflected in the UDTC, has been replaced with

Recognizing. A number of Member States have called for *Noting*, while a number of other Member States have requested the retention of *Affirming*. The new term *Recognizing* aims at striking a balance between the two requested terms.

In PP 15, the term States Members of the United Nations has been replaced by Member States of the United Nations at the request of a Member State.

Article 2: Use of terms

Article 2 of the draft convention reproduces article 2 UDTC, with one modification in paragraph (e) to streamline the definition of service provider: the sequence any public or private entity that was moved from subparagraph (i) to the chapeau of the definition, while deleting any other entity that from subparagraph (ii).

A newly added interpretative note on this provision clarifies the content of the definition with respect to subparagraph (ii), which reflects the understanding of the term service provider under the Council of Europe Convention on Cybercrime,[2] as provided in its Explanatory Report.[3]

Scope of the draft convention: Articles 3; 4; 23, paragraphs 1 to 3; and 35

In view of the strong support of Member States for maintaining the scope of the future Convention as drafted in the UDTC, as expressed by delegations throughout the reconvened concluding session, articles 3; 4; 23, paragraphs 1 to 3; and 35 were retained in the draft convention without further amendment.

The interpretative note on articles 23 and 35 regarding the term criminal investigations has been further clarified through editorial changes. Furthermore, a clarification was added to specify that this term also encompasses those offences established in article 19, on participation and attempt.

Human rights safeguards: Articles 6; 23, paragraph 4; 24

Article 6 of the draft convention implements the Proposal of the Chair on the main pending provisions of the UDTC,[4] which envisaged to modify article 6, paragraph 2 UDTC by including the term and in a manner consistent with before applicable human rights law. As explained during the consideration of the Chairs proposal, this correction merely specifies the obligation to adhere to the human rights obligations applicable to each State Party. Except for the editorial amendments of changing the word freedom to its plural form and the addition of the article the, this paragraph has been retained as drafted in the UDTC.

Article 24 incorporates the proposal of the Chair, with additional modifications. These amendments were made to facilitate consensus by striking a balance between Member States positions regarding the application of article 24 to Chapters IV and V of the Convention, and regarding the clarification of the term judicial or other independent review.

Accordingly, as contained in the Chairs proposal, former paragraph 4 of article 23 UDTC was reformulated and moved to article 24, as a new paragraph 4. This paragraph now clarifies that the safeguards established at the domestic level equally apply when rendering international cooperation. The interpretative note exclusively on article 23 was deleted.

Article 24, paragraph 5 of the draft convention incorporates a reformulated version of article 24, paragraph 2, *in fine*, as contained in the Chairs proposal. The Chairs proposal on this subject was to reformulate the interpretative note on article 24 and move it to this provision, in order to affirm that the review referred to in this article concerns review at the domestic level, and not the establishment of a review body at the international level.

Article 14: Offences related to online child sexual abuse or child sexual exploitation material

The draft convention retains paragraphs 1 and 2 of article 14 UDTC as drafted and incorporates a number of changes in its paragraphs 3 and 4. These changes reflect the discussions of the informal consultations on article 14.

In paragraph 3, the term a real child has been replaced with an existing person to align the wording with the definition of child sexual abuse or child sexual exploitation material, as contained in paragraph 2.

Paragraph 4 incorporates the relevant points contained in the Chairs proposal. Accordingly, in its chapeau, in accordance with their domestic law and consistent with applicable international obligations has been added as a general condition for the optional exceptions under subparagraphs (a) and (b). In subparagraph (a), the sequence as described in paragraph 2 of this article has been deleted to account for a broader approach.

In subparagraph (b), the reference to consensual sexual relationship has been deleted. Moreover, conduct set forth in paragraph 1 of this article, relating to has been deleted and the exempted acts limited to the consensual production, transmission and possession of material [] where the underlying conduct depicted is legal as determined by domestic law.

Article 16: Non-consensual dissemination of intimate images

Article 16 incorporates the Chairs proposal, which was informed by the outcome of the informal consultations on this article. The Chairs proposal was to reformulate and move the interpretative note on article 16 to the text of the draft convention, as new paragraph 6 of article 16. This paragraph merely reiterates the principle that the article sets only a minimum standard for prohibited conduct. States Parties remain free to establish under their domestic law other criminal offences, in accordance with their international obligations.

Article 21: Prosecution, adjudication and sanctions

This article has been retained as drafted in the UDTC, with one amendment in paragraph 4, which was to add applicable to clarify the reference to international obligations of States Parties. This amendment was proposed by a Member State and agreed *ad referendum* by the Committee.

Article 34: Assistance to and protection of victims

In paragraph 4 of this article, the word effective has been added before steps to ensure compliance with requests to remove or render inaccessible the content described in articles 14 and 16 of this Convention. This amendment was elaborated in informal consultations and subsequently agreed *ad referendum* by the Committee.

Article 36: Protection of personal data

Paragraphs 1 and 2 of this article have been retained in the draft convention as drafted in the UDTC. Paragraph 3 was elaborated in informal consultations and subsequently agreed *ad referendum* by the Committee.

Article 40: General principles and procedures relating to mutual legal assistance

Article 40 of the draft convention contains one amendment in paragraph 3(h), namely the deletion of evidentiary items, which was considered to be covered by the broader term evidence. This change was elaborated in informal consultations and later agreed *ad referendum*.

While a number of Member States requested the inclusion of an explicit political offences exception, its omission was deemed important to keep a balance in the text, in particular in view of the number of Member States requesting the deletion of paragraph 22 and due to the fact that requested States Parties, in the context of mutual legal assistance, may rely on the broad grounds for refusal agreed upon in paragraph 21(c).[5]

Article 41: 24/7 network

In paragraph 2 of article 41 of the draft convention, the secretariat function of keeping an updated register of points of contact has been extended with the sentence: and shall annually circulate to the States Parties the updated list of contact points, based on a proposal made by a Member State which was agreed *ad referendum*.

In paragraph 3(c), and has been inserted between the collection of evidence and the provision of legal information. The measures of the locating of suspects have been moved from subparagraph (c) to a standalone provision in subparagraph (d). These changes were elaborated in informal consultations and subsequently agreed *ad referendum* by the Committee.

Article 45: Mutual legal assistance in the real-time collection of traffic data

Article 45 has been retained as drafted in the UDTC, with one change in paragraph 3(c), from which or other illegal act has been deleted to increase the specificity of the provision. This change was elaborated in informal consultations and subsequently agreed *ad referendum* by the Committee.

Article 52: Return and disposal of confiscated proceeds of crime or property

In article 52 of the draft convention, paragraph 4 has been added, taken verbatim from article 57, paragraph 4 of the United Nations Convention against Corruption.[6] This addition reflects the outcome of informal consultations, which was later agreed *ad referendum* by the Committee.

Article 53: Preventive measures

Article 53 has been retained as drafted in the UDTC, with only one change in paragraph 3(e), which reflects the important contributions that security researchers make to the cybersecurity environment. The wording and to the extent permitted by domestic law has been amended to read and to the extent permitted and subject to the conditions prescribed by domestic law, following a proposal by a Member State, which was agreed *ad referendum.*

Article 54: Technical assistance and capacity-building

Article 54 of the draft convention includes three modifications.

In paragraph 1, the term where possible before transfer of technology on mutually agreed terms has been deleted, aligning the wording of this paragraph with that of PP 6.

In paragraph 4, the words international and regional have been included before organization. This change was elaborated in informal consultations and subsequently agreed *ad referendum* by the Committee.

In paragraph 10, concerning voluntary contributions to the United Nations Office on Drugs and Crime for fostering technical assistance and capacity-building, the term consider making has been replaced with shall endeavour to make. This change was elaborated in informal consultations and subsequently agreed *ad referendum* by the Committee.

Article 57: Conference of the States Parties to the Convention

Article 57 of the draft convention, on the Conference of the States Parties (COSP) to the Convention, includes two amendments to the corresponding article of the UDTC.

In paragraph 5(g), a reference to article 62 has been included, given the content of the newly added article 62.

In paragraph 6, the words and regional has been added before organizations. This amendment was elaborated in informal consultations and subsequently agreed *ad referendum* by the Committee.

In paragraph 7 of article 57 of the draft convention, the last sentence, which concerned, within the mechanism reviewing the implementation of the Convention, consultations at the national level with stakeholders, has been deleted. This change aims to balance the divergent positions of Member States, some of which requested deletion of this sentence, while some called for its retention, by aligning its content with that of article 63, paragraph 5 of UNCAC. The consultation of stakeholders for purposes of gathering information is stipulated in article 57, paragraph 5 (b) and (c).

Required number of States Parties for the Convention's entry into force and the adoption of supplementary protocols by the COSP: Articles 62 and 64

The draft convention seeks to reflect a balance between those calling for a low number of ratifications in order to ensure the rapid entry into force of this much-needed instrument, and those supporting a higher number so as to guarantee the inclusivity of future decisions of the COSP on the adoption of a supplementary protocol.

Therefore, article 64 has been retained as drafted in the UDTC, thus requiring forty States Parties for the Conventions entry into force.

The new article 62, regulating the adoption of supplementary protocols, envisages in its paragraph 1 that a supplementary protocol could only be adopted by the future COSP when the Convention has reached a minimum number of sixty States Parties. The COSP shall make every effort to reach consensus on any supplementary protocol and, subsidiarily, take a decision by at least a two-thirds majority of States Parties present and voting. These rules of procedure would thus be similar on decisions on amendments to the draft convention, as contained in its article 66, paragraph 1 (i.e. former article 65 UDTC).

Paragraph 2 of article 62 specifies the right and modality, for regional economic integration organizations, to vote in relation to any supplementary protocol.

Operative paragraph (OP) 5 of the draft Resolution was amended accordingly.

Article 64: Signature, ratification, acceptance, approval and accession

Paragraph 1 of article 64 of the draft convention includes one amendment specifying the date until when the Convention would be open for signature, namely 31 December 2026. This amendment follows the advice of the depositary and is in line with the formulation of the latest treaties that are opened for signature at United Nations Headquarters, following the earliest possible circulation of the

Conventions final text after review by the United Nations Office on Legal Affairs. It also takes into consideration the precedents of the UN Conventions against Transnational Organized Crime[7] and against Corruption, which were open for signatures for about 2 years.

Draft General Assembly resolution

The draft resolution for consideration by the General Assembly, to which the draft convention will be annexed once approved by the Committee, contains a number of amendments to the previous version (A/AC.291/25/Rev.1). In particular, it incorporates the Chairs proposal on the mandate of the Ad Hoc Committee to negotiate an additional protocol, the elaboration of the rules of procedure of the future

COSP as well as the Committees modalities of work and timeline. These changes aim at ensuring a balance between all positions expressed at the reconvened concluding session and ensure an open, inclusive and transparent approach in the work of the Committee.

The title of the draft resolution has been aligned with the title of the draft convention.[8] Similar amendments have been made in preambular paragraphs 3 and 4, as well as in operative paragraphs 1 to 4, 6, 7, 10 and 12. The paragraph numbering was adjusted due to the inclusion of OP 6bis of the Chairs proposal, which was included as OP 7 in the resolution.

In PP 3, the reference to crimes committed through the use of information and communications technology systems has been deleted for the same reason as in PP 4 of the draft convention.

In OP 5, several amendments were made to incorporate the Chairs proposal.

First, with a view to elaborating a draft protocol supplementary to the Convention has been replaced with with a view to negotiating a draft protocol supplementary to the Convention. This amendment seeks to balance the conflicting positions of Member States without prejudging the outcome of future discussions. It seeks to ensure a mandate that is sufficiently determined but also sufficiently open to allow for good faith discussions and deliberations by the Ad Hoc Committee in carrying out its task. Second, the timeframe for these negotiations in an additional session of the Committee has been changed from one year to two years after the adoption of the Convention. This change was made in response to the view of a large majority of Member States that one year would be too early for such negotiations, particularly in view of the resource constraints that might arise from parallel negotiations on the rules of procedure of the future COSP and the need to focus on preparing for the entry into force of the Convention before drafting an additional protocol.

Third, OP 5 has been aligned with the newly included article 62 of the draft convention, which requires at least sixty States Parties to the Convention before any supplementary protocol is considered for adoption by the COSP.

Fourth, in order to account for the three preceding changes, the timeline, which envisaged that the Committee submit the outcome of its work on the supplementary protocol to the COSP at its first session was left open by deleting at its first session.

Finally, in the last line of OP 5, the phrase in accordance with the relevant articles of the Convention has been specified to read in accordance with articles 57, paragraph 5(g), 61 and 62 of the Convention. In OP 6, which concerns the mandate of the Ad Hoc Committee to elaborate the rules of procedure of the future COSP, two amendments were made to structure the timeline as well as the modalities of the Committees work.

Regarding the timeline, instead of meeting well before the convening of the first session of the Conference of the States Parties to the Convention, the Committee would now meet one year after adoption of the Convention. This change ensures a clear timeline and that the rules of procedure will be elaborated before the Committee convenes to negotiate an additional protocol.

With regard to the modalities of work of the Committee, the specification of holding a session mutatis mutandis, in accordance with General Assembly resolutions **74/247** and **75/282** aligns the modalities of work of the Committee in the elaboration of the Convention with those in the elaboration of the rules of procedure.

OP 7 incorporates OP 6bis of the Chairs proposal. It urges Member States to provide voluntary contributions to the United Nations Office on Drugs and Crime, which would be designated by the Secretary-General, pursuant to OP 8 of the draft resolution, as the secretariat for and under the COSP, in order to ensure the participation of representatives of developing countries, in particular those that do not have resident representation in Vienna, in the work of the Ad Hoc Committee.

In OP 12, the date of the Anti-Cybercrime Day has been further specified as the day of the adoption of the Convention by the General Assembly. Should Member States wish a different date, delegations are invited to consult in order to submit a unanimous amendment to the draft resolution to the General Assembly before its adoption.

NOTES

1 Title as orally revised and approved at the 16th meeting of the Ad Hoc Committees reconvened concluding session.
2 ETS No. 185.
3 Council of Europe, Explanatory Report to the Convention on Cybercrime (2001) para. 27, available at https://rm.coe.int/16800cce5b.
4 As circulated on 4 August 2024.
5 See in this regard the Explanatory note on the UDTC, available on the website of the reconvened concluding session.
6 United Nations, Treaty Series, vol. 2349, p. 41.
7 United Nations, Treaty Series, vol. 2225, p. 209.
8 As orally revised and approved at the 16th meeting of the Ad Hoc Committees reconvened concluding session.

Glossary

Advanced persistent threats: A cyber attack that involves gaining unauthorized access to a network and remaining undetected for a long time.

Attribution: The process of identifying the responsible party for a cyber attack.

Autonomous Weapons Systems: Weapons that can identify and engage targets without human control..

Cyber criminals: Hackers and other malicious users who use the Internet to commit crimes such as identity theft, spamming, phishing and other types of frauds.

Cyber diplomacy: The use of diplomatic strategies and tools to address cyber security challenges and opportunities in international relations.

Cyber espionage: Also known as cyber spying, is a cyber attack that involves stealing sensitive information without permission. It can be used for economic gain, political reasons, or to gain an advantage over a competitor.

Cyber power: Encompasses the ability of state and non-state actors to deploy digital technologies for offensive and defensive purposes, affecting everything from essential infrastructure to political discourse.

Cyber security: The protection of computer systems and networks from unauthorized access, use, disclosure, disruption, modification, or destruction.

Cyber warfare: The use of cyber capabilities to achieve military or political objectives.

Critical infrastructure: Systems and assets that is essential for the functioning of society.

Confidence-building measures: Actions or agreements that help reduce tensions and build trust between countries or groups. CBMs can be military, political, or non-military in nature.

Cyber bullying: The use of electronic communication to bully a person, typically by sending messages of an intimidating or threatening nature.

Digital divide: The gap between individuals, groups, or nations in terms of access to information and communication technologies.

Data breaches: Also known as data leakage, it is the unauthorized exposure, disclosure, or loss of personal information.

Data sovereignty: The principle that a nation has jurisdiction over data processed within its borders.

Effective diplomacy: Involves building relationships, promoting dialogue, and seeking common ground to advance shared interests and values.

Internet of Things: Describes devices with sensors, processing ability, software and other technologies that connect and exchange data with other devices and systems over the Internet or other communication networks

Public-private partnerships: Collaboration between a government agency and a private company to deliver a public service or project.

State-sponsored hacking: Cyber attacks conducted by a nation-state or with its knowledge and consent.

Tallinn Manual on the International Law Applicable to Cyber Warfare: An academic, non-binding study on how international law, especially *jus ad bellum* and international humanitarian law, applies to cyber conflicts and cyber warfare.

Track II diplomacy: Informal dialogues among actors such as academics, religious leaders, retired senior officials, and NGO officials that can bring new ideas and new relationships to the official process of diplomacy.

Traditional diplomacy: A type of diplomacy that is based on the formal and official relations between states, and that is conducted by professional and accredited representatives of the states such as diplomats and ambassadors.

Weapons of mass destruction: Devices that can kill or harm many people, or cause damage to the environment. WMDs can be biological, chemical, radiological, or nuclear.

Zero-sum game: A relationship, competition, or business deal where one persons gain is the other persons loss. The phrase zero-sum game comes from game theory and the notion that if one person wins and the other person loses, this produces a net gain of zero.

Bibliography

11. Space and Cyberspace. n.d. SIPRI. https://www.sipri.org/yearbook/2023/11

A, Clare; Deirdre C; Rachael C.; Steve H.;, Greg M.;, Madeline O.;, Stephanie P.; Anissa T.; Bryce W. and Jason L. 2022. Addressing Risks From Non-State Actors Use Of Commercially Available Technologies. https://www.dhs.gov/sites/default/files/2022-09/Addressing%20Risks%20from%20Non-State%20Actors.pdf

Africa at Forefront of Championing Cybersecurity and Digital Transformation in the Global Arena, African Union. n.d. https://au.int/en/pressreleases/20240816/africa-forefront-championing-cybersecurity-and-digital-transformation

African Union Convention on Cyber Security and Personal Data Protection, African Union. n.d. https://au.int/en/treaties/african-union-convention-cyber-security-and-personal-data-protection

Aïmeur, Esma, Sabrine Amri, and Gilles Brassard. 2023. Fake News, Disinformation and Misinformation in Social Media: A Review. *Social Network Analysis and Mining* 13 (1). https://doi.org/10.1007/s13278-023-01028-5

Ajaykumar, Shravishtha. 2023. India: Crucial Cyberwarfare Capabilities Need to Be Upgraded. Orfonline.Org. December 4, 2023. https://www.orfonline.org/expert-speak/india-crucial-cyberwarfare-capabilities-need-to-be-upgraded

Anderson, Janna. 2024. The Future of Truth and Misinformation Online. Pew Research Centre. April 14, 2024. https://www.pewresearch.org/internet/2017/10/19/the-future-of-truth-and-misinformation-online/

ASEAN. 2021. Asean Cybersecurity Cooperation Strategy (2021 2025). *Draft*. https://asean.org/wp-content/uploads/2022/02/

01-ASEAN-Cybersecurity-Cooperation-Paper-2021-2025_final-23-0122.pdf

Basu, Arindrajit and United Nations Institute for Disarmament Research. 2022. Indias International Cyber Operations: Tracing National Doctrine and Capabilities. Report Paper 5. *International Cyber Operations Research Paper Series*. United Nations Institute for Disarmament Research. https://unidir.org/files/2022-12/UNIDIR_India_International_Cyber_Operations.pdf

Broda, Elena, and Jesper Strömbäck. 2024. Misinformation, Disinformation, and Fake News: Lessons from an Interdisciplinary, Systematic Literature Review. *Annals of the International Communication Association* 48 (2): 13966. https://doi.org/10.1080/23808985.2024.2323736

Bronk, Christopher, and Eneken Tikk-Ringas. 2013. The Cyber Attack on Saudi Aramco. *Survival* 55 (2): 8196. doi:10.1080/00396338.2013.784468

Budapest Convention. 2024. Cybercrime. February 8, 2024. https://www.coe.int/en/web/cybercrime/the-budapest-convention

Burton, Joe. 2019. Cyber-Attacks and Freedom of Expression: Coercion, Intimidation and Virtual Occupation. *Baltic Journal of European Studies* 9 (3): 11633. https://doi.org/10.1515/bjes-2019-0025

Caciuloiu, Alexandru. 2019. Tackling Cybercrime in Support of a Safe and Secure AP-IS. Report. *Second Session of the Asia-Pacific Information Superhighway (AP-IS) Steering Committee*. https://www.unescap.org/sites/default/files/UNODC%20tackling%20Cybercrime%20in%20supoprt%20of%20a%20safe%20 and%20secure%20AP-IS.pdf

Callejas, Jorge Flores; Aicha Afifi; Nikolay Lozinskiy; Vincent Hermie; Szilvia Petkov; Hervé Baudat, et al. 2021. Cybersecurity in the United Nations System Organizations. *Report of the Joint Inspection Unit*.

CCDCOE. n.d. https://ccdcoe.org/organisations/osce/

Chinas Cyberattack Strategy Explained. 2024. December 20, 2024. https://www.boozallen.com/insights/cyber/chinas-cyberattack-strategy-explained.html

Clark, Robert. 2020. The Cybersecurity Canon: Tallinn Manual on the International Law Applicable to Cyber Warfare. *Palo Alto Networks Blog*. April 21, 2020. https://www.paloaltonetworks.com/blog/

2015/07/the-cybersecurity-canon-tallinn-manual-on-the-international-law-applicable-to-cyber-warfare/

Connect the Dots on State-Sponsored Cyber Incidents - Compromise of Saudi Aramco and RasGas. n.d. Council on Foreign Relations. https://www.cfr.org/cyber-operations/compromise-saudi-aramco-and-rasgas

Constellation. 2021. The 1999 NASA Cyber Attack, Cyber Consultancy. The 1999 NASA Cyber Attack, Constellation Cyber Consultancy. January 28, 2021. https://thecyberconsultancy.com/hack.html

Cyber Capabilities & Capacity Development Project. n.d. https://www.interpol.int/en/Crimes/Cybercrime/Cyber-capabilities-development/Cyber-Capabilities-Capacity-Development-Project

Cyber Capabilities Development. n.d. https://www.interpol.int/en/Crimes/Cybercrime/Cyber-capabilities-development

Cyber Risk GmbH. n.d. European Cyber Defence Policy. https://www.european-cyber-defence-policy.com/

Cyber Warfare and U.S. Cyber Command, The Heritage Foundation. n.d. The Heritage Foundation. https://www.heritage.org/military-strength/assessment-us-military-power/cyber-warfare-and-us-cyber-command

Cyber-Attack Against Ukrainian Critical Infrastructure. CISA. 2021. Cybersecurity and Infrastructure Security Agency CISA. July 20, 2021. https://www.cisa.gov/news-events/ics-alerts/ir-alert-h-16-056-01

Cybercrime Module 8 Key Issues: International Cooperation on Cybersecurity Matters. n.d.https://sherloc.unodc.org/cld/en/education/tertiary/cybercrime/module-8/key-issues/international-cooperation-on-cybersecurity-matters.html

Cybersecurity and New Technologies, Office of Counter-Terrorism. n.d. https://www.un.org/counterterrorism/cybersecurity

Cybersecurity and Outer Space. n.d. Centre for International Governance Innovation. https://www.cigionline.org/cyber security-and-outer-space/

Cybersecurity Policies. 2025. Shaping Europes Digital Future. January 15, 2025. https://digital-strategy.ec.europa.eu/en/policies/cybersecurity-policies

Dealing With Propaganda, Misinformation and Fake News. 2023.

Democratic Schools for All. October 7, 2023. https://www.coe.int/en/web/campaign-free-to-speak-safe-to-learn/dealing-with-propaganda-misinformation-and-fake-news

Developments in the Field of Information and Telecommunications in the Context of International Security UNODA. n.d. https://disarmament.unoda.org/ict-security/

Digital Watch Observatory. https://dig.watch/resource/un-gge-2021-report

Druet, Dirk; Annika Hansen; Mariana Knaupp; Jenna Russo; Albert Trithart; and International Peace Institute. 2024. Cybersecurity and UN Peace Operations: Evolving Risks and Opportunities. https://www.ipinst.org/wp-content/uploads/2024/03/2403_Cybersecurity-and-UN-Peace-Opsweb.pdf

ETtech. 2022. NotPetya: the cyberattack that shook the world. *The Economic Times*, March 5, 2022. https://economictimes.indiatimes.com/tech/newsletters/ettech-unwrapped/notpetya-the-cyberattack-that-shook-the-world/articleshow/89997076.cms?from=mdr

Fanchiotti, Vittorio and Jean Paul Pierini. 2012. Impact of Cyberspace on Human Rights and Democracy. *2012 4th International Conference on Cyber Conflict*. NATO CCD COE Publications, Tallinn. https://ccdcoe.org/uploads/2012/01/1_4_Fanchiotti_Pierini_ImpactofCyberspaceOnHumanRightsAndDemocracy.pdf

Fruhlinger, Josh. 2022. Stuxnet Explained: The First Known Cyber weapon. CSO Online. August 31, 2022. https://www.csoonline.com/article/562691/stuxnet-explained-the-first-known-cyberweapon.html

Global Data Alliance. 2023. Cross-Border Data Transfers & Cybersecurity Global Data Alliance. *Global Data Alliance*, February 9, 2023. https://globaldataalliance.org/issues/cybersecurity/

Groll, Elias. 2019. Cyberattack Targets Safety System at Saudi Aramco. *Foreign Policy*, July 25, 2019. https://foreignpolicy.com/2017/12/21/cyber-attack-targets-safety-system-at-saudi-aramco/

Guess, Andrew M. 2020. Misinformation, Disinformation, and Online Propaganda. Cambridge Core. September 1, 2020. https://www.cambridge.org/core/books/social-media-and-democracy/misinformation-disinformation-and-online-propaganda/D14406A631AA181839ED896916598500

Guides: International and Foreign Cyberspace Law Research Guide: Tallinn Manual & Primary Law Applicable to Cyber Conflicts. n.d. https://guides.ll.georgetown.edu/cyberspace/cyber-conflicts

Guides: International and Foreign Cyberspace Law Research Guide: IGO, NGO, & U.S. Government Resources. n.d. https://guides.ll.georgetown.edu/cyberspace/cyber-crime-igos-and-ngos.

Hakala, Janne, Jazlyn Melnychuk, and NATO STRATCOM COE. 2021. *Russia's Strategy In Cyberspace. NATO Strategic Communications Centre of Excellence.* NATO Strategic Communications Centre of Excellence. https://stratcomcoe.org/cuploads/pfiles/Nato-Cyber-Report_11-06-2021-4f4ce.pdf

Herzog, Stephen. Revisiting the Estonian Cyber Attacks: Digital Threats and Multinational Responses. *Journal of Strategic Security* 4, no. 2 (2011): 4960. http://www.jstor.org/stable/26463926

Hogeveen, Bart. Australian Strategic Policy Institute, Department of Foreign Affairs, Department of ICT, Office of the President, National Security Council, Ministry of Foreign Affairs, et al. 2022. The UN Norms of Responsible State Behaviour in Cyberspace. https://documents.unoda.org/wp-content/uploads/2022/03/The-UN-norms-of-responsible-state-behaviour-in-cyberspace.pdf

Honstein, Emily. 2024. Organization for Security and Cooperation in Europe. ICNL. January 12, 2024. https://www.icnl.org/resources/civic-freedom-monitor/osce.

Jardine, Eric. 2019. Beware Fake News. Centre for International Governance Innovation. April 2, 2019. https://www.cigion line.org/articles/beware-fake-news/?utm_source =google_ ads&utm_medium=grant&gad_source=1&gclid=CjwK CAi An9a9BhBt EiwAb Kg6frYX QKh7NwFALLbuo8a GktzbCd LpGWiuH7I3dE24 GyvHildmOuiWUho CVKMQAvD_ BwE

Jensen, Eric Talbot. 2017. The Tallinn Manual 2.0: Highlights and Insights. *Georgetown Journal of International Law*. vol. 48. https://www.law.georgetown.edu/international-law-journal/wp-content/uploads/sites/21/2018/05/48-3-The-Tallinn-Manual-2.0.pdf

Kakoti, Ananya Raj, and Gunwant Singh. 2024. The New Cyberspace Doctrines Impact on Indias Security. *Hindustan Times*, July 13, 2024. https://www.hindustantimes.com/ht-insight/future-tech/the-new-cyberspace-doctrine-s-impact-on-indias-security-101720843641057.html

Kerner, Saheed Oladimeji and Sean Michael. 2023. Solar Winds Hack Explained: Everything You Need to Know. *WhatIs*. November 3, 2023. https://www.techtarget.com/whatis/feature/SolarWinds-hack-explained-Everything-you-need-to-know

Kristen E. Eichensehr. *The American Journal of International Law*, 108, no. 3 (2014): 58589. https://doi.org/10.5305/amerjintelaw.108.3.0585

Lukitasari, Diana and Universitas Sebelas Maret Surakarta, Indonesia. 2013. Freedom of Speech in Cyberspace in Human Rights Protection. *International Journal of Business, Economics and Law* 2 (3): 78. https://ijbel.com/wp-content/uploads/2014/07/Freedom-Of-Speech-In-Cyberspace-In-Human-Rights-Protection-Perspective-Freedom-Of-Speech-In-Cyberspace-%E2%80%93-Human-Rights-Perpective-Diana-Lukitasari.pdf

Luo, Han, Meng Cai and Ying Cui. 2021. Spread of Misinformation in Social Networks: Analysis Based on Weibo Tweets. *Security and Communication Networks* 2021 (December): 123. https://doi.org/10.1155/2021/7999760

Lyu Jinghua,. n.d. What Are Chinas Cyber Capabilities and Intentions? Carnegie Endowment for International Peace. https://carnegieendowment.org/posts/2019/04/what-are-chinas-cyber-capabilities-and-intentions?lang=en

Matamis, Joaquin. 2024. The Cyber World and Human Rights: Perspectives on International Accountability. *Stimson Centre*, September. https://www.stimson.org/2024/the-cyber-world-and-human-rights-perspectives-on-international-accountability/

McGuinness, Damien. 2017. How a Cyber Attack Transformed Estonia. *BBC News*. April 27, 2017. https://www.bbc.com/news/39655415

Nadj, Filip. 2024. Organization for Security and Co-operation in Europe, Digital Watch Observatory. Digital Watch Observatory. April 8, 2024. https://dig.watch/actor/organization-security-and-co-operation-europe

Nation-State Cyber Actors, Cybersecurity and Infrastructure Security Agency CISA. n.d. https://www.cisa.gov/topics/cyber-threats-and-advisories/nation-state-cyber-actors

NATO Cooperative Cyber Defence Centre of Excellence Estonian Defence Forces. 2025. Estonian Defence Forces. February 11, 2025. https://mil.ee/en/landforces/ccdcoe/

OII, Spread of Disinformation the Biggest Concern for Internet and Social Media Users Globally Finds New Oxford Study. n.d. https://www.oii.ox.ac.uk/news-events/spread-of-disinformation-the-biggest-concern-for-internet-and-social-media-users-globally-finds-new-oxford-study/

Organization for Security and Co-operation in Europe (OSCE). n.d. https://www.eda.admin.ch/eda/en/fdfa/foreign-policy/international-organizations/osce.html

Organization for Security and Co-operation in Europe. 2023. Submission to UN New Agenda for Peace February 2023. https://dppa.un.org/sites/default/files/osce.pdf

Paganini, Pierluigi, Centre For Cyber Security and International Relations Studies (CCSIRS), Centro Interdipartimentale di Studi Strategici, Internazionali e Imprenditoriali (CCSSII), and Università degli Studi di Firenze. 2022. Non State Actors in Cyberspace: An Attempt to a Taxonomic Classification, Role, Impact and Relations with a States Socio-Economic Structure. https://www.cssii.unifi.it/upload/sub/Pubblicazioni/2022_Paganini_Pierluigi.pdf

Press Release. 2024. ITU. September 10, 2024. https://www.itu.int/en/mediacentre/Pages/PR-2024-09-10-Global-Cybersecurity-Index.aspx

Quinn, Ben, and Charles Arthur. 2020. PlayStation Network Hackers Access Data of 77 Million Users. *The Guardian*, April 16, 2020. https://www.theguardian.com/technology/2011/apr/26/playstation-network-hackers-data

Radchenko, A. N. and E. I. Yurevich. 1972. On definition of artificial intelligence. In *Springer eBooks*, 91101. https://doi.org/10.1007/978-3-662-40393-8_7

Ramen, Aishwarya. 2023. States Use of Non-state Actors in Cyberspace. Orfonline.Org. December 4, 2023. https://www.orfonline.org/expert-speak/states-use-of-non-state-actors-in-cyberspace

Research Guides: FYS1010: Propaganda, Misinformation, Disinformation & Fact Finding Resources. n.d. https://guides.lib.wayne.edu/c.php?g=401320&p=2729574

Richter, Konstanze, and Konstanze Richter. 2025. InterDigital Launches Attack on Disney at Multiple Venues Including UPC. JUVE Patent. February 10, 2025. https://www.juve-patent.com/cases/

interdigital-launches-attack-on-disney-at-multiple-venues-including-upc/

Robert, Wickramatunga. n.d. The Outer Space Treaty. https://www.unoosa.org/oosa/en/ourwork/spacelaw/treaties/introouterspacetreaty.html

Robinson, Rob. 2024. Cyber Diplomacy: A New Frontier in International Relations and Professional Practice. *EDRM*. June 28, 2024. https://edrm.net/2024/06/cyber-diplomacy-a-new-frontier-in-international-relations-and-professional-practice/

Rosenzweig, Paul. 2021. Chinas Cyber Capabilities: Warfare, Espionage, and Implications for the United States. Report. *China's Cyber Capabilities: Warfare, Espionage, and Implications for the United States*. https://www.uscc.gov/sites/default/files/2022-11/Chapter_3_Section_2Chinas_Cyber_Capabilities.pdf

Russell, Martin and European Parliamentary Research Service. 2021. The Organization for Security and Co-operation in Europe (OSCE): A Pillar of the European Security Order. Report PE 696.190. *EPRS, European Parliamentary Research Service*. https://www.europarl.europa.eu/RegData/etudes/BRIE/2021/696190/EPRS_BRI(2021)696190_EN.pdf

Ryan-Mosley, Tate. 2023. How Generative AI Is Boosting the Spread of Disinformation and Propaganda. *MIT Technology Review*, October 3, 2023. https://www.technologyreview.com/2023/10/04/1080801/generative-ai-boosting-disinformation-and-propaganda-freedom-house/

2023b. How Generative AI Is Boosting the Spread of Disinformation and Propaganda. *MIT Technology Review*, October 3, 2023. https://www.technologyreview.com/2023/10/04/1080801/generative-ai-boosting-disinformation-and-propaganda-freedom-house/

2024b. The International Telecommunications Union (ITU) and Cyber Accountability. *Stimson Centre*, September. https://www.stimson.org/2024/the-international-telecommunications-union-itu-and-cyber-accountability/

Salvaggio, Salvino A. and Nahuel González. 2022. The European Framework for Cybersecurity: Strong Assets, Intricate History. *International Cybersecurity Law Review* 4 (1): 13746. https://doi.org/10.1365/s43439-022-00072-9

Schjolberg, Stein. 2017. The Role of INTERPOL in a Geneva Convention or Declaration for Cyberspace. *Report from the INTERPOL Global Cybercrime Expert Group Meeting, and INTERPOL World 2017, Singapore.* https://www.cybercrimelaw.net/documents/The_Role_of_INTERPOL.pdf

Schmitt, Michael N. and Sean Watts. Beyond State-Centrism: International Law and Non-State Actors in Cyberspace. *Journal of Conflict & Security Law* 21, no. 3 (2016): 595611. https://www.jstor.org/stable/26298218

Schmitt, Michael. 2021. The Sixth United Nations GGE and International Law in Cyberspace. *Just Security*. October 8, 2021. https://www.justsecurity.org/76864/the-sixth-united-nations-gge-and-international-law-in-cyberspace/.

Shandler. 2022. The 5×5Non-state Armed Groups in Cyber Conflict - Atlantic Council. Atlantic Council. October 26, 2022. https://www.atlanticcouncil.org/content-series/the-5x5/the-5x5-non-state-armed-groups-in-cyber-conflict/

Sharma, Deepak and Institute for Defence Studies and Analyses (IDSA). n.d. Chinas Cyber Warfare Capability and Indias Concerns. *Journal of Defence Studies*. . April. https://www.idsa.in/system/files/jds_5_2_dsharma.pdf

Sigholm, Johan. 2013. Non-State Actors in Cyberspace Operations. *Journal of Military Studies* 4 (1): 137. https://doi.org/10.1515/jms-2016-0184

Significant Cyber Incidents, CSIS. n.d. https://www.csis.org/programs/strategic-technologies-program/significant-cyber-incidents

Slonopas, Andre. 2024. What Is Cyber Warfare? Various Strategies for Preventing It. American Public University. May 3, 2024. https://www.apu.apus.edu/area-of-study/information-technology/resources/what-is-cyber-warfare/

Special Section: Ukrainian Power Grids Cyberattack - ISA. 2022. Isa.Org. January 31, 2022. https://www.isa.org/intech-home/2017/march-april/features/ukrainian-power-grids-cyberattack

Stellar Safeguards: How Organizations Can Protect Space Assets From Cyberthreats. 2024. *Deloitte Insights*. August 30, 2024. https://www2.deloitte.com/us/en/insights/industry/public-sector/defending-against-cyber-threats-space-systems.html

Stuxnet Definition & Explanation. 2017. September 13, 2017. https://www.kaspersky.com/resource-center/definitions/what-is-stuxnet

Technical Difficulties. n.d. https://2009-2017. state.gov/t/isn/5181.htm

Temple-Raston, Dina. 2021. A Worst Nightmare Cyberattack: The Untold Story of the SolarWinds Hack. *NPR*, April 16, 2021. https://www.npr.org/2021/04/16/985439655/a-worst-nightmare-cyberattack-the-untold-story-of-the-solarwinds-hack

The International Institute for Strategic Studies. n.d. Cyber Capabilities and National Power: A Net Assessment. *The International Institute for Strategic Studies*, 8990. https://www.iiss.org/globalassets/media-librarycontentmigration/files/research-papers/cyber-power-report/cyber-capabilities-and-national-powerchina.pdf

The Tallinn Manual. n.d. https://ccdcoe.org/research/tallinn-manual/

The UN Takes a Big Step Forward on Cybersecurity, Arms Control Association. n.d. https://www.armscontrol.org/act/2013-09/un-takes-big-step-forward-cybersecurity

The United Nations Institute for Disarmament Research, and Camino Kavanagh. 2017. The United Nations, Cyberspace and International Peace and Security: Responding to Complexity in the 21st Century. *Unidir Resources*. https://unidir.org/files/publication/pdfs/the-united-nations-cyberspace-and-international-peace-and-security-en-691.pdf.

To Combat Cross-border Cyber Threats, Cooperation Is Key IBM Policy. 2022. *IBM Policy*. April 15, 2022. https://www.ibm.com/policy/to-combat-cross-border-cyber-threats-cooperation-is-key/

Tools That Fight Disinformation Online. n.d. RAND. https://www.rand.org/research/projects/truth-decay/fighting-disinformation/search.html

Tsagourias, Nicholas. 2012. The Tallinn Manual on the International Law Applicable to Cyber Warfare: A Commentary on Chapter II the Use of Force. December 14, 2012. https://papers.ssrn.com/sol3/papers.cfm?abstract_id=2538191

U.S. Can Respond Decisively to Cyber Threat Posed by China. https://www.defense.gov/News/News-Stories/Article/Article/3663799/us-can-respond-decisively-to-cyber-threat-posed-by-china/

U.S. Department of Defence. n.d. DOD: Its Not Just State Actors Who Pose Cyber Threat to U.S. https://www.defense.gov/News/News-Stories/Article/Article/3039462/dod-its-not-just-state-actors-who-pose-cyber-threat-to-us/

Uberoi, Aditi. n.d. July 2024: Biggest Cyber Attacks, Data Breaches and Ransomware Attacks. https://www.cm-alliance.com/cybersecurity-blog/july-2024-biggest-cyber-attacks-data-breaches-and-ransomware-attacks

UN GGE 2021 Report, Digital Watch Observatory. n.d. Digital Watch Observatory. https://dig.watch/resource/un-gge-2021-report

United Nations. n.d. Countering Disinformation, United Nations. https://www.un.org/en/countering-disinformation

United States Cyber Command. n.d. Command Challenge Problems Guidance. Report. *Command Challenge Problem Set*. https://www.cybercom.mil/Portals/56/Documents/Technical%20Outreach/USCC_CC_Booklet_Final-v2.pdf

United States. 2021. Cyber Capabilities and National Power: A Net Assessment. Report. The International Institute for Strategic Studies. https://www.iiss.org/globalassets/media-library contentmigration/files/research-papers/cyber-power-report/cyber-capabilities-and-national-powerunited-states.pdf

UNODC ITU. 2011. Cybersecurity for ALL. Conference proceedings. https://www.unodc.org/roseap/uploads/archive/documents/2011/09/cybercrime-workshop/ppt/Ashish_ITU_Cybersecurity_General_an_f1.pdf

What is an Advanced Persistent Threat (APT)? 2024. *Cisco*. August 21, 2024. https://www.cisco.com/c/en/us/products/security/advanced-persistent-threat.html

Why Space Cyber? 2021. Centre for Space Cyber Strategy and CyberSecurity - University of Buffalo. March 4, 2021. https://www.buffalo.edu/space-cybersecurity/center/why-space-cyber.html

Wolff, Josephine. 2021. How The NotPetya Attack Is Reshaping Cyber Insurance. *Brookings*, December 1, 2021. https://www.brookings.edu/articles/how-the-notpetya-attack-is-reshaping-cyber-insurance/

Zouheiry, Ziad. 2024. Cyber Attacks on Human Rights and the Role of Cyber Governance. *International Journal of Science and Research (IJSR)* 13 (1): 39197. https://doi.org/10.21275/sr24104133608

Index